AutoCAD
Onstage

A Computer-Aided Design Handbook
for Theater, Film, and Television

Rich Rose

BETTERWAY PUBLICATIONS, INC.
WHITE HALL, VIRGINIA

Published by Betterway Publications, Inc.
P.O. Box 219
Crozet, VA 22932
(804) 823-5661

Cover design by Susan Riley
Typography by Park Lane Typography

Library of Congress Cataloging-in-Publication Data

Rose, Rich
  AutoCAD Onstage : A Computer-Aided Design Handbook for Theater,
Film, and Television / by Rich Rose.
    p. cm.
  Includes index.
  ISBN 1-55870-165-6 : $29.95. — ISBN 1-55870-164-8 (pbk.) : $19.95
  1. Theaters--Stage-setting and scenery—Computer programs.
2. Motion pictures--Setting and scenery—Computer programs.
3. Television--Stage-setting and scenery—Computer programs.
4. Stage lighting--Computer programs. 5. Costume design—Computer
programs. 6. AutoCad (Computer program)   I. Title.
PN2091.S8R584 1990
791.4'0285--dc20   90-38825
                                                      CIP

Printed in the United States of America
0 9 8 7 6 5 4 3 2 1

To Melissa

ACKNOWLEDGMENTS

Thank you to all of my students who have provided me with the opportunity to learn just how AutoCAD might best be used to enhance the Theater and Film/Television designer's art. A particular thank you to those students who contributed their drawings to use as examples: William R. Bathgate, Nadja Brost, Teresa Enroth, Rachel Hauck, Daniel Jue, David Namba, Craig Pierce, Dan Poirier, Ian McIntosh, Natalie Rigolet, Vickie Scott and Peter Yesair.

Thank you to the professional designers who believed in this project and donated their experiences as well as their drawings: Lighting designer Bob Heller; CBS Television Art Director Bill Hulstrum; Lighting Designer Bill Klages of the Klages Group; Scenic Designer Joanne McMaster; Assistant Professor Phyllis Bell Miller of Mississippi State University; and Software Developer and Costume Designer Stephanie Schoelzel.

Let me also add a personal thank you to the UCLA School of Theater, Film and Television including Theater Chair Bill Ward, Property Master and Author Thurston James, former head of the Laboratory for Technology in the Arts Phil Middleman, Software Designer Jim Pickrell and the faculty and staff of UCLA Theater. Thank you to the very supportive Robert & Jackie Hostage and Hilary Swinson of Betterway Publications. Most significantly, I would like to express my appreciation to the people at Autodesk Inc., especially Jim Purcell, Kathleen Batty and Mark Sturges for their long term continued encouragement and tangible support that continue to make it possible to develop CAD applications in this area.

CONTENTS

INTRODUCTION

A First Word

CAD, computer aided; drafting, design, drawing. It's all of those things and more. CAD is to drafting, designing, and drawing as word processing is to writing. The easy manipulation of words available in Microsoft Word™ or WordPerfect™ becomes the quick and easy electronic manipulation of lines, drawings, and symbols in AutoCAD®.

As a teacher of the AutoCAD software program for many years, to both students and professionals in the fields of theater and film/television design, I have been frustrated by the lack of a guide specifically written for these unique areas. If you've tried to learn from the AutoCAD manual, you quickly came to realize that it is not an AutoCAD primer but rather an excellent encyclopedia for looking up information in its alphabetically arranged pages. You can certainly learn the software from any number of other good books out there and I have used them in my own classes, but I found that my students experienced a rough transition period when it came to relating their new-found knowledge to scenic or lighting design. Their productivity ground to a halt. *AutoCAD Onstage* addresses this issue by combining a basic understanding of the AutoCAD program with connections and strategy links to production design. This is accomplished by presenting practical examples and drawing approach tactics that are unique to entertainment design.

What and Why CAD

AutoCAD is the world's biggest seller in the field of PC-based computer-aided design software. As a matter of fact, it outsells all of the other PC CAD software combined. This is the top reason we chose it to use at UCLA in the School of Theater, Film and Television. I wanted to make sure that the CAD program my students learned was the one they were most likely to encounter in the "outside world."

Another top reason for choosing this software package over others is its versatility and adaptability. As you will see, AutoCAD is being used in areas as diverse as architecture (where it has become a standard in many firms) and engineering as well as the design fields relating to theater, film, and television. And even in this field it is adaptable to such diverse disciplines as scenic, lighting, and costume design. There are many, many other CAD programs for the PC. AutoCAD has become the one that each of the other programs compares itself to. It has virtually become the standard.

After learning any CAD program it is not too difficult to learn another CAD program. Most of us who have been around computers for a while have learned two or three word processing programs. The first one might have been a "bear" to learn but the others came a lot quicker. When I was in elementary school I learned the trumpet and played in the band. As I progressed in school, the trumpet section was encouraged to learn the other less popular brass instruments in order to fill out the orchestra. Some went to the tuba, others went to the French horn, piccolo trumpet, etc. Many (a lot!) of the concepts and commands among the different CAD programs are quite similar. If you do decide that AutoCAD isn't your cup of tea, or maybe you've learned another CAD program and found out that AutoCAD is what you needed to really do the job right, then converting or learning the new program won't really be too painful.

An advantage that CAD has over traditional pencil and paper techniques is the time saved. Drawings done with CAD on a previous project can quickly be retrieved from memory and inserted into a new drawing. Think about that; after a number of shows have been CAD-drafted you decide with this particular design to use a scenic unit from a past show. It is a simple matter to take the unit out of memory and place it right in the new drawing. There is no need to redraw the scenery. It is for this reason that I now consider drawing anything without the computer a waste of time. Pencil and paper drawings can't easily be used again. This principle lays the foundation for building up your own libraries of symbols. You can collect all of your doors, windows, lighting instruments, etc. into libraries from which you can pick and choose for future CAD projects. Many libraries are commercially available for AutoCAD. These symbol libraries range from bathroom fixtures to lighting instruments to landscape symbols.

Another time- and labor-saving feature is copying. Parts of a current drawing that need to be duplicated many times in the drawing, such as windows on a wall, can be drawn in seconds. Symmetrical objects can be drawn as a half and then turned into a whole.

Another advantage is the precision that CAD programs impose on drawing. With pencil and paper you might draw a line that is intended to be 10′ long but you draw it 3″ longer because that's where the pencil stopped. You dimension it at 10′ and no one is the wiser. CAD drawing doesn't allow that. You must make the line 10′ long, it's that simple. The result is precision in your drafting like you have never known.

All of these time-saving features mean that you can work closer to production time. I have often been frustrated in having to plan and draft well before the first rehearsal in order to take advantage of shop time. By some time around the middle of the rehearsal period, some of the set has become irrelevant to the show. With AutoCAD I can draw more quickly and make changes quite effortlessly. By working later in the process — closer to first rehearsal — the design can be more in tune with the director's most current thoughts and objectives. Maybe CAD drawing doesn't make you a better designer, but perhaps in this way it can make your design better.

Operating Systems, Computers, and AutoCAD Releases

Autodesk has written different versions of the AutoCAD program for MS-DOS computers, the Apple Macintosh II, and UNIX computers. If you've learned it on the PC but will be using it on the Mac, don't worry. Everything that you learned applies to any of the other operating systems. As a matter of fact, your drawing disks can go from one system to another with no problem (if you follow a few rules). The different systems do have a few different capabilities, but it is a simple matter to learn the extra features of AutoCAD unique to each system.

From time to time a newer edition of AutoCAD comes out, called a Release. Each Release is a little different from previous Releases. Some of the terms, menus, and dialog boxes that you find in this book may be slightly different than the version of AutoCAD that you are using. Be patient. A second or two of investigation on your part will allow you to find a similar path to accomplishing the same task on most operating systems and most AutoCAD releases.

Learning CAD

Learning to draw with CAD really is simple if it is handled one step at a time. At first, CAD drawing will take two or three times the amount of time that it would have taken if you had done it with pencil and paper. But after a while you will pick up speed. This initial period of "really slow" drawing seems to be related to dragging the old traditional pencil and paper techniques to the computer. The new computerized methods require that you approach and think about a project in a whole new way. This seems to take two or three projects before you really kick into gear. It's like learning to drive a car. At first you learned the commands (key in, foot on brake, release emergency brake, look around . . .) as separate mechanical steps that were unnatural to you. Later, as you gained more driving experience everything "clicked" into place. Now driving has become almost like breathing. You barely have to think about it. I sometimes get to work in the morning with a complete lack of memory of passing through certain parts of town. It is like I blacked out over entire stretches of the L.A. freeway system. Well, I haven't really blacked out. What has happened is that driving a car has become intuitive. This is exactly what happens with computer-aided drafting and design. At first it is quite awkward and mechanical, very deliberate and quite slow. But suddenly there is a day when it has seemingly infiltrated your bloodstream and is at your finger tips.

If you stick with it, you will experience this phenomenon soon enough. Until then you may get quite frustrated with your pace. I do not recommend undertaking your *first* CAD project or design if you are under a tight deadline. These first couple of projects with AutoCAD should be ones where you have plenty of time to get the job done. Allow perhaps twice the time that it would take you to complete the project with pencil and paper.

This book is structured to suit the needs of the designer or draftsperson in the field of entertainment. It should be followed in the order presented. It is important to you not to skip over anything that you don't understand. Don't count on "getting it later." All the information in the subsequent sections of the book builds upon the information covered in the earlier parts of the book. Don't allow anything to get away from you that you don't completely understand.

As You Get Started

Throughout the book, the text will refer to certain keyboard keys. These keys will be presented in bold face capital letters. For example, the **ENTER** key or the **F1** key.

AutoCAD commands and Tablet and Pull Down Menu areas will be typeset differently in order to distinguish them from descriptive text. These items will be in small capital letters. For example, the SAVE command or the EDIT area of the Tablet Menu. Command options will be in bold letters. They will be in the same mix of capital and lower case letters that you will encounter in the program. Examples include **Window** or **nExt**.

Drawing titles will be distinguished by underlined capital letters — just as they would be designated in any normal drafting assignment. For example, ELEVATION or STAGING PLAN.

You will find that these chapters make many assumptions about your knowledge of drafting. This book presumes that you have already learned to draft and have a good understanding of PLANS, ELEVATIONS, line weights, lettering, etc. If not, I would recommend my companion book, *Drafting Scenery for Theater, Film, and Television*. This "pencil-and-paper" drafting manual is available through Betterway Publications, Inc. as well.

With those formalities out of the way your "tour" of AutoCAD begins. AutoCAD commands and issues that will not concern the production designer are not covered in this book. Some issues that relate in a more peripheral way are briefly touched on. For more information and fuller explanations of any aspects of AutoCAD, you should always consult the *AutoCAD Reference Manual* that came with your software.

PART I

THE THEATER AND FILM/TELEVISION DESIGNER'S CAD WORKSTATION

MICRO COMPUTERS
INPUT DEVICES
OUTPUT DEVICES

1 SETTING UP A CAD WORKSTATION

FUNCTION: If the workstation is not properly fitted, in terms of both equipment and comfort, your drawing sessions will not be the pleasant, creative, and efficient experiences that they should be. Take time to figure out precisely what your hardware and software needs are. Plan an efficient CAD office space that takes into account both your comfort and your long term health.

Here is a survey of some of the equipment that you will need to set up your CAD workstation. Where choices are presented (in pointing devices for instance) think hard about what seems to suit your natural way of doing things. The recommendations made in this book are based on a couple of years of both drafting in CAD and teaching CAD to hundreds of university students and professionals.

The Monitor

The monitor is your window to communicating with the computer and is, at the same time, your electronic drawing surface.

Most monitors have an on/off button that you push or a knob that you turn. These are located on the front or side of the monitor. Usually there is a pilot light that lights up if the monitor is on. IBM has pioneered several monitor formats over the years: EGA, VGA, etc. My recommendation is that you go with the latest of these — VGA. The latest releases of AutoCAD are designed to take advantage of the VGA monitor's color and detail.

The Computer

The brain of the computer workstation is the large box that your monitor is most likely resting on right now. Sometimes this box is of a tower design that stands somewhere near the work area. The on/off switch for this box is located on the front of the computer but may also be found on the side. The older PC/XT/AT style IBM computers and many of their clones have this switch not on the side but at the very back of the computer (often resulting in scratched up knuckles).

Your IBM or clone computer should be a 386 or 286 based computer. This number refers to the code number of the computer chip that IBM puts in its computers to process information. The IBM PS/2 model 50z is an example of a moderately priced 286 computer. AutoCAD is also available in a specialized 386 version. This edition is designed to work on computers that have a 386 chip such as the IBM model 70 computer. The 386 computer contains more memory and will work much faster than a 286 based machine. The 386 is especially important for lighting designers. Your computer should have a fixed or hard disk information storage device of at least 20 megabytes; 30 megabytes and more is better if your budget allows.

The Keyboard

The typewriter style keyboard is one of the ways that you will communicate with the computer while using AutoCAD. It is very much like a typewriter. Most of the keys are laid out in the same QWERTY style. If you can touch type, you will be ahead of the game. But don't go and take a course in typing. Most of your information will be fed into the computer in other ways.

There are many keys on this keyboard that are not found on your typewriter. The **ENTER** key takes the place of the Carriage Return key on your typewriter. After typing a command or some other instruction that you want the computer to carry out, you press the **ENTER** key. Only then will the computer "see" the instruction. Even if you select a command with the mouse or digitizing tablet, you must press the **ENTER** key. The IBM/Microsoft style mouse and most digitizing tablet pucks include a button that acts as the **ENTER** key. This convenience allows you to keep your hand on the mouse, trackball, or puck. You don't have to stop, go to the keyboard to hit **ENTER**, and then go back to your work.

Your typewriter doesn't have function keys on it either. These keys run along the top or left side of most computer keyboards. They are labeled **F1** through **F12** on the IBM style keyboard. The function keys perform various shortcut tasks that are specific to each program being run. The same function key will do one thing in AutoCAD and quite a different thing in a word processing program. AutoCAD takes advantage of only five of these keys. More on that in the chapters ahead.

To the right of the function keys on the IBM style keyboard are nine other keys. They are:

PRINT SCREEN	PAGE UP
SCROLL LOCK	DELETE
PAUSE	END
INSERT	PAGE DOWN
HOME	

Of these keys, AutoCAD uses only **PRINT SCREEN** (to print any text on the screen).

Mouse/ Trackball

This is the most common non-keyboard method of communicating with your computer. Looking very much like its namesake, the mouse is used to point at things on the screen and draw lines, circles, etc. To do this you simply roll the mouse around on a table top and watch the monitor screen while a pointer moves accordingly. Move the mouse to the right and the pointer moves to the right. Move the mouse to the left and the pointer moves to the left.

The Microsoft/IBM type mouse has two buttons. One button (the left one) is used to pick menu items from the screen. The other button (right button) acts very much like the **ENTER** or **RETURN** key on the keyboard. You also use these buttons to indicate the beginnings and endings of lines, circles, etc. while drawing.

The Macintosh mouse has only one button. Pushing down on the button selects the item (like the left button on the other mouse) and letting go of the button carries out the selection (like the right button).

Because the mouse rolls around on your desk top, it can get clogged up with dirt, hair, coffee, oil, and whatever else might be lurking in your work area. These things sometimes cause the mouse to stick or jump. The ball can be removed and cleaned with much difficulty and questionable success. It's a good idea to buy a mouse pad. This is a little rubber pad that sits on your desk top on which you roll your mouse. Put it away after each session and it will greatly reduce the amount of mouse cleaning in your life. The special rubber surface is ideally suited for the mouse and completely eliminates skips and jumps which occur on even the cleanest desk tops.

The trackball is essentially a "belly-up" mouse. Some designers prefer it because you don't need to clear desk space for the mouse to travel in. It stays stationary while you roll the ball. Two buttons on either side can be programmed to simulate either the dual IBM/Microsoft mouse buttons or the single Mac button.

Digitizing Tablet

The digitizing tablet is another method of communicating information to the computer while using AutoCAD. It has a mouse-like device called a "puck," which is used to draw with like an electronic pen. The puck has no moving parts, no rolling ball. Instead there is a coil of wire which interacts with the magnetized field of the digitizing tablet (don't rest your disks here!). The computer knows where the puck is at all times (as long as it is on the tablet) by sensing the location of the magnetic interaction of the puck and the tablet.

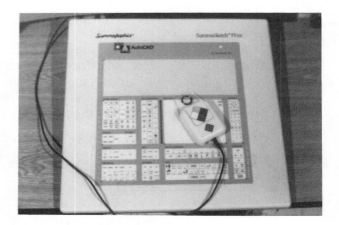

The puck also has several buttons. Like the mouse it has a "pick" button for choosing the item that you are pointing to, or for indicating the beginning and ending of lines, circles, etc. Unlike the Macintosh mouse but like the Microsoft/IBM type mice, there is an "enter" button that acts much like the **ENTER** or **RETURN** key on the keyboard. And unlike either mouse, there are 2, 3, 4, or more buttons which execute commands, emulate other keys on the keyboard, or make pull down menus appear on the screen. On the common four-button puck the third button will "pull down" the OSNAP menu. The fourth button invokes the CANCEL command. The more buttons you have, the more time you will save and the easier your drawing sessions can be.

Another pointing option with the tablet is a stylus, which looks very much like an ordinary pen. Pushing down on the pen depresses a tiny "pick" button. Another button on the side of the stylus is the "enter" or "return" button. The stylus' disadvantages include its tendency to be shaky and the fatigue it brings on from holding it. The puck rests on the tablet all by itself and needs merely to be pushed around. No energy is spent holding it in place.

Any lines drawn on the tablet with either the puck or the stylus appear directly on the monitor and not on the tablet.

The tablet will have an overlay or template made of plastic that is attached directly to the tablet. The overlay is partitioned into many different areas. One area of the template has been designated as the area where you do your drawing. Other areas on the template have command names written on them. By pointing to a command and "clicking" with the puck, you can quickly execute that command. This is much quicker than using a mouse and going through multiple pull down menus. A command may be buried in two or three or more layers of menus but may be instantly available on the tablet with just a "click."

The most common tablet size for AutoCAD is 12" x 12". I realize that this seems wrong; after all your drawing is going to be something more like 24" x 36" when it is blueprinted. The drawing is accomplished proportionally, however, don't worry! You will be able to have your much larger blueprint. Larger tablets (including 24" x 36") are available, but they are really for taking an existing drawing and tracing it with the puck or stylus in order to have a computerized or "digitized" version of the drawing. The area partitioned on the template overlay for your actual drawing is actually only 4" x 3½". You can set the tablet up for digitizing existing drawings of up to 12" x 12" if you wish.

The 12" x 12" command template is available directly through Autodesk Inc., the makers of AutoCAD, and is made available to you once you purchase and register your copy of AutoCAD with them.

The speed advantages of instant access to commands with the digitizing tablet and AutoCAD's template overlay, combined with the built-in extra features and convenience of the multi-button puck, make it the hands down favorite in the pointing device race. Designers who are in love with their mice should strongly consider the tablet as a faster alternative.

Disks

Most computers have at least two memory storage devices. One is called the hard disk drive (sometimes called the fixed disk) and the other is the floppy disk drive. Both disk drives record your information, computations, data, drawings, etc. onto a recording medium. This is very much like recording your voice onto recording tape. As a matter of fact the actual recording medium is almost identical.

Let's talk about the floppy disk drive first. Your IBM compatible computer will most likely refer to this drive as the A drive. The floppy disk drive records your work onto a small, round flexible disk of this recording medium. There are two disk sizes currently available for personal use.

The oldest of the two is the larger 5¼" diameter disk. The disk itself is permanently encased in a protective jacket made of stiff paper or flexible plastic. As the disk drive records (writes) and plays (reads) the disk, it spins it around inside the jacket like a record on a turntable. The jacket has holes in it for the disk drive head to gain access to the floppy disk. When the disk is out of the disk drive it is stored in a protective sleeve, also made of paper or plastic. This second paper sleeve is necessary because the access holes in the paper jacket make the disk vulnerable to dust, dirt, oils, and other foreign matter which might ruin the disk or the disk drive itself. These disks must be carefully handled to avoid such hazards. Because the disks are only protected by paper, they must be stored in tough cases to keep them from being bent. A 5¼" disk is ruined if it can't spin freely inside the jacket due to a crease or bend.

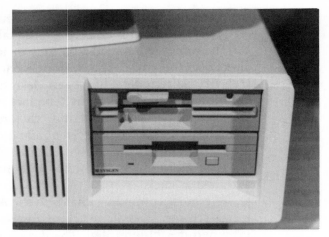

The other, newer size is a smaller 3½" diameter floppy disk. This disk is encased in a hard plastic jacket. Its disk drive access hole is covered by a sliding aluminum gate. The gate is opened by the disk drive only after it has been inserted in the disk drive. No other protective sleeve is needed. If you are able to choose between the two sizes, choose the more convenient 3½" disk drive. The diskette will easily fit in your shirt pocket and it is very difficult to damage it. And no, the smaller disks don't hold less information. They actually hold more!

You will most likely be using high density (as opposed to single or double density) disks in your computer. If you use an IBM AT or PS/2 computer (or clone) they are required. They can be harder to find in the stores than the other types, so be careful. Many sales people will try to tell you that they are the same as double density and that you can use double density disks in order to save some money. They *aren't* the same; spend your money and hunt down the right disk. But just in case you made a mistake, as with all computer hardware and software purchases, save your receipts.

The hard disk drive reads and writes information also. Your IBM compatible computer will refer to this disk drive as the C drive. Prior to using AutoCAD, you will transfer the contents of the many program disks onto your hard disk drive. If you didn't do this, you would have to be constantly swapping floppy disks during your drawing sessions as the computer needed instructions from different parts of AutoCAD spread out over the assorted disks.

cessed by your computer. For this reason, if you are working on your own computer, it is also a good idea to store your drawings on your hard drive as you work on them. Use your floppy drive for making backup copies of your work. After opening night, you should remove the drawings from your disk drive in order to free up disk memory (disk space). Always copy drawings onto floppies before removing them from the hard drive.

If you have more than one hard or floppy disk drive on your computer, the references to A drive and C drive may conflict. For instance, your computer may have a B drive and even a D drive! Ignore these references if you are in this situation and refer to the manuals that come with your computer.

Printer Plotters

All dot-matrix style printing devices are called printer plotters in the world of CAD. Printer plotters are one of the ways to get your electronic drawings onto paper.

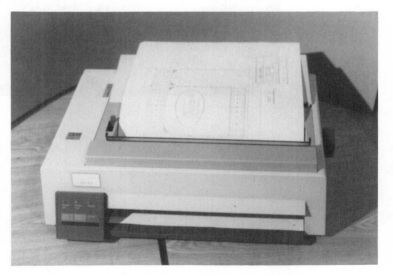

Printers tend to be slow and make circles and curved lines a bit jagged — stair stepped. A "home size" dot matrix printer is one such printer plotter. It isn't the printing device of choice because you are limited to small pieces of paper. Although individual ELEVATIONS could be printed out, large FLOOR PLANS or an entire sheet of ELEVATIONS could not.

A better alternative is a wide carriage printer. These printers have a 14"

wide carriage which will print out small sheets of <u>ELEVATIONS</u> and ¼" <u>FLOOR PLANS</u> of smaller spaces. Even larger printer plotters are available that will plot out on C size paper and will even print in color.

Plotters

Plotters actually draw your work with colored pens. They can plot out your drawings on 48" paper and can do so much quicker than any printer plotter can.

A wide variety of pens is available for plotters — felt tip, fiber tip, technical drawing, and others. You can plot onto vellum for making blueprint copies, or you can plot onto special plotter bond for making photocopies. You can even plot onto acetate. One company makes a pencil plotter. With pencil plots you can edit the drawing even after it has been plotted.

Multiple copies of a drawing should be photocopied or blueprinted from your plot. Plotting several sets of working drawings in color can take hours and hours. Although the plotter is the fastest of the output devices, one complex drawing can take thirty minutes to plot.

If you can afford a pen plotter, it is the output device of choice. The plot that results is the closest to a hand drafted look. If you can't afford one, most graphic service companies in large cities will make a plot for you when you bring your disk in. There are also many plot services that will receive your disk through the mail and send it back with your plot in the next day or so.

Ergonomics

Not long after deciding *where* you are going to set up your work station you should begin to think about *how* you are going to position everything. You will soon be spending hundreds and hundreds of hours at your computer. Computer-related injuries are on the rise. Many private companies as well as government agencies are spending thousands and thousands of dollars researching the ergonomics of the computer operator and his or her environment. Millions are being spent on redesigning the computerized office. It is very important that you place yourself and all of your equipment in a comfortable relationship that will keep you healthy for years to come.

One of the most important factors that you can use as a guideline is comfort. If you find your back aching after an hour at the computer then something is wrong. But comfort can't be your only criterion. Many injuries won't be detected for several years — injuries that are so severe that therapy and/or surgery may be necessary in your hands, arms, eyes, or back.

The American National Standards Institute (ANSI) has described some other factors to consider when you begin to set up your CAD station. Here are some of those factors.

Chair

A good CAD chair is a rolling multi-adjustable typing-style chair. Adjustability is a requirement that cannot be compromised. Both the seat height and back height should be fully adjustable, as should the back tilt angle. Seat height adjustment range should be from a height of 16" to 20½". Seat width should be at least 18.2". The seat depth should be a minimum of 12". The seat back should be centered on your lower back. Avoid armchairs. Arms are not a good idea since they can inhibit arm movement.

Draw with your feet flat on the floor. The height of the chair seat should be adjusted to allow you to place your feet on the floor with your legs bent at a 90° angle. If your feet don't reach the floor don't cheat and bend your legs at an angle more than 90°. Instead, use a footrest.

Your back should be straight up and down at a 90° angle with the lower back fully and solidly supported.

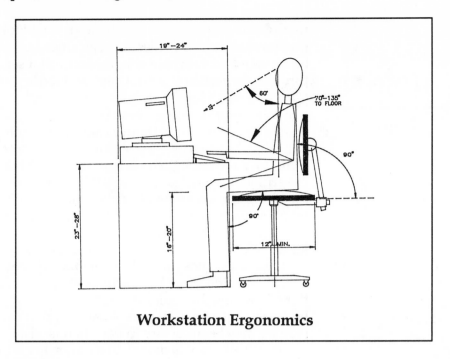

Workstation Ergonomics

Input device table

The keyboard and tablet or mouse area should be arranged on your table or desk so that as you work, your lower arms are at an angle somewhere between 70° and 135° to the floor; 90° (parallel to the floor) should be your goal. Your legs must be able to move around freely under the desk. A typical desk height should be somewhere between 23" and 28". A minimum width is 24". This is for the keyboard alone. More width is required depending on whether you are using a mouse (about 12 additional inches) or a digitizing tablet (about 24 additional inches). A minimum depth is 19"-24".

Monitor

The monitor should be placed so that, as you work, the top of the screen is never higher than eye level. Looking somewhat down at the screen is acceptable (60° maximum). However, you should never find yourself looking up at the screen. Tilt stands are available for most monitors if yours didn't come with one.

In most cases the monitor is placed on top of the computer box (central processing unit or CPU) just behind the keyboard. If this puts the monitor too high for you, then move the CPU to the side or below your desk on its side. Special mounts are available that hold your computer in this position.

Avoid glare on the screen. Low table lamps or drafting type lamps in the room are better than ceiling fixtures. Turn off all overhead lighting! Glare screens are available that will help considerably. Avoid shadows on the keyboard and digitizing tablet by having several light sources on in the room.

Take a break every hour for at least ten minutes. Studies show that many computer-related eye injuries are the result of the static-focus environment of the computer work station. During your break, do some focus therapy. Alternately look at things close to you and then farther away. Your eyes will be the first part of your body to tell you to quit working when you still have three sheets of drafting to do. Take good care of them during your drafting sessions and you should go away from each session healthy and less fatigued.

Platform Support (Release 11)

This table shows you all of the computer systems that AutoCAD will run on. It is important to note each platform's operating system level. For instance, the Macintosh must have a 6.0.3 (or higher) operating system in order to support AutoCAD. Many machines also require additional math co-processors. Consult a dealer who is familiar with AutoCAD when designing your own workstation.

Workstation	Operating System
AutoCAD 386	DOS 3.3+
AutoCAD 286	DOS 2.0+
Sun Sparc	Sun OS 4.0+
DEC 3100	Ultrix
Macintosh	System 6.0.3+
OS/2	OS/2 PM 1.1/1.2
Xenix	Xenix
Apollo	Aegis 9.7+
DEC VAX	VMS 4.0+
Sun 386i	Sun OS 4.0+
Sun 3	Sun OS 4.0+

PART II

THE CAD ENVIRONMENT

DRAWING COMMANDS
EDITING COMMANDS
DISPLAY COMMANDS
DIMENSIONING
PROTOTYPE DRAWINGS

2 AutoCAD's DRAWING ENVIRONMENT

> **FUNCTION**: To explore AutoCAD's drawing environment. AutoCAD is a world with its own rules and language. Before actually drawing anything, take time to get acquainted with this system of specific protocol and multiple menus.

As you will soon begin to see, AutoCAD is quite complex but not difficult to learn. It is complex in the sense that there is so much to it. It does just about anything you might want a CAD program to do. To get it to do all of these things you must learn its "language" of commands. You will be learning a new vocabulary in order to communicate with the program and the computer. But here's the good news — it's all in English! To draw a line for instance, it couldn't be any simpler. The first step is to select the DRAW command, and the second step is to select the LINE command. Then you start drawing with your puck or mouse. That's it! There are no complex secret codes to type in such as **SHIFT D — <- — F5 — BACKSPACE**. Since drawing lines is what you will be doing most of the time with AutoCAD, you're well on your way to mastering the program.

By the way, as you read on, you will notice some words, such as LINE or DRAW, printed in a special way. This special type style refers to an AutoCAD menu selection. If an instruction in this book tells you to ". . . pick LINE . . ." it is telling you to find that command in either the pull-down menus, Screen Menu Area, or tablet overlay and select it with your mouse or puck.

Formatting Floppy Disks

A floppy disk must be formatted — electronically organizationally prepared — before it is ready to record your data. The disk is sold to you unformatted. That is because any floppy disk may be used in any computer, whether it is a Mac or an IBM. You don't usually buy Mac disks or IBM disks (although these pre-formatted disks do exist). Instead you buy a disk by the size and density required (see your computer manual for the specifications for your particular computer) and customize it for your computer by having its DOS do the formatting. Different disk operating systems like their disks formatted in different ways.

You see, each drawing on your disk is stored as a file — a drawing file or a backup file. The computer needs an organized filing cabinet before it can begin sorting these files for you. Formatting a floppy disk is like preparing an empty filing cabinet with hanging files and file folders.

Formatting a floppy disk is a rather simple task and it must be performed on each new disk. You may want to get into the habit of formatting your entire box of new disks all at once. If you prefer to format one or two disks at a time, avoid confusion by placing the adhesive disk label on the formatted disks only.

Formatting erases everything on a disk permanently. For this reason it should only be done to an empty floppy disk or to a disk that you want to "erase." Read your computer's DOS manual to find out how to format a disk for your computer. Each disk operating system has a unique method for doing this.

If you are using an IBM or compatible computer using IBM DOS:

At the C:\> type:

C:\>format a: (ENTER)

or if you are in the drawing editor screen, type SHELL first. This command allows you to perform DOS functions without leaving your drawing session. In about a minute the computer will ask if you want to format another disk. That's all there is to it.

| N O T E ! | The a: in the above command is very important. If that were left off and you simply were to type C:\>format the contents of the hard disk would be erased. This would wipe out any and all programs previously loaded onto the disk. Be careful! |

In order to distinguish formatted from unformatted disks put an adhesive label on all of your formatted disks. For the purposes of the exercises in this book you will need to have two disks always ready and formatted. Label one WORK DISK and label the other BACKUP DISK. You will be saving your work on both disks at all times.

Once your IBM DOS formatted disk has been formatted on your IBM or compatible computer, it can be used on any similar IBM or compatible computer. Once your Mac disk has been formatted it can be used on any similar Mac. If you attempt to use a disk that has not been formatted, the computer will tell you right away. The message will not be as simple as DISK NOT FORMATTED. Instead it will be something a bit more cryptic such as:

General error reading drive A:

Abort? Retry? Ignore?

Format your floppy disks now, before going any further. You're about to start using AutoCAD and you will need these disks right away.

Entering the AutoCAD Environment

On IBM compatible computers you will see C> once you have gotten past the preliminary startup routine. This is called the C prompt. This tells you that the C drive (hard drive) is waiting for a command; it is ready to do your bidding. The flashing line or box is called the cursor. The cursor indicates where any typing that you do will be seen. You can usually move the position of the cursor with the arrow keys.

To activate the AutoCAD program, type ACAD.

MEMO

If you are not already in the AutoCAD directory, or if you haven't created a batch file that automatically changes to your AutoCAD directory, you need to first type:

CD\ACAD

See your *AutoCAD Reference Manual* or *Installation Guide* for more information on this.

Next, to get this or any other command to take effect, push the **ENTER** key (this key is the **RETURN** key on some computers).

After some information flashes by on the screen and a couple of **ENTER** key presses pass by you (as directed by the program) the AutoCAD Main Menu will appear on the screen. This special menu is the only menu called the Main Menu. Although you will encounter many menus in your AutoCAD travels, this is the only menu called the Main Menu. Note that the Main Menu options may vary depending on your particular AutoCAD Release. Release 11 for instance provides a drawing recovery feature that is not a part of earlier versions of AutoCAD.

From the Main Menu you can make certain things happen. You can:

---

0. Exit AutoCAD
1. Begin a NEW drawing
2. Edit an EXISTING drawing
3. Plot a drawing
4. Printer Plot a drawing
5. Configure AutoCAD
6. File Utilities
7. Compile shape/font description files
8. Convert old drawing file
9. Recover damaged drawing

In order to begin drawing, you need to select

1. Begin a NEW drawing.

To do this, you simply press the **1** key and then press the **ENTER** key. All of the menu items on the Main Menu are selected by simply entering the number that precedes it.

AutoCAD now asks you for the name of your new drawing.

MEMO

A computer running IBM DOS cannot have a drawing name longer than eight letters, numbers, or symbols. The letters A-Z and the numbers 0-9 can be used as well as the symbols $ - _

The Macintosh II has no such drawing name restriction. However, if you keep the name confined to eight figures and add a .dwg file designation, drawings done on the Mac can be read on IBM and compatible computers. Additionally, any drawing created on an IBM or compatible computer can be read on a Macintosh II computer without any further alteration or translation.

Before you name the drawing you must decide if you are going to save the drawing on the hard drive or on a floppy disk. If you will be using the same computer each time you work on a drawing, then the hard drive would be your choice. If you are in a computer lab or an office where you may be continuing your drawing at a later date, possibly on one of the other computers, then you should make your work portable by saving it on a floppy disk — the A drive.

Let's put this drawing on a floppy disk.

1. Insert your formatted floppy work disk into the computer.

2. To let the computer know that you want this drawing saved on the floppy disk you should type A: in front of the name of the drawing.

3. Name the drawing TEST1.

4. Type in A:TEST1

5. Press the **ENTER** key.

A blank Drawing Editor screen should now appear. If you had wanted to save this drawing onto the hard drive it would not have been necessary to type C: in front of the drawing name. Instead you would simply have typed:

TEST1

> WHY? The hard drive is the default drive. That means that if you don't specify a drive, the computer will always assume that you mean the C drive.

In a few seconds a new screen should appear. This is called the drawing editor. Here is where you will be spending most of your time creating new drawings or editing existing ones.

Giving AutoCAD a Command

Let's actually give AutoCAD a command. Let's go through the steps necessary to draw a circle. These steps are called the command structure.

The command for drawing a circle is CIRCLE. You can find the CIRCLE command in one of three places:

1. One of the places commands are located is in the Screen Menu Area along the right side of the screen.

   The menu currently being displayed in the Screen Menu Area is the Root Menu. The Root Menu commands are:

   SETUP, BLOCKS, DIM, DISPLAY, DRAW, EDIT, INQUIRE, LAYER, SETTINGS, PLOT, UCS, UTILITY, 3D, ASHADE, SAVE.

   Notice that although there are many commands listed here, CIRCLE isn't one of them. This is called the Root Menu because *all* of the AutoCAD commands "branch" out from one of these primary commands. To draw a circle, you must first go through a few related menus. This idea of commands branching off of other commands is called a menu hierarchy. If you are using a mouse or trackball you will rely heavily on the Screen Menu area to access commands. Using the Screen Menu area requires that you memorize AutoCAD's menu hierarchy. Don't be frightened off by this idea. It is quite logical and with very little effort on your part you will find yourself having memorized it without even realizing it.

   Investigate the circle menu hierarchy by sitting down at your computer and going through these next few steps.

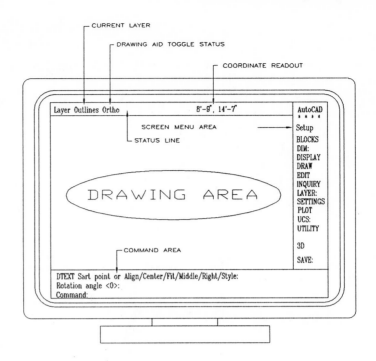

```
AutoCAD
* * * *
Setup

BLOCKS
DIM:
DISPLAY
DRAW
EDIT
INQUIRY
LAYER:
SETTINGS
PLOT
UCS:
UTILITY

3D

SAVE:
```

```
AutoCAD
* * * *
ARC
ATTDEF:
CIRCLE:
DONUT:
DTEXT:
ELLIPSE:
HATCH:
INSERT:
LINE:
MINSERT:
OFFSET:
PLINE:

next

_LAST_
DRAW
EDIT
```

```
AutoCAD
* * * *
CIRCLE

CEN,RAD:
CEN,DIA:
2 POINT:
3 POINT
TTR:
```

```
_LAST_
DRAW
EDIT
```

a. To draw a circle, you must first select the DRAW menu. Highlight DRAW with your pointing device (puck, mouse, or stylus).

b. Select or "pick" this menu by pressing the pick button or pushing down on your stylus.

The Root Menu should now be replaced by the DRAW menu. CIRCLE is one of the many drawing commands found on this DRAW menu.

Some options and variations of commands cannot be found here. If this is your menu selection method, you may want to occasionally mix one of the features that can only be found in the Pull Down Menus.

c. Select CIRCLE.

The DRAW menu has now been replaced with the CIRCLE menu. This menu gives you a choice of several methods to draw a circle — CEN,RAD; CEN,DIA; 2POINT; 3POINT; TTR (we'll discuss these options in detail later on). To actually begin drawing the circle, you would then select one of these options.

MEMO

Commands are always followed by a ":". Other menu items (CIRCLE, for instance) lead you to a command (CEN,RAD:, for example.)

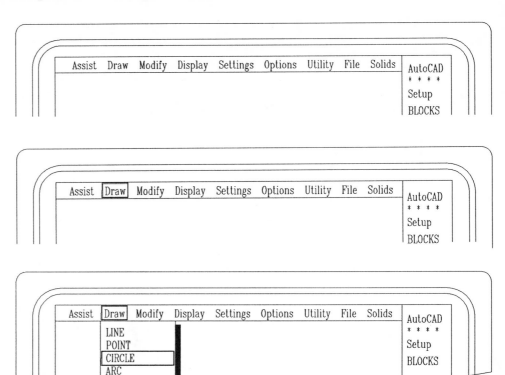

2. Commands can also be invoked from the Pull Down Menu Bar at the top of the screen.

   To activate the CIRCLE function, you would:

   a. Highlight the Pull Down Menu bar by moving your crosshairs to the top of the screen.

   b. Highlight and then pick DRAW.

   c. Highlight and then pick CIRCLE.

      Now you can begin drawing circles. Not all commands and their options can be found here. You will have to use the Screen Menu Area some of the time.

3. If you have a digitizing tablet, the CIRCLE command can be found in the Draw Commands area of the tablet. There is even a picture of a circle to make things quicker. Not all commands can be found on the digitizing tablet. Therefore it's a good idea to familiarize yourself with the Screen Menu hierarchy as well as the Pull Down Menus.

Of course you can also type in any command. If you are a "power typist" you may find this method preferable to memorizing the menu hierarchy.

In general, the Tablet Menu method is the quickest way to draw in AutoCAD. The Screen Menu method is the slowest. Invoking the CIRCLE command took three steps. The Pull Down Menu method can be a one or two or more step process, but generally speaking it will be quicker than the Screen Menu method.

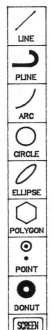

MEMO

This book will not describe each command selection method for every command and every input selection device. After the first couple of commands, the text will simply read "Select CIRCLE." You will be on your own to go through the steps involved with the method you have chosen.

You should familiarize yourself with all three options for selecting commands and decide which of the three you prefer, based on your particular input selection device.

You have just been indoctrinated into AutoCAD's menu hierarchy system. To return to the Root Menu, select AUTOCAD (always at the top of the Root Menu and every Screen Menu) at any time.

It's important to keep an eye on the Command Prompt Area at the bottom of the screen. Many times you will be frustrated because you have selected a command but AutoCAD doesn't seem to be cooperating. This is usually because the command, although selected, hasn't loaded into the Command Prompt Line. This is often due to AutoCAD waiting for more instructions about a previously selected command. Only after the selected command appears in the Command Prompt Line will it be possible to use it. AutoCAD often prompts you for more information. It does not like to proceed if it hasn't been given the information that it needs. You must check the Command Prompt Area whenever you are selecting commands in order to know how to proceed properly.

Quitting

AutoCAD gives you three options for ending a drawing session. You can simply end the drawing session without saving it. You can save the drawing without ending the session. Or you can end the session and save it simultaneously while at the same time making a special backup file copy of your drawing on your disk. The next section of the book will explain all of these options to you. To get out of this current drawing session and return to the Main Menu, select QUIT and answer yes to the follow-up question that AutoCAD will pose to you.

QUIT can be found in the FILE Pull Down Menu located at the top of the screen. It can also be found after selecting UTILITY on the Root Menu. You can also find a QUIT box on the Tablet Menu. You may find that simply typing QUIT at the command prompt is the quickest and easiest method.

3 LEAVING AutoCAD'S DRAWING ENVIRONMENT

> **FUNCTION**: Leaving the drawing environment must be done in a very particular way. The QUIT and END commands discussed in this chapter are used when you want to end an AutoCAD drawing session. The SAVE command can be used to periodically record your work during a drawing session.

Although it might seem that these three commands accomplish similar tasks — getting you out of and/or saving the drawing session — they each function quite differently. It is important that you understand these differences and choose the proper command at the right time. Being careless about these commands can result in the loss of a drawing that took many hours to complete.

QUIT

QUIT ends your drawing session and takes you back to the Main Menu.

Locating the QUIT command
- the Root Menu under UTILITY
- the Pull Down Menu under FILE
- the Tablet Menu

As is the case with all AutoCAD commands, it can also be typed in.

Here's how QUIT works

1. After selecting QUIT AutoCAD will ask if you:

   Really want to discard all changes to drawing?

2. Type Y if you don't want to save any of your work. Type N if you want to save any changes you have made since your last SAVE.

3. If you typed Y, AutoCAD will return to the black and white Main Menu.

4. When you are back at the Main Menu after choosing QUIT, you can then select: 0 Exit AutoCAD in order to exit the AutoCAD program.

The QUIT command discards any new work that you have done in that drawing session and it discards any editing or updating that you may have done if the drawing is an existing one. IT DOES NOT SAVE ANY OF YOUR WORK!

SAVE

SAVE records any drawing or updating that you have done up to that moment onto your hard or floppy disk. You can continue to work on your drawing after you SAVE. SAVE does not end your drawing session. It does not exit you from the drawing editor and return you to the Main Menu.

Locating the SAVE command
- the Root Menu Area
- the Pull Down Menu under FILE
- the Tablet Menu

One method of ending a drawing session is to follow the SAVE command with the QUIT command. When you do so AutoCAD will ask you if you:

Really want to discard all changes to drawing?

You may be too frightened to move at this point since it looks like you're about to lose everything. The question is really an incomplete one. It is really asking you if you want to discard your work since the last time you SAVEd. Since you just SAVEd and haven't done any more work between SAVE and QUIT, you can rest assured that nothing will be discarded.

The SAVE command makes a new drawing file (.dwg) that replaces any existing files of the same name. Any backup files (.bak) are cycled as in the END command (see END).

I recommend that you set an alarm that will go off every 15-30 minutes. Each time the alarm rings SAVE your work. If some disaster does occur during a drawing session, the most time you will have to make up is 15-30 minutes.

END

END saves your work and returns you to the Main Menu.

Locating the END command

- the Root Menu under UTILITY
- the Pull Down Menu under FILE
- the Tablet Menu

END combines the two previous commands. When you choose END, AutoCAD will save your work and then return you to the Main Menu. You can then select:

0 Exit AutoCAD

in order to leave the AutoCAD program completely.

At the same time that your work is saved with the END command, AutoCAD will make a backup file (.bak) of your drawing and save it on your disk. For instance, a regular drawing file is saved as TEST1.dwg. When you use END another file is made and is filed as TEST1.bak. Every time you work on this drawing TEST1 and then save it using the END command, it is saved as TEST1.dwg. The previous version of the drawing, the one you had on disk from your session yesterday, is also saved but is renamed TEST1.bak. The AutoCAD manual refers to this "roll over" process as "cycling." It occurs each time you END a drawing.

If a disaster occurs in which AutoCAD will not allow you to access your drawing (and believe me these things do happen — particularly if your disk has become overloaded), there is hope of at least partial recovery with a .bak file.

To access a .bak file, go to the Main Menu and select choice number 6, File Utilities. The secret is to utilize the *renaming* feature of this utility. To use this element, you must first throw out that inaccessible .dwg file — *delete* the file. Next, you rename your TEST1.bak file as TEST1.dwg. That old and out of date drawing can then be used to start picking up the pieces. A disaster yes, but starting from scratch would be an even bigger one.

The very best solution to keeping yourself out of these messes is to keep up-to-date backup floppies! SAVE on a floppy backup every fifteen minutes.

MEMO

Knowing how to use these three commands correctly can save you hours of recovering accidentally erased <u>PLANS</u> and <u>LIGHT PLOTS</u>.

AutoCAD often warns you if a command you are about to issue could have disastrous results. This warning usually contains the message **Are you sure?**

If you see this warning in the command area after you have selected a command, it means that what you are about to do could be catastrophic to the drawing. Stop and think about what you are doing before you go any further.

---

4 FIRST DRAWING SESSION — DRAWING LINES

> **FUNCTION**: The LINE command allows you to draw a single line or a series of connected lines. The line may be continuous, dashed, dotted, a center line, or a host of other variations. It may represent the outline of a flat, lighting instrument, or costume pattern.

Lines are an important fundamental drawing component to just about everything that you plan to accomplish with AutoCAD. It is one of the most important commands to master.

LINE

As with all other AutoCAD commands, the LINE command deals with a menu structure — a sequence of steps that must be followed in an exact order. In each case these steps involve highlighting command names (or pointing to them on a tablet) found in a list called a menu. This is followed by selecting the command in a technique called picking.

Let's draw our first line. Between the two lines drawn below, find the method that you will be using to draw with AutoCAD.

> ### MEMO
> Your AutoCAD program is not set up to deal with feet and inches yet. You may have noticed that all measurements are in a strange decimal increment. Don't worry! You'll soon be able to draw ½" scale PLANS and LIGHT PLOTS. Right now though, play along with this system until you're ready to set up feet and inches.

Mouse/Puck Root Menu Method
    a. From the Root Menu pick DRAW.
    b. pick LINE.

Mouse/Puck Pull Down Menu Method
    a. Make the Pull Down Menu bar appear by moving your cross hairs to the top of the screen.
    b. pick DRAW.
    c. pick LINE.

Tablet Method
    a. pick LINE.

The Command Prompt Line now says:

    Line from point:

AutoCAD is telling you that before it can draw your line, it must know the location of the beginning of the line. In response:

1. Move your pointing device (mouse, puck, or stylus) in order to place the cross hairs where you intend to start your line.

2. Pick a point.

    "Pick" is a mouse/puck/stylus term. When the book tells you to pick a point or an object, it means to put the cross hairs on the desired location of the screen and hit your pick button. It can also mean to invoke a command by highlighting it on a menu and then hitting your pick button to select it.

The Command Prompt Line says:

    To point:

AutoCAD is asking you where the end of your line is going to be. In response:

3. Move your pointing device (mouse, puck, or stylus) in order to place the cross hairs where you intend to end your line. Moving the end of the line around like this is called "dragging" the line. As you drag the end of the line you will notice the line getting longer and shorter. This is called the "rubber band" effect.

4. Pick the end of the line. You have now drawn your first line.

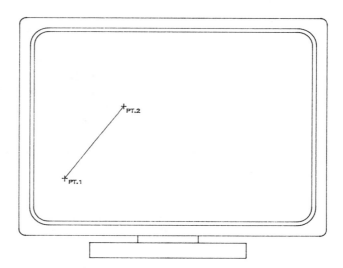

Notice that the rubber banding is still in effect. AutoCAD is ready to draw another line connected to the one you just drew. The Command Prompt says:

    to point:

5. To draw a line connected to this one pick another point on the screen. AutoCAD again says:

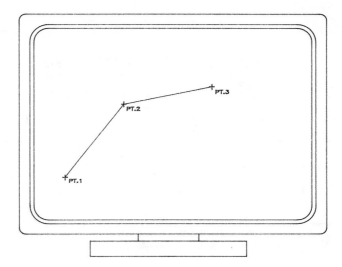

to point:

6. Push the **ENTER** button on your pointing device (or hit the **ENTER** key on your keyboard) to "break" the rubber band. It should now be blank after the Command Prompt. AutoCAD is waiting for your next command.

7. Select QUIT in order to get back to the Main Menu. Remember that you must always go through the Main Menu when beginning and ending a drawing (or editing) session.

MEMO

Here is a reminder about how the QUIT command works. After you choose QUIT AutoCAD will ask you if you Really want to discard all changes? This is a warning to you that if you go any further with the command, AutoCAD will toss it out forever. QUIT does not save your work. If you want to save your work then you want to use either the SAVE or END commands.

It is safe to QUIT after first using SAVE as long as you have not altered the drawing in any way between the two commands.

As you can see, the Command Prompt Area is a terrific guide through a command's structure. AutoCAD novices often get stuck trying to figure out what the next step is and forget to look at the Command Prompt resulting in many wasted minutes staring at the screen — frozen. If you're not sure what the next step is in any command, AutoCAD is usually prompting you on the Command Prompt Line.

MEMO

You can change your mind after selecting a command.
a. If you've typed in the command on the command line but haven't hit the **ENTER** key, you can use the **BACKSPACE** key.
b. If you have hit the **ENTER** key after issuing a command but suddenly realize it's not the command you want, you can CANCEL the command by pushing the **CONTROL** and C keys simultaneously.

There is also a CANCEL area on the Tablet Menu. One of the buttons on the puck is a CANCEL button as well.

Entities

Earlier, when you drew your first line, you also created your first entity. Entity is a special term that AutoCAD uses to describe a basic editable drawing unit. A line is a basic editable drawing unit. So is a circle. Two lines are two entities. Two lines connected to each other are two entities. A square drawn with the LINE command is four entities.

Complex drawings are made up of many entities. For instance, a circle inside of a square is composed of five entities — the four sides of the square and the circle. The concept of the entity becomes important when you go to edit the drawing. If you later decide that you want to erase the square from your drawing and leave only the circle, you will need to be sure to pick all four entities that make up the square. You see, AutoCAD doesn't understand that there is a square there at all, it only understands that there are four lines connected together.

There *is* a way to make a single entity square. By using the POLYGON command, you can make a four-sided polygon (a square). AutoCAD does understand that a multi-sided polygon is a single entity.

Which system is better for making the square? Well, it all depends. If you think that you might want to eliminate one of the sides of the square later on, then the LINE command is the one to use. If you know that you would never be doing that type of editing but you think that you might move the square around on your drawing until the placement is just right, then POLYGON is the command of choice. When it comes time to move the square, you can pick just one side and the entire polygon will react. If you tried that with your LINE-command square then only the side that you picked would move.

It's important to plan carefully, in advance, the method you will use for creating equilateral multi-sided geometric shapes. Using the right command can save you many minutes later on.

Project 1

LINE

1. At the Main Menu select 1 Begin a New Drawing. Name this new drawing a:PROJ1. Another way of saying this is that the file name will be a:PROJ1.

2. In the center of the drawing area, draw a series of connected lines representing a simple FLOOR PLAN (see example below).

3. On the right and left sides of the screen draw a series of single unconnected lines. These will represent tormentors (legs) for masking the sides of the stage.

4. SAVE this drawing on your work disk.

5. Swap disks. SAVE this drawing again on your backup disk.

6. Swap disks again. Your work disk should be in the computer when you exit this drawing.

7. Select QUIT.

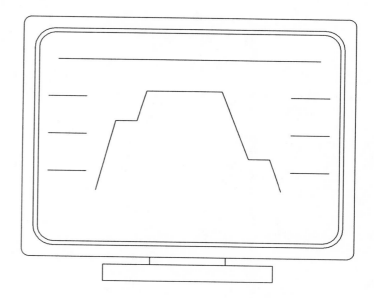

5 ORGANIZING YOUR DRAWING DISKS

> **FUNCTION**: The menus and commands explained in this section are all designed to keep your AutoCAD world in order. Before too long you will have dozens of drawings and dozens of floppy disks filled with your drawings. Locating old drawings for incorporation into new designs or trying to recover from a crashed disk crisis can be a nightmare if you aren't organized from the very beginning. Study this section very carefully and don't leave it until you fully understand it. Struggling to unearth a long lost drawing from poorly organized files can be like trying to find a needle in an electronic haystack.

The Main Menu

The Main Menu is the black and white menu you must first use before doing anything with the AutoCAD program. With it you can do a host of functions from leaving the program to plotting out your drawings. Let's take a look at the options in the Main Menu and what they mean.

Main Menu options

0. Exit AutoCAD

> After leaving a drawing session, you will return to the Main Menu and then select this option before exiting the AutoCAD program.

1. Begin a NEW drawing

> You select this option when you are ready to start a new drawing on a blank drawing screen, or from a prototype drawing.

2. Edit an EXISTING drawing

> This is the menu option you use to edit or continue to work on a drawing that already exists.

3. Plot a drawing

> This selection is for plotting out your drawing on a pen plotter.

4. Printer Plot a drawing

> This selection is for printing out your drawing on a dot matrix printer.

5. Configure AutoCAD

> Choosing this allows you to tell AutoCAD what hardware you are going to be using (printer model, digitizing tablet size, etc.). You must configure AutoCAD when you first install the program on your computer and every time you add, delete, or change hardware.

6. File Utilities

> Selecting File Utilities takes you right into another menu — the File Utilities Menu. File Utilities allows you to perform organizational

functions such as looking at the names of your drawings, copying files, renaming files, etc.

7. Compile shape/font description files

This complex and advanced utility allows you to load and name AutoCAD-recognizable custom shape patterns and fonts.

8. Convert old drawing file

This selection converts AutoCAD drawings that were made on one version (Release) of AutoCAD for use on your current version.

9. Recover drawing file (on AutoCAD Release 11 and beyond)

This selection helps you recover "damaged" drawing files. Refer to the AutoCAD manual for assistance.

You will be trying out these various options from time to time as you go through the exercises in this book.

File Utilities Menu

The File Utilities Menu has been singled out because it is your primary organizational tool. Let's inspect the File Utilities Menu and see how its options can benefit you.

File Utilities Menu options

0. Exit File Utilities Menu

When you are finished with a File Utilities session, select this option to return to the Main Menu.

1. List Drawing files

Select this option when you want to see a list of your .dwg (drawing) files.

2. List user specified files

With this option you can see a listing of files that you specify. Option #1 allows you to look at .dwg files only, but with this option you can specify and search for backup (.bak) files as well.

3. Delete files

Use this option to get rid of a file.

4. Rename files

This is the option you use to rename a file. You might want to change the name of a file for reasons of clarity. Or you may have had to delete a crashed file that could not be retrieved and now need to transform the .bak version of the file into the .dwg version.

5. Copy file

Use the Copy file option to copy a file from one disk to another — hard to floppy or floppy to hard.

6. Unlock file (on some later AutoCAD Releases)

Used to unlock drawing files.

Here are some typical functions that you will need to perform from time to time using the File Utilities Menu.

List your drawing files

To see what drawing files are on your hard disk drive:
(Hit the **ENTER** key to complete each step)

1. Type 1

2. AutoCAD says: Enter drive or directory:

   Type a:

   This will give you a list of drawing files on your floppy disk. Type c: or hit **ENTER** to see those on your hard drive.

Copy a file from floppy disk to hard disk

To transfer a drawing file:

1. Type 5

2. AutoCAD says: Enter name of source file:

   Type a:name.dwg

3. AutoCAD says: Enter name of destination file:

   Type c:name.dwg

   To copy a file from your hard disk to your floppy disk, type c: in Step #2 and a: in Step #3.

Throwing out a crashed drawing file and replacing it with its backup

First of all there is no reason to find yourself in this terrifying situation. These predicaments are completely avoidable — MAKE BACKUPS! To make a backup:

a. If you are drawing on your hard disk, SAVE on both your hard disk drive and a floppy disk every 15-30 minutes.

b. If you are drawing and SAVEing on a floppy disk, SAVE on a WORK and a BACKUP floppy disk every 15-30 minutes.

If you have gotten yourself into an "I've got to recover the only .bak file of the only copy of my drawing in existence" quandary, here are some steps that you might try.

1. The first thing to do is to get rid of the crashed file that AutoCAD refuses to have anything to do with. (Let's call this file a:name.dwg.)

   If you feel that you can't part with it or are in such a panic that you can't think straight and aren't really sure that the file is irretrievable, then make a copy of it on a floppy disk. (An empty floppy is preferable since most of these complications are caused by floppy disks that are stuffed to the gills with drawings.)

   Before doing any of this, however, you need to see if there is a .bak version of a:name.dwg.

Select option #2 List user specified files.

2. AutoCAD says: Enter file search specification:

3. Type .bak

   AutoCAD will now list all of your .bak files. Is there an a:name.bak file? If not — DON'T GO ANY FURTHER!! If so, go to the next step.

4. Now you need to be able to look at and draw on this drawing. To do so you must make it a drawing file (you can't draw on a backup file).

   Select the Rename files option.

   Type #4

5. AutoCAD says: Enter current file name:

   Type a:name.bak

6. AutoCAD says: Enter new file name:

   type a:name.dwg

   Now you have a new a:name drawing. Hopefully it's not too old. Backup (.bak) files are created whenever you end a drawing session.

   It is actually the old drawing that was made obsolete by your ended update. Rather than completely deleting these old drawings, AutoCAD tucks them away and renames them as backup files.

FILES

The FILES command is a shortcut to the File Utilities Menu. You see, with all of the other choices in the Main Menu, you must leave your drawing in order to access the Main Menu. Choice #6, File Utilities, has a shortcut — the FILES command. By typing FILES at the command prompt on your drawing screen, you will instantaneously be taken out of your drawing session and brought directly into the File Utilities Menu. The return trip back to your drawing session is just as simple and just as speedy; press the **F1** (flip screen) toggle key.

PROJECT 2

FILE ORGANIZATION

1. Look up the titles of the drawing files in the hard disk drive AutoCAD directory.

2. Copy two of them to your BACKUP floppy.

3. Rename one of these drawings on your floppy a:MIZPLAN.dwg

4. Rename the other a:MIZELEV1.dwg

5. Delete MIZPLAN.

6 MAKING GEOMETRIC SHAPES

> **FUNCTION**: POLYGON draws complex geometric shapes quite easily. This command is helpful for drawing geometric fabric patterns, newel posts in a PLAN, or any number of lighting symbols for the light plot.

POLYGON

The POLYGON command is used to draw multi-sided equilateral polygons. This includes the triangle and the square. You probably won't use the command too often, but it is a convenient one to know. If you have tried drawing these shapes in manual pencil and paper drafting, you know what a nightmare it can be.

A polygon that has been created with the POLYGON command is a single entity.

Here is the command sequence for finding and using the POLYGON command.

Mouse/Puck Root Menu Method
- a. From the Root Menu pick DRAW.
- b. pick next.
- c. pick POLYGON.

Mouse/Puck Pull Down Menu Method
(Release 11 and beyond only)
- a. pick DRAW
- b. pick POLYGON

Tablet Method
- a. pick POLYGON from the DRAW area

The Command Prompt Line now says:

Polygon number of sides?

AutoCAD is telling you that before it can go any further it must know the number of sides that you want your polygon to have. In response:

1. Type in 3 and then push the **ENTER** button on the keyboard.

2. AutoCAD responds with:

Edge/<Center> of Polygon

This means that AutoCAD draws a polygon in one of two ways — by specifying the edge placement on your drawing first or by specifying the center placement first. Multiple options such as these are typical of many AutoCAD command structures. To choose one or the other you type the capitalized letters in the choice statement. In this case it would be the E or the C. You can usually find these choices in the Menu Area also. In these cases you simply highlight your choice and then pick it.

Notice that the <Center> choice is contained in brackets. If your choice is the one found in the brackets, you don't need to type it in or highlight it. In this case you would begin placing the center of the polygon on your drawing immediately. Choices in brackets are called the default choices. Default choices are the choices that most people would select. If you were to opt for Edge, then the next time you chose this command you would find that <Edge> is the new default. In this way AutoCAD customizes itself to your needs to make each drawing session go a little faster.

3. Using the CENTER option, our next step is to move the cross hairs to where we want the center of the polygon to be. Since CENTER is the default we don't need to select it.

4. In the Command Area AutoCAD says:

    <Center of polygon>

AutoCAD is asking you to pick the center point of the polygon. To do so move your cross hairs to the correct position and pick that point (pt. 1).

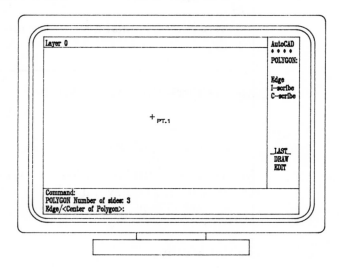

5. In the Command Area AutoCAD says: Inscribed in circle / Circumscribed about circle (I/C):

Neither of these choices is in brackets. You must make a choice by picking or typing one or the other.

Inscribed in circle means that in relation to a circle, our pentagon would be drawn with its points touching the circle if we chose this option. Circumscribed about circle means that the center of each edge of the pentagon would be touching the circle.

If you were placing a 3-sided periaktoid on a 4' diameter turntable in a PLAN then you would select Inscribed. If the turntable needs to rotate inside our 3-sided piece of scenery then you would want to select Circumscribed.

6. We want to place our 3-sided unit on top of the 4' turntable so select I for Inscribed:

    Select I

7. AutoCAD responds with:

    Radius of circle?

8. Type in 4 and **ENTER**. (You will be working with feet and inches a little later on. For now, continue to work in decimal inches.)

MEMO

The little white crosses you see are blips. AutoCAD puts them there for you to use as a reference. For instance, the center of the imaginary circle is marked if you need to reference other scenery to it. It is not a part of the drawing and will soon go away. This feature is called blipmode and can be turned off. To do so select the SETTINGS pull down menu. Then select DRAWING AIDS or DRAWING TOOLS (depending on your AutoCAD version). You will see a box labeled Blips. A check in the box turns blipmode on and no check in the box turns it off. Un-check the box by moving the arrow to the box and picking it. Finally, pick the OK box.

You can clear your drawing of blips from time to time by one of several methods. One method is to select the REDRAW bar on the Tablet Menu. Another method is to type in REDRAW at the Command Prompt. A third way is to access the REDRAW command by first picking the DISPLAY menu in the Root Menu. A fourth method is to hit the **F7** (grid toggle) key twice.

You could also drag the radius with your stylus, mouse, or puck, watch the pentagon get larger and smaller on the screen, and then pick the radius (pt. 2). AutoCAD doesn't show you a 4' circle. It relates the polygon to an *imaginary* circle.

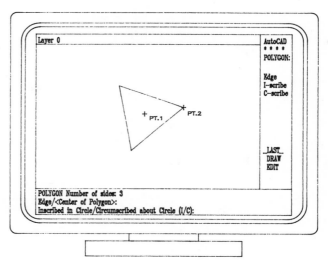

POLYGON

1. Begin a new drawing called a:PROJ3.

2. Use the POLYGON command to draw a triangle. Use the Center and Iscribe options. Use a radius of about 1.5.

3. Draw the following additional shapes using the options and radii described below:

   SQUARE Edge (place the first edge corner in the upper right corner of the screen, place the second edge corner at the bottom of the screen).

   PENTAGON Center Iscribe about 2

   HEXAGON Center Circum about 1.5

   HEPTAGON Center Iscribe about 1.5

   OCTAGON Center Circum about 1.5

Example:

4. SAVE on your WORK disk.

5. SAVE on your BACKUP disk.

6. Put your WORK disk back in the computer.

7. QUIT.

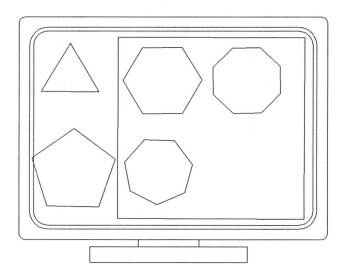

7 DISPLAY TECHNIQUES PART I

> **FUNCTION**: The display commands are designed to help you manipulate how you see what's on the screen. With these commands you will be able to zoom in or out on any part of your drawing and pan side to side or up and down. You will even be able to save any of these views for instant future reference. You can zoom in on an individual ELEVATION and recall that same display later on in the drawing session.

ZOOM

Using this command is like placing a zoom lens on your monitor. It is an important command and one that you are likely to use more than all others. It may seem inconceivable to create detailed scenic, lighting, or costume drawings on a small 12" monitor. A typical ½" scale LIGHT PLOT is almost 3′ x 4′ when plotted out. Working on LIGHT PLOTS, PLANS, ELEVATIONS, or costume pattern drafting in such a tiny format requires the ability to magnify portions of the screen many times the original display size. The ZOOM command is the solution to this problem.

Locating the ZOOM command
- the Root Menu under DISPLAY
- the Pull Down Menu under DISPLAY
- the Tablet Menu

Exploring the ZOOM command
To survey the ZOOM command you will need an existing drawing up on your screen. Call up PROJECT 3.

AutoCAD provides several ZOOM options. They all are designed to accomplish the same task — to zoom in or out of a particular part of your drawing. Let's look at the options that will be the most helpful to you.

Window
With this option you will zoom to a full screen view of the part of the drawing that you enclose in a window.

Since the aspect ratio of the window you create is most likely not the same as the aspect ratio of your monitor, what you see in your zoomed view will not be precisely what you included in your zoom window.

Previous
Takes you back to the previous screen zoom display.

All
Zooms back to show you all of the drawing.

Dynamic
Choosing this option shows you the entire drawing and a floating zoom box. The box is made larger or smaller and then placed on the part of the

drawing that you want to zoom to.

An "X" on the zoom box means that you can move it around on your drawing. Hitting your pick button turns the "X" into an ->. This symbol means that you can now enlarge or shrink the box by moving your pointing device. When you have your box sized, hit the pick button again. Position the box and then hit **ENTER** to make the zoom.

The zoom box has the same aspect ratio as your monitor. What you include in your zoom box will be precisely what you see on the monitor screen.

Lines and brackets around the edge of the screen show you your limits and extents. An hourglass will appear if your zoom will take extra regeneration time.

Extents

This option zooms you to a drawing that is defined by the area taken up by your drawing entities. This can include anything that is outside of your drawing limits. It may also produce a view that is much smaller than your limits if the entities are well within that boundary.

Some other zoom options that you are not likely to use are:

number
Type in a magnification number relative to the All zoom.
numberX
Type in a magnification number relative to the current zoom display.
Center
Pick a zoom center point and then a display height.
Left
Indicate a lower left corner for the display and a display height.

Using ZOOM **Window** (the ZOOM option you will use the most) works like this:

1. Select ZOOM **Window**.

2. AutoCAD says:

First corner:

Pick a lower left corner point for your zoom window.

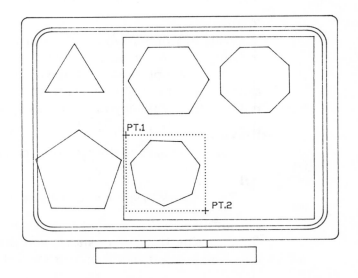

3. AutoCAD says:

Other corner:

Pick the upper right corner.

The display that results should be close to what you selected in your window. Now try ZOOM **Previous** and then the other options.

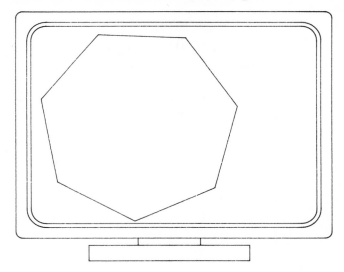

PAN

PAN moves your drawing while you are zoomed in. It is important to understand that the screen doesn't move, it's the drawing that's moving. This command allows you to work in, or check, an area adjacent to your current zoom display without having to zoom back and forth to see that area. You can always get back to your original zoom with the ZOOM **Previous** option.

Locating the PAN command
- the Root Menu under DISPLAY
- the Pull Down Menu under DISPLAY
- the Tablet Menu

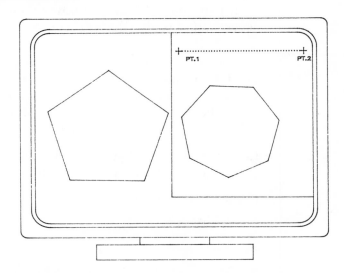

Here's how PAN works

1. Select PAN.

2. AutoCAD says: PAN displacement:

This is asking you for the point where you will grab your drawing paper before moving it, relative to your drawing screen.

Pick.

3. AutoCAD says: Second point:

AutoCAD is really asking you to show it the direction that you want your paper to move. If you want to PAN to the left (remember, this really means moving your paper to the right), pick a point (with Ortho on) to the right of your first displacement point. The distance that you will pan is the distance between your two pick points.

Pick.

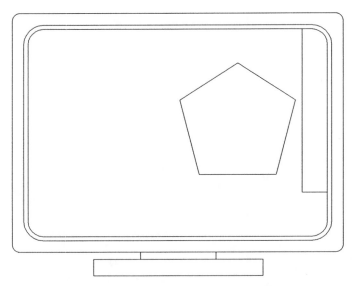

You now have panned to the left. You will find that it is helpful to leave a *part* of a "panned away" object on the screen as a reference. If you do this for each pan you will always know where you are on the drawing. Practice this several times until it doesn't seem too awkward.

VIEW This command allows you to save any of your zoom displays. You name them and later recall them at any time. You could save a zoomed view of all of your ELEVATIONS or each of your electrics or certain patterns. Being able to recall these "favorite" zooms instantly is convenient and can save you lots of drawing time by eliminating a ZOOM **All** between each zoom.

Locating the VIEW command
• the Root Menu under DISPLAY

How VIEW works

1. ZOOM **All.**

2. Select VIEW.

3. AutoCAD says: ?/Delete/Restore/Save/Window:

Select **Window**.

4. AutoCAD says: View name to save:

   Type in your <u>ELEVATION</u> marker letter, electric number, or pattern part name.

5. AutoCAD says: First corner:

   Pick a zoom window corner for your view.

6. AutoCAD says: Other corner:

   Pick.

To call up your view

1. Select VIEW.

2. AutoCAD says: ?/Delete/Restore/Save/Window:

   Select **Restore**.

3. AutoCAD says: View name to restore:

   Type in your view name.

AutoCAD has zoomed to your view.

VIEW Options

The VIEW options are:
  ?/Delete/Restore/Save/Window:
  You know what **Restore**, **Save**, and **Window** do. The other options are:
?
Shows you a list of all of your views.
Delete
Deletes a view.

PROJECT 4

ZOOM, PAN, VIEW

1. Delete MIZELEV1 from your BACKUP floppy disk.

2. Zoom in on each of the five parts of your PROJECT 3 drawing as designated in the example.

3. Save each of the zooms as a view.

4. Restore the ZOOM 2 view.

5. Pan away from the ZOOM 2 view half a screen width toward ZOOM 3.

6. Save that new display as a view for a total of six saved views.

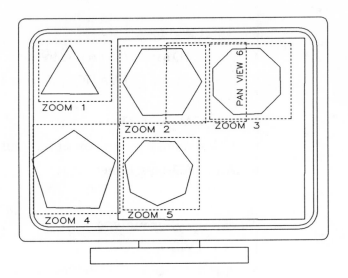

8 DISPLAY TECHNIQUES PART II

FUNCTION: This command breaks your screen up into several "mini-screens" called viewports. Each viewport can have a different part of your drawing or another zoom magnification of the same drawing. This command gives you the capability of looking at and working on one view of a scenic element, while in another viewport looking at and working on a zoomed-in detail of that same element — all at the same time. You can also plot multiple viewports.

VPORTS

Many times different views of the same object are separated by some distance on your drafting paper. AutoCAD's viewport capability helps alleviate this type of inconvenience. Being able to look at a zoomed-in front view and side view of the same piece of scenery at the same time makes VPORTS a handy command.

Locating the VPORTS command
- the Root Menu under SETTINGS
- the Pull Down Menu under DISPLAY
- the Tablet Menu (in Release 10)

Setting up viewports with VPORTS

Before you begin, have a drawing called up on your screen. Call up PROJECT 3.

1. Select VPORTS from the Tablet Menu or Root Menu.

2. AutoCAD says:

    Save/Restore/Delete/Join/SIngle/?/2/ <3>/4:

    Select the number of viewports. AutoCAD places 3 in brackets (default) = 3 viewports

    Hit **ENTER.**

3. AutoCAD says: Horizontal/Vertical/Above/Below/Left/<Right>:

    Let's select a dominant (largest) viewport position. AutoCAD suggests that the right half of the screen become the dominant viewport.

    Hit **ENTER.**

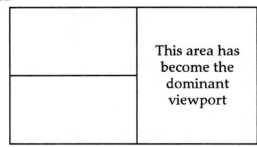

This area has become the dominant viewport

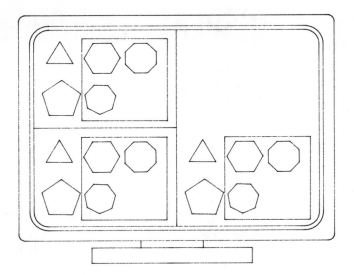

AutoCAD now divides the screen into 3 viewports. A miniature copy of your drawing appears in each of the viewports.

Other viewport combinations are possible. Many of them can be seen in a dialog box in the Pull Down Menu. You will find the 3 Right configuration to be the most useful.

4. Draw a small square in the viewport that currently has cross hairs.

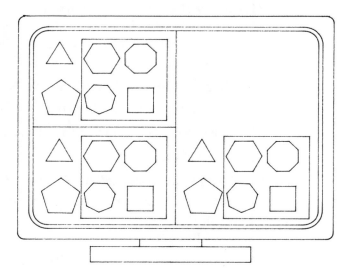

5. Move to another viewport.

6. ZOOM in on your new square in that other viewport. To do so:

   • Pick anywhere in that viewport.

   • The arrow changes to cross hairs.

   • ZOOM in on the square.

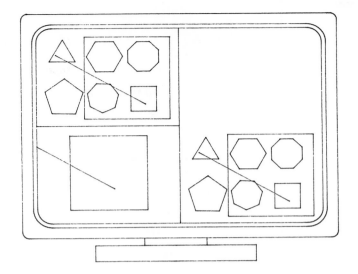

7. Move to the third viewport.

8. ZOOM in on the triangle.

9. Move back to the right dominant viewport. Make it current.

   The viewport that you are currently working in is called the "current" viewport. It is the only viewport where cross hairs will appear.

10. Draw a line from the triangle to the new square. The results show up on all three viewports.

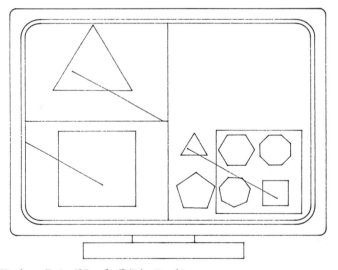

VIEWPORT Options

Save/Restore/Delete/Join/SIngle/?/2/<3>/4

Save

You can name and then Save the current viewport configuration.

Restore

For retrieving previously saved viewport configurations.

Delete

Deletes previously saved viewport configurations.

Join

Combines two viewports into one.

Single
Fills the screen with the current viewport. All other viewports are tossed out.
?
Lists all saved viewport names.
2
Makes two viewports.
3
Makes three viewports.
4
Makes four viewports.

You can name and then SAVE the current viewport configuration.

PROJECT 5

VIEWPORTS

1. Call up PROJECT 3.

2. Set up viewports using the Pull Down Menu.

3. Repeat steps 4-10 in this chapter.

9 CREATING A PROTOTYPE DRAWING PART I

ELECTRONIC DRAFTING PAPER

> **FUNCTION**: AutoCAD contains the ability to customize your drawing style and annotation preferences in dozens and dozens of ways. To "load-in" these instructions at each drawing session would be quite time consuming. By starting each drawing not from scratch but from a prototype, you can save hours of work and bring uniformity and standardization to your drawings. The commands in this chapter help you create your own prototype drawings.

Before you can do any real professional quality drawings with AutoCAD you need paper to create a prototype. Your prototype will be your electronic drafting. It will be encoded with all of your AutoCAD drafting preferences: the size of the paper you will print your drawing out on, the system of measurement (feet and inches), Grid spacing, Snap spacing, the type of dimension arrows you prefer, and dozens of other features. A pencil and paper analogy (and a poor one at that) of a prototype would be drafting vellum that has a grid and title block and border printed right on the paper. An AutoCAD prototype is much more sophisticated and "intelligent" than that. Its counterpart in word processing programs is the style sheet.

After your prototype has been assembled you will call upon it to create your next <u>LIGHT PLOT</u>, <u>FLOOR PLAN</u>, etc.

Creating a Prototype — UNITS

Before going any further, follow these steps to create your personal prototype drawings. As you will see in step #3, you will most likely need to create several prototypes for different situations. You will need to repeat all of these steps for each one of your prototype drawings.

1. Invoke the UNITS command. It is found under SETTINGS in the Root Menu.

   Notice that your screen has "flipped" to text mode. AutoCAD gives you two screen modes, text and drawing.

   In going through the command you will be asked to make several choices regarding your unit preferences. Without going into a complete discussion and description, each choice will be accompanied by a recommendation for the option that is best for the theatrical and film/television type of drawing that you will be doing.

System of Units
Establishes your unit of measurement.
Select Architectural Units.

Denominator of Smallest Fraction
Sets the fraction denominator (if any) to be displayed during drawing sessions and in the dimension command. For ¼" or ½" scale drawings, use no fractions

(denominator of 1). For FULL scale drawings such as details or costume patterns you should select the smallest fraction (largest denominator) that suits your needs. Selecting 16 for instance allows you to draw in $\frac{1}{16}$ths of an inch. Select a denominator of 1.

System of Angle Measurement
Select the one that you are familiar with and fits the drawing.
Select decimal degrees.

Number of Fractional Places for Display of Angles
Unless you are drawing something in great detail, you will not need fractional degrees.
Select 0 fractions.

Direction for Angle 0
Use AutoCAD's defaults here. In brief they are:

> A line drawn from left to right is said to be at angle 0. A line from down to up is said to be at 90°. Angle 0 is therefore at 3:00. Angle 90 is at 12:00.

Select 0.
Select counterclockwise.

   These selections will match your prototype 0 direction with the chart found on the AutoCAD Tablet Menu in the numeric area.

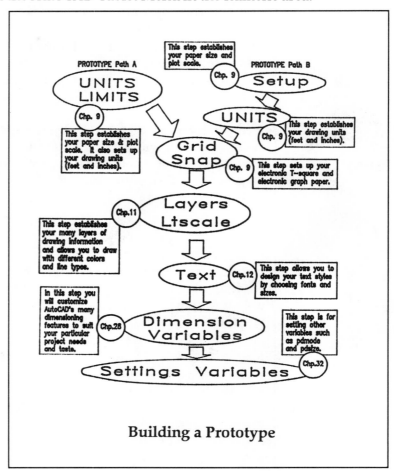

Building a Prototype

2. "Flip" back to the drawing editor by hitting the **F1** key. This is the Flip Screen Toggle.

LIMITS 3. Select the LIMITS command. It too can be found under the SETTINGS command in the Root Menu.

With this command you are telling your prototype what paper size you will be printing on. You will need to make a prototype for each paper size that you use and for each scale on each paper size that you use.

For instance, if you draft <u>ELEVATIONS</u> in ½" scale on 24" x 36" paper, you will create a prototype for those situations. If you also draft at ¼" scale on the same paper size, you will create another prototype for that situation. If you draft in ½" scale on 17" x 22" paper that will be a third prototype. And if you sometimes draft in ¼" scale on the same size paper, you will need to create a fourth prototype.

You can see that this can become complicated real fast. It's best to keep things simple (at least in the beginning). Stick to one paper size from now on.

A lighting designer will most likely be working in ½" scale on the same large sheet. Here too only one prototype will be needed. Most scenic drafters work primarily in three scales: ¼", ½", and FULL. By sticking to one sheet size, only three prototype drawings will be necessary. Here are the three prototype drawing suggestions.

QUARPROT — your ¼" scale prototype

HALFPROT — your ½" scale prototype

FULLPROT — your full scale prototype

Note that all of the above prototype drawings are for one paper size, 24" x 36". If you have different paper sizes for each of these scales, you may want to identify them in a different way. Here are two examples:

2436HALF — your 24" x 36" ½" scale prototype

1722HALF — your 17" x 22" ½" scale prototype

4. Select the LIMITS command. LIMITS establishes what the electronic boundaries of your drawing will be. Another way to say this is that in setting LIMITS you are telling AutoCAD how big the paper will be onto which you will eventually plot your drawing.

AutoCAD says:

Lower left corner 0'0",0'0".

This part of the LIMITS command positions the "paper" on the screen. You will want to use as much of the screen as possible, so tell AutoCAD that you do want the lower left corner to be 0'0",0'0". Remember that all points on the AutoCAD screen need to be positioned with two coordinates — a left/right coordinate (X), and an up/down coordinate (Y). And all coordinates are in relation to the lower left corner of the screen. In this case we want the lower left corner of our paper (lower left limit) to be in the lower left corner of the screen. Another way to say this is that the lower left corner of the paper is not to the left or right (X) of the lower left screen corner any inches (0'0") and not up or down (Y) of the lower left screen corner. We want the two corners to match up.

5. Select 0'0" or simply hit **ENTER** since it is the default.

AutoCAD says:

Upper right corner.

6. Establishing the upper right corner of our limits (telling AutoCAD how big your paper is going to be) requires a bit of fourth grade math, so hold on!

   a. Establish the width (left/right) dimension of the paper you are going to plot onto.

   b. Multiply this dimension by the denominator of the scale fraction you intend this drawing to be measured at (4 for ¼", 2 for ½", etc.).

   c. That number (in feet) will be your X coordinate.

   d. Take the height (up/down) dimension of the paper you are going to plot onto.

   e. Multiply this dimension by the same number you used in step b.

   f. That number (in feet) will be your Y coordinate.

   Example: You will be plotting onto a 24" x 36" sheet of paper and you intend the drawing to be read at ½" scale:

   a. 36" wide paper

   b. 36 x 2 = 72

   c. X = 72'

   d. 24" high paper

   e. 24 x 2 = 48

   f. Y = 48'

   The upper right corner limit would be 72',48'. Type in your upper right corner. In this case you would type in:

   > 72',48'

   (You could have typed 72'0",48'0" but AutoCAD doesn't need inches if they are zero.)

   ### MEMO

   AutoCAD usually displays measurements with a dash between the feet and the inches. However, AutoCAD does not ever allow *you* to type a dash between feet and inches. 4'-7" must be typed in as 4'7". Many an AutoCAD novice has been brought to the brink with this little AutoCADism. Be careful!

STATUS

7. Select STATUS. This command is found under INQUIRY in the Root Menu. This command allows you to quickly check the things you have just set on your prototype and a number of others. STATUS shows you:

   • the status of your limits

   • the range covered (drawing uses) by your drawing within (or outside of) its set limits

- what your display is showing you (limit coordinates of any zooms)

- Grid setting — gives you an electronic graph paper option (more about this in the next chapter)

- Snap setting — forces you to draw in specific increment divisions (more about this in the next chapter)

- and a host of other important pieces of drawing tool information that you will be learning about later on.

8. Establish Grid and Snap settings as a permanent part of your prototype drawings. For your 24" x 36" prototype drawings follow these recommendations:

½" scale	¼" scale
Grid = 1′	Grid = 2′
Snap = 3"	Snap = 3"

To set each of these, type in the command (GRID, SNAP) and then type in the recommended setting.

9. Be sure and SAVE your drawing before going on to set up your next prototype.

MEMO

AutoCAD has come up with a less complicated way to get a prototype going. It is called the SETUP command. SETUP does away with all of the math. You pick from a choice of paper sizes or you can type in your own. You select a scale for the drawing, and you select the units (architectural) — that's it! The drawback with this method is that it doesn't allow you to fine tune the prototype in terms of fractions, degrees, etc.

You could (and should) after using the SETUP command, take the extra time to go through the UNITS command in order to establish those important extra choices.

SETUP draws the outline of the paper on your screen. This outline will print out on your drawing. If you are going to draw a border in from the edges of the paper I recommend you erase what will become a second border.

Creating a New Drawing from a Prototype

To call upon your prototype to create a new <u>LIGHT PLOT</u>, <u>FLOOR PLAN</u>, or <u>COSTUME PATTERN</u>, use the

1. Begin a new drawing

option found in the Main Menu.

Type in the name of the new drawing followed by the name of the appropriate prototype drawing. For example:

CURSE1=QUARPROT

or

a:CURSE1=a:QUARPROT

This will allow you to begin a brand new <u>FLOOR PLAN</u> drawing for *Curse of the Starving Class* called CURSE1 from the ¼" scale 24" x 36" prototype drawing. This new drawing will automatically contain all of your custom drawing preferences.

MEMO

If you are storing your drawings on floppy disks, you must be careful not to overload a disk. As a rule of thumb, limit the amount of prototype-based drawings to four per floppy (including backup files). This should help eliminate FATAL ERROR messages and damaged drawing files.

PROJECT 6

STARTING A PROTOTYPE DRAWING

1. Begin your prototype drawings. Establish the paper size(s) and scale(s) that you will be using from now on in addition to ¼", ½", and full scale prototypes. You will have at least three prototypes as a result of this project.

2. Create a prototype for each of these by going through the procedures outlined in this chapter.

3. Base your prototype drawing names on the suggestions included in this chapter.

10 HELP IN DRAWING MORE ACCURATELY

> **FUNCTION**: These commands and options are designed to make your drawing sessions much easier. For instance, REDRAW allows you to occasionally "clean up" your screen. The DRAWING TOOLS and function keys are like an electronic combination of the drafting machine, adjustable triangle, and scale rule.

AutoCAD provides a number of useful tools to make your drawing session easier. These are called DRAWING TOOLS. You have already looked at one such DRAWING TOOL — blips.

DRAWING TOOLS

The DRAWING TOOLS (called DRAWING AIDS prior to Release 11) are located in the SETTINGS Pull Down Menu. In the upper right hand corner of the box you see six option boxes. Some of them can be instantaneously toggled on and off with function keys. These TOOLS are Grid, Snap, Axis, Ortho, Blips, Isoplane, and Coordinates. Let's take a look at what they do.

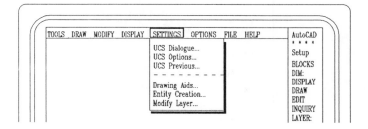

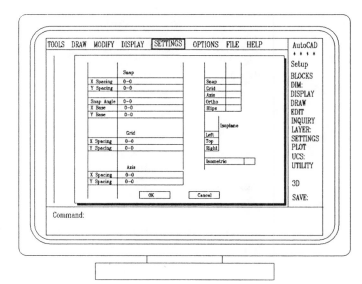

Grid

Using this TOOL turns your screen into electronic graph paper. Instead of a line grid however, AutoCAD shows you just the intersections of those lines. They are shown to you as dots (which are not part of your drawing and would never print out).

The Grid can be set at any size. Every 6" or every 6' for instance. You can also have a *rectangular* Grid with the increments set at 6" horizontally and 1' vertically.

To set up Grid spacing, you need to make use of the Grid Spacing boxes on the left side of this dialog box. To set up the horizontal spacing, move your arrow to the X Spacing box (horizontal is always the X direction in AutoCAD), pick it, and type in 6". The Y Spacing box automatically duplicates the spacing set up in the X Spacing box. To set up a different vertical spacing you need to repeat the process used for the X spacing box in the Y Spacing box with a new measurement (vertical is always the Y direction in AutoCAD).

Pick the OK box to return to the drawing screen.

Grid can also be toggled (turned on and off) by pressing the **F7** function key.

Snap

Snap allows you to only draw lines of a specific increment division. For instance, setting the Snap at 6" with our 6" Grid will result in lines that can be drawn from Grid point to Grid point only. This example would result in perfectly accurate 6" or 1'-0" or 1'-6" etc. lines.

You could also set Snap at 3" with a 6" Grid and be able to draw to points midway between the Grid points.

Snap can also be toggled by pressing the **F9** function key.

Axis

Axis places a ruler at the edges of the screen. You can set the ruler to any increment. This TOOL is not particularly helpful to scenery and lighting drawings, whereas Snap, Grid, and Ortho are invaluable.

Ortho

With Ortho on, you can only draw vertical and horizontal lines. Lines of any other angle are impossible to draw. This is particularly helpful when drawing scenery <u>ELEVATIONS</u> that consist mainly of rectangular flats or elements.

Ortho can also be toggled pressing the **F8** function key.

Blips

With Blips selected, a little white cross appears on the screen wherever you have used your pick button. The crosses do not print out and are not a part of your drawing. They can be removed from time to time by invoking the REDRAW command.

Isoplane

This feature allows you to turn your Grid into isometric graph paper. It is invaluable when making isometric drawings. To use Isoplane:

1. Call up the SNAP command by typing it in at the keyboard.

2. Toggle the Grid on (**F7**).

3. Select **Rotate**.

4. Hit **ENTER** to select the default base point of 0,0.

5. Type 45 for rotation angle.

   You can now draw in Isometric mode. Use the Isoplane DRAWING TOOL box to toggle between the different Isoplane faces as needed.

6. Return to a normal Grid by repeating steps 1-4. Type 0 for rotation angle in step 5.

Coordinates

A DRAWING TOOL that does not appear in this dialog box is Coordinates. It is toggled on and off with the **F6** function key. This function key controls the coordinate display on the status line at the top of the screen. It has two or three different readout functions depending on the computer that you are using. Each time that you toggle the function key it will invoke either:

Coordinates ON Mode

Locks on and gives you a constant X,Y readout of where your cross hairs are at all times. When you then choose a command and pick a point, it changes to a readout in polar coordinates showing the distance and angle the cross hairs are moving at all times since that point was picked.

Coordinates ON Mode 2

Locks on and gives a constant X,Y readout of where your crosshairs are at all times. The coordinates do not change to polar coordinates when a point is picked.

Coordinates OFF Mode

Locks off and gives you only the coordinates of the last point that you picked. Each time you pick a new point the readout will change to show you those coordinates.

One of these three coordinate modes is always in effect — you can never get rid of them. You can only change from one of the modes to another.

Controlling Toggles

Here is a brief review of the function keys that the AutoCAD program uses as well as the **CTRL** key combinations that perform the same tasks.

F1
FLIP SCREEN TOGGLE

F6 or **CTRL + D**
COORDINATES TOGGLE

F7 or **CTRL + G**
GRID TOGGLE

F8 or **CTRL + O**
ORTHO TOGGLE

F9 or **CTRL + B**
SNAP TOGGLE

The Status Line Area at the top of the screen will always indicate whenever any of these functions is in effect. If you have trouble remembering which function key does what, make a template (strip of paper) that lies above your function keys and reveals what each of the keys is for.

SNAP — Rotating the Grid

The pencil and paper draftsperson uses an adjustable triangle or adjusts the drafting machine in order to draw parallel lines at angles other than 0° or 90°.

In AutoCAD you accomplish this same task by rotating the Grid. To rotate the Grid, select the SNAP command. Don't confuse the SNAP command with the Snap DRAWING TOOL. Select the Rotate option after you have selected the command. When AutoCAD asks for the base point, choose the end point of the angled line that you want to draw parallel to. For angle, select the other end of the line. The Grid will rotate automatically.

When you are finished and want to draw lines straight across and up and down again, select SNAP. Type in 0,0 for the base point and 0° for the angle. The Grid will return to normal.

PROJECT 7

DRAWING TOOLS

1. Create a PROJECT 7 drawing from your ½" scale prototype drawing. For example, at the

    1. Begin a New Drawing

    option of the Main Menu, type a:PROJ7=a:HALFPROT.

2. Copy these <u>ELEVATION</u> drawings from *The Misanthrope*.

    Be sure to toggle the various DRAWING TOOLS on and off when appropriate so that your drawing has professional quality accuracy and precision.

3. Don't include the text or the dimensions (since you don't know how to do that yet).

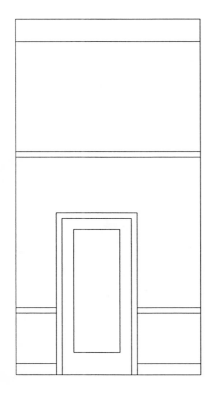

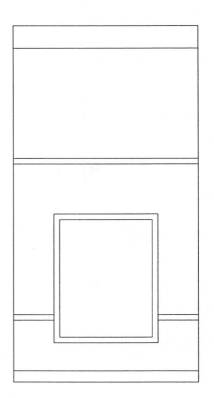

ELEVATION Ⓐ

ELEVATION Ⓑ

11 CREATING A PROTOTYPE DRAWING PART II

SEPARATING DRAWING ELEMENTS

> **FUNCTION**: As you continue to build upon your prototype drawing(s) with each of the *Prototype* chapters, you will bring more and more precision and versatility to the drawings created from these prototypes. This chapter supplements your prototype by adding AutoCAD's LAYER feature. Layers separate drawing elements so that they can be easily duplicated, eliminated, or edited in other ways without disturbing the integrity of the remainder of the drawing. They also allow you to work with different linetypes, colors, and line widths on the same drawing. For the lighting designer one layer may represent the instruments, another layer may represent the hanging positions, and a third may be instrument notations.

Layering

Layering is an extremely important AutoCAD feature. It is one of the functions of CAD drawing that makes it powerful and far superior to pencil and paper drawing. With manual pencil and paper drafting you have no choice but to combine all of the elements of the drawing onto one piece of paper. This makes editing (correcting mistakes, duplicating elements, copying certain data from one drawing to the next, etc.) almost impossible.

AutoCAD separates all of these various elements into different layers. It's as if you were drawing on many overlapping sheets of "clear electronic acetate." Each sheet contains a separate drawing element. This allows you to work on one "sheet" at a time and later on to produce drawing variations that contain one, several, or all of the layers. What are these drawing elements? Among the twenty or so that you might eventually create are:

OUTLINES
- the architecture of the theater, sound stage, or studio
- the title block
- the outlines of the scenery
- the lighting instruments
- the hanging positions
- the costume pattern outline
- audience seating

HIDDEN OUTLINES
- alternate scenery positions
- flown scenery
- pattern notation
- hidden scenic elements
- stage draperies

TEXT
- title block information
- drawing titles

— 77 —

- materials lists
- instructional notes

DIMENSIONS
- scenic element dimensions
- electric batten heights
- pattern dimensions

Each "sheet" or layer can have a different linetype — but only one linetype per layer. You might assign one layer to represent the outline of a scenic element using a continuous line. Another layer may represent structural elements that are hidden from view, yet are nonetheless important to indicate to the shop carpenters. This layer would be in a dashed, hidden outline linetype. For purposes of clarity on the monitor, you can even assign each layer a different color — say white for the outline and green for hidden. Plotted line width can be controlled through layering also. Each layer can be plotted with the same or a different line width. More about that in Chapter 15, but as a rule of thumb, keep all elements that are to be plotted in lightweight lines (dimensions, text, etc.) on separate layers.

Later on, after your FLOOR PLAN is complete, you can produce several versions for different people for different reasons. A complete PLAN, including the entire stage, audience, set, notes, and measurements would be required for the carpenters, of course. For purposes of blocking, the director and stage manager would need only the acting space. I would not need to plot out the layers containing construction information, measurements for placement of the set, the audience seating, etc. The rigging technicians may only need to see the layers that have all of the rigging/flying information. Many of the people to whom I have given these "reduced information" drawings find them clearer and easier to understand. The primary use of color in CAD drafting is to help you distinguish the many parts of a complicated drawing on a little monitor screen. You can plot in color, but if you make multiple copies for distribution using a blueprint or photocopy machine, the color will not copy. Think of color as an aid to you while you are drafting to help you distinguish different layers.

I suggest that you make many layers. The more layers you have, the easier the drawing and especially the editing process will go. Here are some ideas for creating your own layers. It is important that you decide on a set of layers that stays consistent with other drawings that you create. This is especially important if you will be sharing your drawing disk with other designers. It is quite a nightmare if your layers don't "synch up" with each other.

Layer Suggestions for the Scenic Designer

Here is the layering system that I use for all of my drawings and include as a part of all of my prototypes. Many of my students have adapted it for their own prototypes. With very little effort it can be adapted for use by the lighting designer.

The layer will be described by:
1. The name of the layer (OUTLINES).
2. The linetype (CONTINUOUS).
3. The monitor/plotting pen color (WHITE/BLACK).
4. The intended plotted-line pen width (medium weight).

OUTLINES   continuous   White/Black   medium weight

For drawing the outline of all scenery that would be drawn manually with a medium weight line.

HIDDENOUTLINES   hidden   White/Black   medium weight

Lines in an <u>ELEVATION</u> that represent scenery or other structural elements hidden behind the drawn surface. Or in a <u>PLAN</u>, hidden represents scenic elements above the cutting plane line.

DIMENSIONS   continuous   Blue   light weight

All dimensions including the dimension numbers, extension lines, and dimension lines. Blue was chosen for this layer because it tends to recede. A White scenic outline on the monitor next to a blue dimension line stands out quite clearly. You would not mistake a dimension line for an outline.

TEXT   continuous   green   light weight

All text.

FURNITURE   continuous   red   medium weight

Used only in the <u>FLOOR PLAN</u>.

DETAILS1   continuous   magenta   medium weight

Details on a flat in an <u>ELEVATION</u> including hatch patterns, or perhaps something in a <u>FLOOR PLAN</u> such as plants.

DETAILS2   continuous   cyan   medium weight

Detail on top of detail.

STAGE   continuous   yellow   medium weight

The architecture of the stage itself. The yellow color was chosen because it recedes in the blueprint or photocopy.

HIDDENSTAGE   dashed   yellow   medium weight

Features of the architecture that require a dashed line are drawn in this layer: a doorway, catwalks, traps, etc.

PLATFORMS   continuous   magenta   medium weight

All platforming is drawn on this layer. This layer is helpful for developing a <u>PLATFORM PLAN</u> later on. Other layers can be turned off while plotting the platform layers.

HIDDENPLATFORMS   hidden   magenta   medium weight

Platforms hidden by other platforms are drawn with this layer.

SETDRESSING   continuous   red   medium weight

Used to indicate such things in a <u>PLAN</u> as rugs, important props, etc.

SIGHTLINES   dot   cyan   light weight

A really light weight line is difficult to achieve with a plotter. AutoCAD's special dot line comes the closest to achieving this quality.

CENTERLINE   center   yellow   medium weight

For drawing the center line in a <u>FLOOR PLAN</u>.

DRAPERY   continuous   red   heavy weight

For drawing masking in the <u>FLOOR PLAN</u>.

SEATS   continuous   red   medium weight

For drawing audience seating or at least the extreme sightline seats.

LAYOUT   continuous   cyan   not to be plotted

This layer is the equivalent of the layout line you would use when planning or laying out a pencil and paper drafting project. In pencil and paper drafting, this is sometimes done with a non-repro blue pencil. It is used to work out placement and proportion and then is drawn over with the appropriate final layer(s). It does not need to be erased but merely turned off before plotting (more on that in Chapter 37).

FIRECLEARANCE   continuous   cyan   not to be plotted

This layer is used to check and draw fire egress lines when performance space and scenery mix and mingle — as in a television studio or alternative non-traditional theatrical performance space.

ACTCURTAIN   dashed   red   heavy weight

FLY   dashed   cyan   medium weight

All flown scenery in a <u>FLOOR PLAN</u>.

ELEVATIONMARKER   continuous   green   medium weight

Used for the markers found on a <u>PLAN</u> that "key" the <u>PLAN</u> to the <u>ELEVATIONS</u>.

MEMO

Heavy weight lines, medium weight lines, thick lines, thin lines — these terms all get a bit muddled and confused in AutoCAD. In the sample list of layers the line weight refers to the eventual *plotted* thickness of the line and not necessarily how it will appear on the screen as you draw it.

To get a thin (light weight) line, you will put a thin pen such as a roller ball in the plotter. Lines intended to be thin do not appear thin on your monitor.

You can achieve an extra thick (heavy weight) line by putting a thick pen in the plotter for those layers that require it or better yet, you can actually draw wider lines (that appear wide on both the monitor and the plot) with the PLINE command discussed in Chapter 29.

Creating a Layer — SETTINGS

Creating a layer from the SETTINGS Pull Down Menu is the simplest method of setting up a layer. Here's how to go about it.

1. Pick the SETTINGS Pull Down Menu.

2. Pick the Layer control option.

A dialog box will appear.

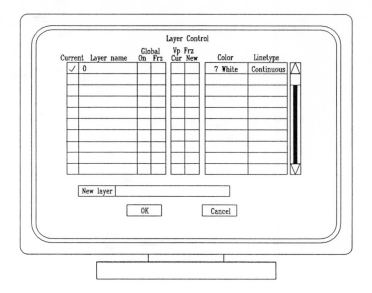

3. Take the pointer to New Layer and pick it.

4. Type in the name of your new layer.

   In making the OUTLINES layer you would:

   a. Type in OUTLINES

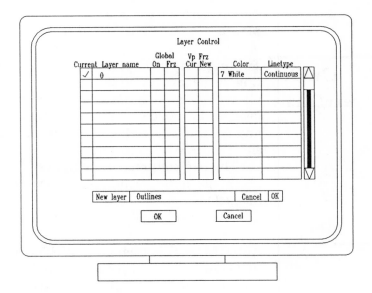

   b. Select the OK box.

   c. Select White as the color.

   d. The linetype is already set to CONTINUOUS. If you needed to change the linetype you would follow a special procedure described later in this chapter.

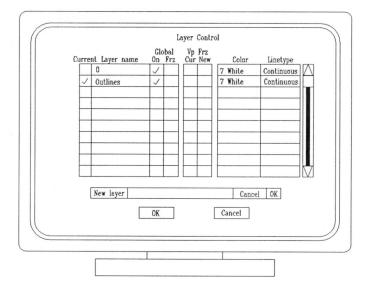

To draw with this layer you need to make sure that the CURRENT box in the first column is checked. Only one layer can be CURRENT at a time. To make a layer CURRENT you must go to this dialog box and check the layer. Pick the OK box to return to your drawing session.

When you return to your drawing you will notice that in the upper left hand corner of the screen on the status line the current layer name is displayed.

On/Off/ Freeze/Thaw

Turning a layer off prevents it from being seen on the screen and from plotting. If the layer is off it cannot be altered in any way. Freezing has the same effect — except that it is a little more off than off. The difference between an off layer and a frozen layer is that AutoCAD will think about the layer if it is off and not think about it if it is frozen. Freezing makes the program work quicker since AutoCAD ignores the information on that layer completely.

The two columns to the right of ON and FRZ control layers in viewports. (Tilemode must be off. See Freezing Layers in Viewports in the *Reference Manual*.)

The slider bar allows you to scroll through your layers.

Color

AutoCAD makes each layer WHITE by default. To change a layer color, pick that layer's Pull Down Menu color box. Check your color choice or type in the color code number and then pick the OK box. Besides the standard WHITE, BLUE, RED, YELLOW, CYAN, MAGENTA, and GREEN, you can access a number of other colors. Select the **Chroma** option from the LAYER Screen Menu to see the range of colors available on your particular computer. Here is a chart with the additional colors and code numbers that are available on an IBM PS/2 with VGA graphics.

CODE	COLOR
8	Dk. Gray
9	Dk. Red
10	Brown
11	Dk. Green
12	Dk. Cyan
13	Dk. Blue
14	Dk. Magenta
15	Med. Gray

The LTYPE (Linetype) Option

LTYPE is one of the LAYER command options. The LTYPE option allows you to set one of 25 different linetypes. You may have noticed that if you pick any of the linetype boxes, not all are available. There really are several other linetypes available and four of these will be very handy to you. They are:

CONTINUOUS
A continuous line.

HIDDEN
A dashed line with short dashes. This line is appropriate for showing hidden construction.

DASHED
A longer dashed line. This line is appropriate for indicating plaster, ceiling, set, and proscenium lines.

CENTER
A typical center line.

DOT
A series of dots. AutoCAD's closest equivalent to the lightweight line. This linetype is excellent for drawing sightlines.

PHANTOM
A special dashed line that works well for indicating cut-through views.
    Except for CONTINUOUS, each linetype has two size variations.

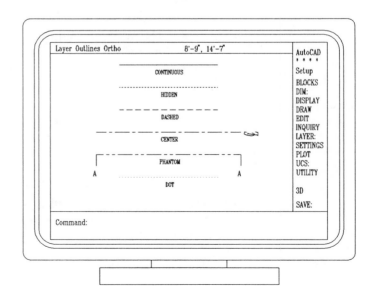

Loading non-continuous linetypes

Not all linetypes are loaded into the dialog box. To use linetypes not loaded in, you use must load them in via the LAYER Screen Menu. Once a linetype has been loaded, however, it can easily be picked from the list in the linetype box, in the same way that you assign layer colors. Load in non-continuous linetypes only after the layers themselves have been created. Here are the steps involved in loading a linetype.

1. Select the LAYER command from the Screen Menu.

2. Select LTYPE. AutoCAD says: Linetype (or?) <CONTINUOUS>:

3. Highlight and pick HIDDEN from the Screen Menu. AutoCAD says: Layer name(s) for Linetype HIDDEN:

4. Type HIDDENOUTLINES.

5. Hit **ENTER**.

6. Get out of the command loop (AutoCAD assumes that you want to keep loading in linetypes). Either:

    a. choose **CANCEL** from the Tablet Menu

    OR

    b. hold down the **CTRL** (control) and **C** keys at the same time.

    The command prompt should have returned to the command line.

    HIDDENOUTLINES is now a part of your line choices in the dialog box. Go ahead and check it!

    AutoCAD novices often forget to change the layer to suit the drawing element. Check your layer status, in the Status Line Area, often. Don't mix different drawing functions (outlines and dimensions for instance) on the same layer.

LTSCALE

LTSCALE is a special command designed to ensure that the dashes between lines and dimension figures, lines and arrows will all print properly and at the correct size regardless of the scale at which you intend to eventually plot your drawing. The LTSCALE command (line type scale) works hand in hand with line type and dimensions. If you intend to plot your drawing out at ½" scale but a stage manager needs it at ¼" scale for a blocking/prompt book, setting the LTSCALE properly will guarantee that the dimensioning and dash spaces keep their intended proportions. A dimension figure (not the object's dimension itself) that is supposed to be ⅛" high will stay that high no matter what scale you print out at.

Locating the LTSCALE command

*   The Root Menu under SETTINGS

1. Setting the LTSCALE keeps all dashes and spaces between dashes at ANSI (American National Standards Institute) standards. It requires using this simple formula to arrive at the scale factor:

    The prototype that we are currently building is for ½" scale plotting . . . or . . . ½" = 1'-0" . . . or . . . 1" = 24" . . . or . . . 1/24 (½" scale is 1/24" scale)

Take the reciprocal and divide by 2.

$^{24}/_2 = 12$

12 is the LTSCALE factor for a ½" scale drawing.

2. For a ¼" scale drawing:

   ¼" = 1'-0" . . . or . . . 1" = 48" . . . or . . . ¹/₄₈ (¼" scale is ¹/₄₈" scale)

   Take the reciprocal and divide by 2.

   $^{48}/_2 = 24$

   24 is the LTSCALE factor for a ¼" scale drawing.

3. When setting the LTSCALE, use 12 and 24 for the ½" or ¼" scale factors. For all other scales use this formula to determine the proper setting.

PROJECT 8

LAYERS

1. Call up your prototype(s).

2. Load in all of your layers.

3. Assign each layer the appropriate color and linetype.

4. Make sure that each layer is on and thawed.

5. Set the proper LTSCALE for each of your prototype drawings.

6. Draw a border on each of your prototype drawings. It should be 2' in from the limits on a ½" scale prototype, 4' in for a ¼" prototype, and 1" in for a full scale prototype.

7. Save your prototype drawings as you complete each one.

12 CREATING A PROTOTYPE DRAWING PART III

ADDING TEXT TO YOUR DRAWINGS

> **FUNCTION**: Theatrical or film/television drawing is not made up of lines exclusively. Text is always needed to explain what the lines cannot. The host of commands associated with writing text allows you to customize styles, size, and placement to suit your needs.

DTEXT

With AutoCAD's dynamic text feature (DTEXT), you can see the text appear on the screen on your drawing where you want it as you type it. DTEXT works very much like a simple word processing program.

Locating the DTEXT command
- the Root Menu under DRAW
- the Pull Down Menu under DRAW
- the Tablet Menu under TEXT

When selecting DTEXT you are presented with six or twelve choices (depending on your version of AutoCAD) for the way that the words can appear on the drawing.

MEMO

As a rule of thumb, all drafting lettering should be one size: 1/8" high letters for all dimensions and most text. The exception is titles — titles of drawings, sheets, and productions. A second exception (optional) might be the title of the show in the title block; many drafters like to have letters of up to an inch high in displaying the show title.

With this in mind, your prototype needs to have at least three styles loaded into it. A **TEXT** style of 1/8" high letters, a **DIMENSIONS** style of 0" high letters (yes, 0", more about this in Chapter 27), and a **TITLES** style of 1/4" high letters.

BE CAREFUL HERE! If you were to type in 1/4" for your title height letters, the result would be letters that were too small to read. It is important always to keep in mind that when working with AutoCAD you are always working in full scale. A 12' high piece of scenery *scales down* to 6" high when plotted in 1/2" scale. A tiny 1/4" high letter would *scale down* to the size of a gnat!

To achieve 1/4" high letters in a 1/2" scale drawing, specify that you want 6" high letters. They scale down, when plotted, to 1/4" high. I actually use 5" high letters. They save space and look better.

Here are my letter height recommendations for your prototypes:

½" scale
    ¼" letters specify 5"
    ⅛" letters specify 2"
¼" scale
    ¼" letters specify 11"
    ⅛" letters specify 5"

DTEXT options for horizontal text alignment

Justify — Justifies text with the following options:

TL (top left)
TC (top center)
TR (top right)
ML (middle left)
MC (middle center)
MR (middle right)
BL (bottom left)
BC (bottom center)
BR (bottom right)

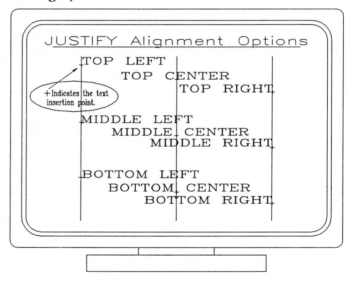

DTEXT options for horizontal and vertical text alignment

Center

Pick where the center point of the line of text should be. The text is automatically centered on that point. The bottom of the line of text is even with the pick point.

Right

Pick a point where the line of text must end. Type the text, and it is placed to the left of that point.

Align

This option allows you to angle the text at an alignment that you specify by picking points. The text height is adjusted proportionally to the length of the text string.

Middle

Pick where the center point of the line of text should be. The text is automatically centered on that point. The vertical middle of the line of text will be even with the pick point.

Fit
Pick the beginning and ending points of the line of text. The text is expanded or compressed to stay within those limits. The text height is not adjusted proportionally to the length of the text string.

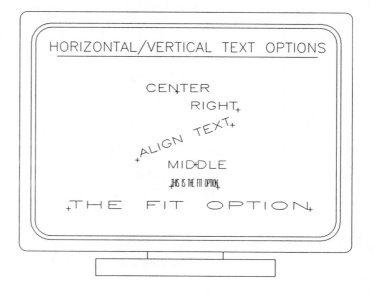

STYLE AutoCAD gives you a choice of text styles to choose from.

Locating the STYLE command
- the Root Menu under SETTINGS
- the Root Menu under DRAW, DTEXT
- the Pull Down Menu under OPTIONS

There is quite a range of styles available going from very simple letters to quite complex styles.

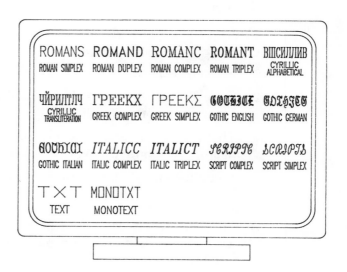

Your prototype should contain three styles:
The TITLES text style is used for all ¼" high text and dimension letters and numbers.

The TEXT text style is used for all ⅛" high sheet, drawing, and show titles.

The DIMENSIONS text style is used for all dimensions.

Creating a text style

Let's create your TITLES text style in the ½" scale prototype.

1. Select STYLE. AutoCAD says: Text style name.

2. Type in TITLES. AutoCAD requests: Font file

3. Type in Romand (Roman Duplex).

   Use Romans (Roman Simplex) for your TEXT and DIMENSIONS styles.

   AutoCAD now wants the height.

5. Type in 5". AutoCAD requests width factor:

   A width factor of 1 means that the width will equal the height. A width factor of 2 will give us a letter that is twice as wide as it is high. I suggest 1.25.

6. Type in 1.25

   AutoCAD now wants an obliquing angle:

   This refers to a slant on the letters. We want them straight up and down.

7. Type in 0

   AutoCAD now wants to know if we want the letters to print backwards:

8. Type in NO

   Now you are being asked if you want the letters to print upside down.

9. Type in NO

   Do you want your letters to print sideways and vertically?

AutoCAD should now tell you that TITLES is the current text style.

(Remember that all heights will be different for your ¼" prototype; refer to the memo box.)

Calling up a text style

Calling up a text style (changing from one style to another) is quite simple.

1. Select STYLE.

2. Type TITLES (if it isn't the default). Hit **ENTER** eight times as you cycle through the pre-set options.

3. The TITLES style is now the current style. Until you change the style again, everything that you type will be in that style.

4. If you haven't already done so, make the TEXT layer current!

Enhancing your text

At times you will need to embellish your text in one way or another. For instance, titles in drafting always need to be underlined. To underline your text in AutoCAD:

Type %%u (as in Hey! Hey! Underline!) just before the text (no space). For example, to have the text ELEVATION B underlined you need to type %%uELEVATION B

Other enhancements available include:

%%o — results in a line over the text

%%c — results in a circle diameter symbol

%%d — results in a degree symbol

%%p — results in a plus/minus symbol

%%% — results in a percent symbol

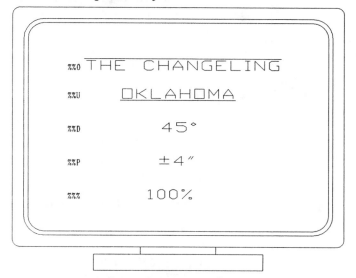

QTEXT

QTEXT is the quick text command. If your drawings are getting complex and slowing down, use QTEXT to regain some of your speed. In general, all text slows down your drawing. Letters are made up of lots of little lines with lots of little curves. Curves are among the biggest "memory eaters." Stick with the simplest font style that you can live with (such as Roman Simplex). The more complex styles are impressive, but they can bog down — even crash your drawing — if used too extensively. Save the fancy styles for title blocks.

Locating the QTEXT command
- the Root Menu under SETTINGS
- the Tablet Menu (Release 11)

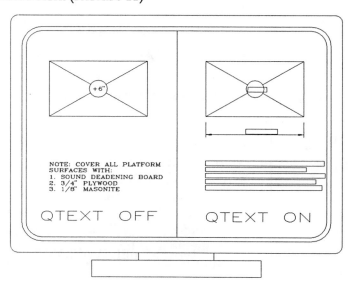

You can greatly speed up your drawing time by using the QTEXT command. It solves the problem of text slowing down your drawing session by getting rid of it! QTEXT is either on or off.

Off
all text is in place and looks normal.

On
QTEXT makes the text invisible but draws a rectangle indicating where the text is on the screen. If your drawings are getting complex and slowing down, use QTEXT to regain some of your speed.

CHANGE-ing Notes and Titles

One of the many, many uses of the CHANGE command is changing your mind about the text you have placed on the screen. For instance, if after drafting and notating your latest PLATFORM PLAN drawing you decide to change from a ¼" plywood surface to ⅛" Masonite, it is a simple matter to change your ¼" ply note-text without erasing it or starting over.

Locating the CHANGE command
- the Root Menu under EDIT
- the Tablet Menu

Here's how to use CHANGE in this situation

1. To alter this text:

NOTE: USE STOCK 4 X 8 PLATFORMS AND
COVER WITH ¼" PLYWOOD. PLACE
1 X 6'S FOR THICKNESS AT ALL VISIBLE
EDGES.

2. Pick the text to be changed.

    CHANGE alters text a line at a time. Pick the second line of the above text.

3. Cycle through the CHANGE options (by pressing **ENTER**) until you see

    NEW TEXT.

4. Type:

    COVER WITH ⅛" MASONITE. PLACE

The text has been corrected.

Dialog boxes also allow you to edit your text. Scroll bars allow you to move through your entry quite quickly.

Completing Your Prototypes

Your prototype drawings are now well underway. You should have a ¼" prototype as well as a ½" prototype for each paper size that you use. Each prototype should have its LIMITS, UNITS, LAYERS, LINETYPES, LINETYPE SCALES, and TEXT STYLES all preset.

You will be adding more features to your prototype drawings a little later on. In the meantime, however, they are quite adequate to assist you in developing some new computer drawing skills.

Remember to be sure to begin all of your example and project work with the appropriate prototype. Always select — 1. begin a new drawing. — from the Main Menu. Then follow the name of your new drawing with the appropriate prototype separated by an equal sign.

     PROJECTX=HALFPROT

This example creates a new drawing called PROJECTX from a prototype called HALFPROT.

PROJECT 9

TEXT

1. Create a TITLES, TEXT, and DIMENSIONS text style for each of your prototype drawings.

2. Design a title block and draw it in the lower right hand corner of each of your prototype drawings.

3. Start a new PROJ9 drawing from your HALFPROT.

4. Use the various DTEXT options suggested and copy the sample text below. Use the TITLES style.

5. Repeat using the TEXT style.

DTEXT option	Text Sample
Justify BL or Left/Cont.	USE ¾" PLY. FOR ALL PLATFORMS
Justify BL or Center	FLOOR PLAN
Justify BR or Right	ELEVATION A
Aligned (place at angle)	COVER FLATS WITH GRAY DUVATENE
Justify MC or Middle	REVISED MAY 4
Fit	ALL UNITS MUST CLEAR LOADING DOOR HEIGHT OF 20'-0"

13 DRAWING CURVES

> **FUNCTION**: This chapter introduces you to the basic curve drawing commands. With the help of these commands you can draw turntables, lighting areas, costume patterns, and many other freeform shapes.

CIRCLE

CIRCLE is the AutoCAD command that you will use to draw all of your circles.

Locating the CIRCLE command
- the Root Menu under DRAW
- the Pull Down Menu under DRAW
- the Tablet Menu

CIRCLE options

The circle command gives you several options for creating a circle:

CEN/RAD — Pick the position of the center of the circle and then either drag or type in a radius. If you drag the radius you can watch your progress by keeping an eye on the status bar at the top of the screen. The angle readout that you see is the angle of the dragging radius. You will use this and the CEN, DIA options 99% of the time. The others are a bit obscure for our purposes.

CEN,DIA — Pick the position of the center of the circle and then either drag or type in a diameter.

2POINT — Pick two points of the diameter and the circle forms between them.

3POINT — Pick three points and the circle will form between them.

TTR (tangent, tangent, radius) — Pick two lines that you want the circle to touch. Specify the radius by typing in a dimension or drawing a radius line anywhere on the sheet. The circle will form at the two tangent points. This might be used for finding the best place to install a 10′ turntable between two flats. Take the time to experiment with each of these options in order to get a sense of how they function.

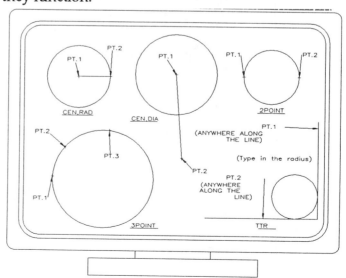

ARC The ARC command gives you a number of options for drawing arcs and undulating lines.

Locating the ARC command
- the Root Menu under DRAW
- the Pull Down Menu under DRAW
- the Tablet Menu

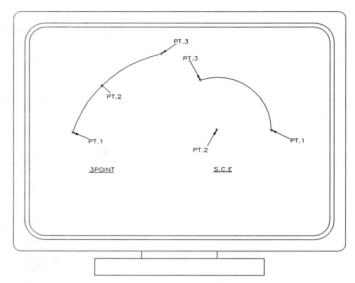

The ARC command gives you several options for creating an arc:

3POINT
Pick three points and the arc will form between them. Start point, second point, and drag the arc line to determine the third point. This is the arc option that you will use the most.

S,C,E (start, center, end)
Pick the beginning of the arc, then the center of the radius of the arc, and finally the end point. An arc will form that travels away from the start point in a counterclockwise direction. This is the arc option to use for drawing a door swing arc in a floor plan.

Here are the other ARC options available to you. Rarely will you use any of them in your theater or film/television drafting. However, you should experiment and become familiar with them. Who knows, one of them may someday be the ARC option that saves your life.

S,C,A	(start, center, included angle)
S,C,L	(start, center, length of chord)
S,E,R	(start, end, radius)
S,E,A	(start, end, included angle)
S,E,D	(start, end, starting direction)
C,S,E	(center, start, end)
C,S,A	(center, start, included angle)
C,S,L	(center, start, length of chord)

By selecting the continuous option you can begin a new arc where the last left off. This allows you to get smooth, fluid compound arcs.

ELLIPSE

ELLIPSE makes effortless work out of drawing an ellipse. This is especially good news if you've ever been confronted with an ellipse drawing problem in manual drafting and were consequently frustrated by never having had the right ellipse template.

Locating the ELLIPSE command
- the Root Menu under DRAW
- the Tablet Menu under DRAW

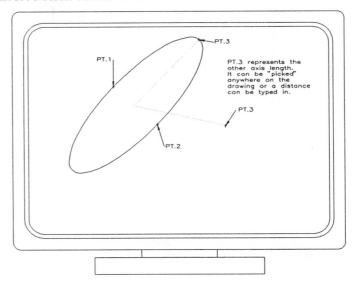

Here's how the ELLIPSE command works

1. Pick ELLIPSE.

    AutoCAD asks you for both axis end points of the ellipse one at a time.

2. Pick the axis end points.

3. AutoCAD then asks you for other axis distance. This is the distance between the sides of the ellipse at their greatest point apart.

    Type in or drag this distance.

    That's all the information AutoCAD needs to quickly produce the ellipse on the screen for you.

ISO

The ISO command is used to draw isometric circles in the isometric drawing mode. See the isoplane drawing mode discussion in Chapter 10.

PROJECT 10

CURVES AND CIRCLES

1. Create a PROJ10 drawing from your PROJ7 drawing (a:PROJ10=a:PROJ7).

2. Using ELLIPSE, CIRCLE, ARC, and LINE add the detail shown in the example below to ELEVATION C.

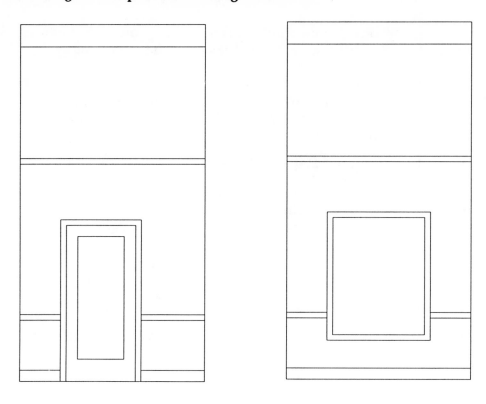

ELEVATION Ⓐ   ELEVATION Ⓑ

ELEVATION Ⓒ

THE MISANTHROPE				
DIRECTED BY: LESLIE SULLIVANT				
UCLA THEATER FREUD PLAYHOUSE				

	Start Cons.	Set Up Date	Production Date	Approval	Scale 1/2" = 1'—0"
	R I C H R O S E				Sheet No.
	scenic design				4
	production design art direction				

14 EDITING YOUR WORK PART I

FUNCTION: Here are some basic editing commands that you will need to begin using right away. They are the electronic equivalent of the eraser and drafting brush. Some of these commands act more like a time machine than an eraser. They can take you all the way back to the beginning of your drawing session.

ERASE

With the ERASE command you can only erase entire entities or groups of entities. To erase part of an entity, half of a line, or one side of a square created with POLYGON for example, you must first break the entity up into smaller entities. That power, and those commands, will be explored later. First, let's master the more basic and most commonly used EDIT commands.

Locating the ERASE command
- the Root Menu Area under EDIT
- the Pull Down Menu bar under MODIFY
- the Tablet Menu

Here's how ERASE works
Before you begin, call up PROJECT 1.

1. Select ERASE and AutoCAD says: Select objects.

2. Move your pointing device and you see that your cross hairs have been replaced by a small square called the pick box. One method of erasing is to "select objects" by picking them with this pick box. The pick box picks entities one at a time.

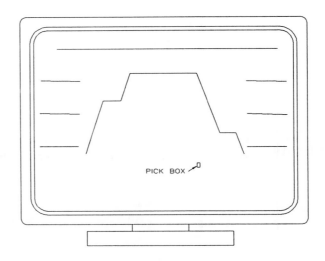

PICK BOX

3. Go ahead and pick all of the masking in your <u>FLOOR PLAN</u>. As you do so you will notice that each line becomes dashed. This is to show you that you haven't erased it yet but it will be soon unless you take action now.

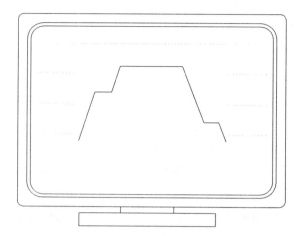

4. Hit the **ENTER** key. All the lines have disappeared leaving only the pick blips.

5. Use the ARC and LINE commands to add a curved cyclorama to your drawing.

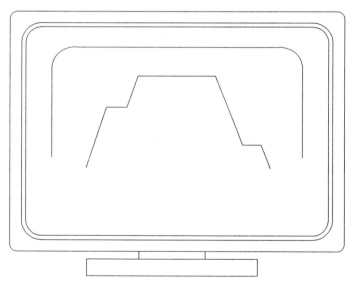

ERASE Options

Window — Using the pick box is one way of erasing objects. The ERASE command gives you a choice of several other options to make the job quicker. **Window** is one of them.

Here's how it works

1. After selecting this option, AutoCAD asks you for: First corner.

   We're going to "lasso" the entire object at once this time with a strange rectangular "rope."

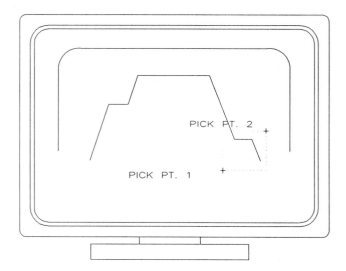

Move your cross hairs to "pick pt. 1" indicated in the illustration.

2. Pick that point. AutoCAD says: Other corner

3. Move your crosshairs to "pick point 2."

    As you do so you will notice that a window is growing.

4. Pick that point. The walls enclosed in the window are now dashed.

    Window will not erase any entities that the window box crosses.

5. AutoCAD now says: Select objects.

    If you wanted to erase other objects, you could now pick or window other objects to your heart's content. I call this the *Select Objects Loop*.

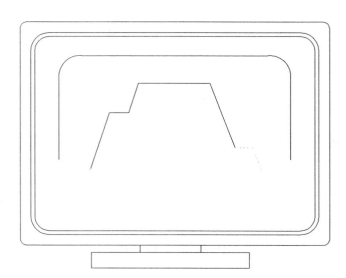

6. Hit the **ENTER** key. This will take you out of the Select Objects loop. All of your dashed objects should now be erased.

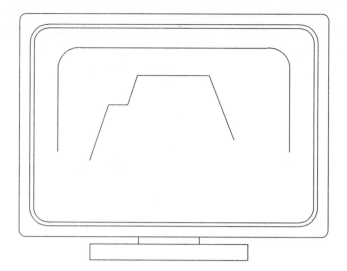

Crossing

The **Crossing** option also uses a window. And this option works almost identically to the **Window** option. The difference is that any entity that the box crosses *will* be erased — right along with all of the objects within the box.

Add/Remove

With the **Add** and **Remove** options you can add and remove objects from what will finally be erased (before you hit **ENTER**). You simply select **Add** or **Remove** and then pick (or window or crossing) the entity that you want to add or remove from the group to be erased.

Undo

(Not to confused with UNDO) — **Undo** also removes entities from the group (before you hit **ENTER**). However, it removes them in the order in which they were picked beginning with the last one you picked.

Oops

If after erasing an object you suddenly realize that you have erased the *wrong* object, you can change your mind. Select **Oops** and the object will reappear. Try *that* on your drafting table at home! **Oops** only works if you have not entered another command since the ERASE. You can't draw something else and then decide that the lighting instrument you erased ten minutes ago should have stayed there after all. **Oops** has a very, very short memory.

U U is a time machine. It takes your drawing session (including all editing) back in time one step at a time. If you are drawing a flat with a door, and after drawing the door trim you decide that you don't like it and want to start over from the point where you started drawing the trim, you can U back one command step at a time.

Locating the U command
- the Root Menu Area under * * * *
- the Pull Down Menu under UTILITY (under TOOLS in Release 10)
- the Tablet Menu

UNDO The UNDO command is a slightly more powerful time machine. It can undo whole groups of commands at once.

Locating the UNDO command
- the Root Menu Area under EDIT
- the Pull Down Menu under UTILITY
- the Tablet Menu (on newer AutoCAD Releases)

To tap into the power of the UNDO command, AutoCAD gives you several UNDO options. The ones that you probably will use the most are:

Number

After selecting this option you type in a number. Executing this command will then UNDO that many steps. A REDO after an UNDO **Number** will restore back that many steps.

Mark

This option places an "electronic bookmark" in your drawing session. For example, if after you had erased the masking but before drawing the cyc you had placed a **Mark**, you could easily have returned to that point in your drawing session by selecting UNDO and then the **Back** option.

Back

Takes you back in your drawing session to the point where you inserted an "electronic bookmark" with the **Mark** option.

Other less used options are **Auto, Control, End,** and **Group.** Experiment with each of them in order to understand their functions fully.

REDO

REDO undoes the last U or UNDO. It cancels the effect of the last U or UNDO and recovers the command(s).

Locating the REDO command
- the Root Menu Area under * * * *
- the Pull Down Menu bar under UTILITY (under TOOLS in Release 10)
- the Tablet Menu

QUIT your drawing session so that PROJECT 1 remains unaltered.

PROJECT 11

ERASE, U, UNDO, REDO

1. Call up your PROJ1 drawing.
2. ERASE all of your masking.
3. Put a **Mark** in the drawing session at this point.
4. Draw a curved cyc around the set.
5. Draw in the forestage and the proscenium.
6. Select U.
7. Select REDO.
8. Select UNDO **Back.**
9. Select REDO.
10. Select U until you get back to the beginning of your drawing session.

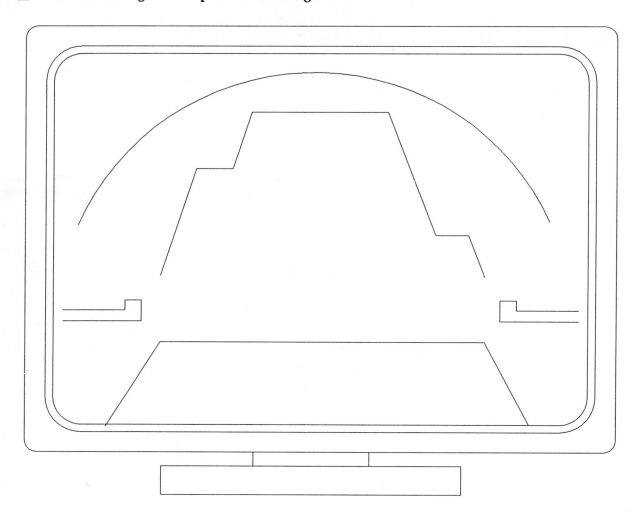

15 PUTTING YOUR DRAWINGS ON PAPER

> **FUNCTION**: Plotting is the CAD term for putting your work onto paper. Whether it be with a pen, pencil, or dot matrix printer, PLOT and printer plot are the commands that do the job. These commands are filled with many customizing options that you need to understand thoroughly.

Student CAD competitions are regularly held across the country. Students from high school level on up compete to draw in the most efficient manner with the fewest keystrokes. Most of these students have become quite proficient at computer assisted drawing and editing techniques. Plotting out their work, however, is where they fall down. The complexity of plotting techniques and options should not be underestimated. Plotting is an art that must be practiced many times to be mastered.

PLOT

Let's plot your 24" x 36" ½" scale a:PROJ10 drawing.

1. To plot your drawing choose PLOT A DRAWING from the Main Menu. You can also plot from the drawing editor during or after a drawing session. To do so select PLOT from the Root Menu under PLOT. This command can also be accessed on the Tablet Menu or the Pull Down Menus under FILE.

2. In this case the drawing will be a:PROJ10.

3. AutoCAD will ask you to:

   Specify the part of the drawing to be plotted by entering: **Display, Extents, Limits, View,** or **Window** <D>.

   You are going to plot your entire 24" x 36" drawing on a large plotter in ½" scale; select **Limits**.

   If you are plotting only part of your drawing onto a small plotter, select **Display**.

   (If you selected PLOT while in the drawing editor, you would have to have zoomed in on the part of the drawing you wanted to plot before going to the PLOT **Display** command option. If you selected PLOT from the Main Menu, you would have to have zoomed in on the drawing you wanted to PLOT and then saved it before going to the PLOT command.)

4. AutoCAD will show you some information that it assumes to be true about how you want your plot to be plotted. Rarely will any of this be correct, especially if other people share your plotter. Type in Y (YES) so that you can "set up" the plotter for your drawing.

5. Now AutoCAD shows you a chart explaining pen assignments, line types, pen speed, and more.

```
            A U T O C A D
Copyright (C) 1982,83,84,85,86,87,88 Autodesk, Inc.
Release 10 c2 (10/26/88) IBM PC
Advanced Drafting Extensions 3
Serial Number:  79-243801
NOT FOR RESALE
Current drawing:  B:23-SC-7

Specify the part of the drawing to be plotted by entering:
Display, Extents, Limits, View, or Window <L>:

Plot will NOT be written to a selected file
Sizes are in Inches
Plot origin is at (0.00,0.00)
Plotting area is 10.73 wide by 7.53 high (MAX size)
2D Plots are rotated 90 degrees clockwise
Pen width is 0.010
Area fill will NOT be adjusted for pen width
Hidden lines will NOT be removed
Plot will be scaled to fit available area

Do you want to change anything? <N>
```

```
Area fill will NOT be adjusted for pen width
Hidden lines will NOT be removed
Plot will be scaled to fit available area

Do you want to change anything? <N> y
```

Entity Color	Pen No.	Line Type	Pen Speed	Entity Color	Pen No.	Line Type	Pen Speed
1 (red)	7	0	25	9	1	0	36
2 (yellow)	7	0	36	10	1	0	36
3 (green)	7	0	36	11	1	0	36
4 (cyan)	7	0	36	12	1	0	36
5 (blue)	7	0	36	13	1	0	36
6 (magenta)	7	0	36	14	1	0	36
7 (white)	7	0	36	15	1	0	36
8	7	0	36				

```
Line types   0 = continuous line
             1 = ...........................
             2 = ----    ----    ----    ----
             3 = -----    -----    -----    -----
             4 = -------.  -------.  -------.  -------.
             5 = ---- -    ---- -    ---- -    ---- -
             6 = --- - -  --- - -  --- - -  --- - -
Do you want to change any of the above parameters? <N>
```

At the bottom of this chart it says:
Do you want to change any of the above parameters?

Type Y (YES)

The only parameter you will be concerned about on this chart is **Pen no.** assignments. If you are plotting in color, make sure that the Entity Color list (think of this as LAYER color list) is coordinated with your pen holder. In other words:

Entity Color 1 (red) — or the red layer — will plot with whatever pen it is assigned to. If the chart says that it is assigned to pen no. 1, and there is a red pen in position #1 of the holder, then anything that is on a red drawing layer will print red on the plot.

You could just as easily have put a black pen in position #1, and then anything that is on a red drawing layer will print black on the plot.

Another option is to put a red pen in position #6 in the holder. In that case if you wanted red drawing layers to be plotted red, you would assign Entity Color 1 (red) to pen no. 6.

If you are plotting with medium and thin pen widths, you need to pay close attention to getting your thin layers (TEXT and DIMENSIONS) assigned to holder positions which have not only the color you want but also a thinner plotter pen.

6. Type in the pen no. assignments. Each entity inquiry will also ask you for linetype and pen speed. Simply hit **ENTER** in order to accept the defaults.

To go back to an entity that you have assigned incorrectly, say entity no. 3, type C3.

When you have finished assigning pens, type X to exit this chart.

If you have set up your PROTOTYPE layers according to the layer suggestions in Chapter 11, you should set up your Entity Pen no. assignments and your pen holder in the following configuration:

Entity Color	Pen No.	Pen Holder
1 (red)	1	red
2 (yellow)	2	yellow
3 (green)	3	green
4 (cyan)	4	cyan
5 (blue)	5	blue
6 (magenta)	6	magenta
7 (white)	7	black

Use a thin (.3mm roller ball) pen in the green and blue positions. I recommend using .3mm fiber tip pens for all other layers.

```
Enter values, blank=Next value, Cn=Color n, S=Show current values, X=Exit

 Layer        Pen  Line  Pen
 Color        No.  Type  Speed
 1 (red)       7    0     25      Line type <0>: x
Write the plot to a file? <N>
Size units (Inches or Millimeters) <I>:
Plot origin in Inches <0.00,0.00>:

Standard values for plotting size

Size    Width    Height
MAX     10.73     7.53

Enter the Size or Width,Height (in Inches) <MAX>:
Rotate 2D plots 90 degrees clockwise? <Y>
Pen width <0.010>:
Adjust area fill boundaries for pen width? <N>
Remove hidden lines? <N>

Specify scale by entering:
Plotted Inches=Drawing Units or Fit or ? <F>:
Effective plotting area:  9.74 wide by 7.53 high
Position paper in plotter.
Press RETURN to continue or S to Stop for hardware setup
```

7. AutoCAD next asks about size units.

   Specify inches.

8. Plot origin is the next question.

   This should be 0,0.

9. AutoCAD now asks how big your paper is.

   The width is 36" and the height is 24".

10. Do you want to rotate your drawing 90°?

    NO

11. Pen width?

    Select the default — hit **ENTER**.

12. Adjust fill areas . . .?

    NO

13. Remove hidden lines? (a 3D drawing question)

    NO

14. Plot scale?

    Type 1" = 2′ — or — .5" = 1′

(The **FIT** option will simply place any drawing nicely onto your paper. It will not be a scaled drawing. It could never be given to a shop or crew to work from.)

15. Hit **ENTER**.

You should now be plotting.

PRINTER PLOT

You can also plot on a dot matrix printer, even your everyday letter writing dot matrix printer. The steps are similar to the ones we just went through but you will not have to deal with Entity and Pen assignments.

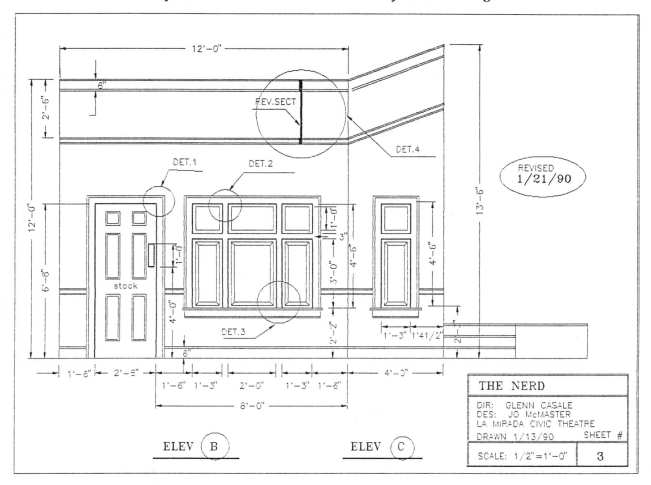

16 QUICK COMMAND REFERENCE

> **FUNCTION**: Basic command and prompt information that you may have forgotten or are unsure of is only a few keystrokes away. The HELP command can come to your rescue at any time as often as you need it. By seeking HELP you can save time by avoiding delays caused by looking up basic information in your book or the AutoCAD manual — and you don't even have to leave your drawing session.

HELP If you don't know or aren't sure of how a particular command or option works, select HELP (by typing it in or picking it from a menu area).

Locating the HELP command
- the Root Menu under INQUIRY
- the Pull Down Menu under ASSIST (under INQUIRY pre-Release 11)
- the Tablet Menu

Here's how the HELP command works

1. Type in, or select from a menu, the name of the command that you are having trouble with.

2. Select HELP.

   A description of the command will appear as well as where you can look it up in the manual for more information.

3. Hit **F1** or select REDRAW to return to drawing mode and your command.

   Get help also by Selecting HELP and then type the command name.

```
The ERASE command lets you delete selected entities from the drawing.

Format: Erase    Select objects: (select)

You can easily erase just the last object you draw by responding to
the "Select objects" prompt with "L".

The        OOPS    command can be used to retrieve the last thing you erased.

See also:        Section 5.1 of the Reference Manual.

Command:
```

PROJECT 12

HELP

1. Seek HELP with a command that you are having trouble with or are unsure about.

2. Print the screen information out on your printer. You will need to consult your computer's manual to perform this step. On IBM and compatible computers this is done by hitting the **PRINT SCREEN** key.

3. Study your printout and practice that command.

4. Repeat for other commands that you are having problems with.

17 AutoCAD's COORDINATE SYSTEM

FUNCTION: There are many times when drawing specific lines at specific angles with a pointing device is not adequate or accurate. If you can't solve the problem by ZOOMing in or out, you will need to enter the information through the keyboard. These situations are infrequent, but when they occur, keyboard coordinate entry is often the only way to input that precise data. It is well worth your time and effort to learn keyboard coordinate entry.

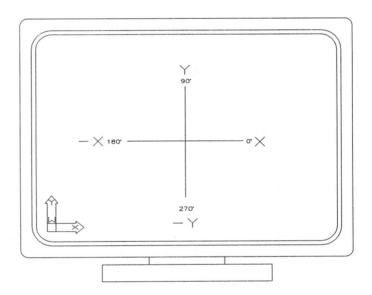

The diagram above illustrates AutoCAD's coordinate system. The symbol found in the lower left corner of the drawing editor screen is called the coordinate system icon. It is a reminder of the coordinate system that you are currently working in. Right now you are working with the World Coordinate System where Y is up and X is to the right. The "W" in the icon is a reference to this system. Later on, when you work in 3D, you will be defining your own coordinate systems. A "U" is in the icon when you are using a user-defined system.

If you are familiar with mathematical terms, you may recognize the World system as the Cartesian Coordinate System. It is important to understand this Cartesian Coordinate system for the polar coordinate keyboard entry system.

The intersection of the arrows in the diagram above represents the lower left corner of your prototype (0'-0", 0'-0").

There are three techniques for entering coordinates via the keyboard. All three systems of keyboard entry will yield the same result. The decision you make as to which one to use will be based on what information is available on your drawing at the time that you need to draw your line.

Absolute Coordinate Entry

Absolute refers to the fact that every point on your drawing screen has an "address." The lower left corner of your screen is 0'-0", 0'-0" and the upper right hand corner of your 24" x 36" ½" scale prototype is 48'-0", 72'-0". These are all *absolute* points.

With this absolute coordinate system of coordinate entry you type:

1. The absolute address of where the line is to start X,Y

2. The absolute coordinate of where it is to end X,Y

Absolute coordinate entry uses the , (comma) symbol to separate the X and Y coordinates representing specific places on the screen. An example — at the LINE command type:

> from point: 5',5'

(Pick your beginning point on the screen by typing in the exact coordinates. If you know where you want to start drawing but don't know the absolute coordinates of that point, you can identify it with the ID command.)

> to point: 5',15'

AutoCAD will draw a line 10'-0" long going straight up.
Erase the line you just drew.

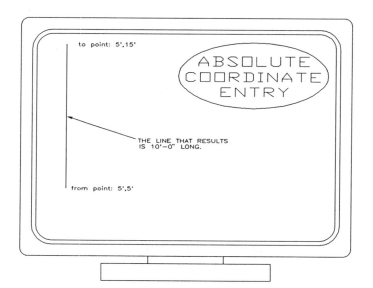

Relative Coordinate Entry

Relative coordinate entry refers to the fact that you will indicate the exact "address" of the starting point of your line, but you will indicate the end point in *relative* terms, not with a specific X,Y address but rather with its X,Y *distance*.

Relative coordinate entry uses the , (comma) symbol to indicate specific X,Y points on the screen and the @ symbol to represent the distance and angle away in relation to that point. In the example below, 0',10' does not refer to the exact "address" of the point. It says that the end point of the line is 0' to the right, and 10' straight up.

An example — at the LINE command type:

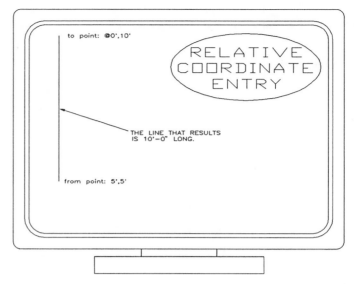

(Pick your beginning point on the screen by typing in the exact coordinates. The coordinate can be identified using the ID command.)

to point: 0',10'

AutoCAD draws the same line 10'-0" long going straight up.

Erase the line.

Polar Coordinate Entry

This is the system that you will probably use the most. With polar coordinate entry you first type in the coordinates of the beginning of the line and then type in the distance away the end of the line will be in feet and inches — followed by the angle at which the line is to be drawn.

Polar coordinate entry uses the @ symbol and the < (angle) symbol.

An example — at the LINE command type:

from point: 5',5'

(Pick your beginning point on the screen by typing in the exact coordinates. The coordinate can be identified using the ID command)

to point: 10'<90

AutoCAD will again draw the same 10'-0" long line going straight up.

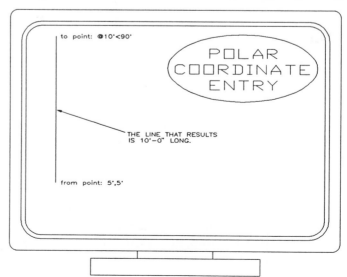

COORDINATES

1. Draw <u>ELEVATION A</u> from the example below using relative coordinate entry.

2. Draw only the outlines of the door flat.

3. Advanced AutoCADers might try drawing the baseboard detail.

4. Draw <u>ELEVATION B</u> using polar coordinate entry.

5. Draw only the outline of the window wall.

6. Advanced AutoCADers might try drawing the window and baseboard details.

7. The first point of each <u>ELEVATION</u> may be picked with a pointing device.

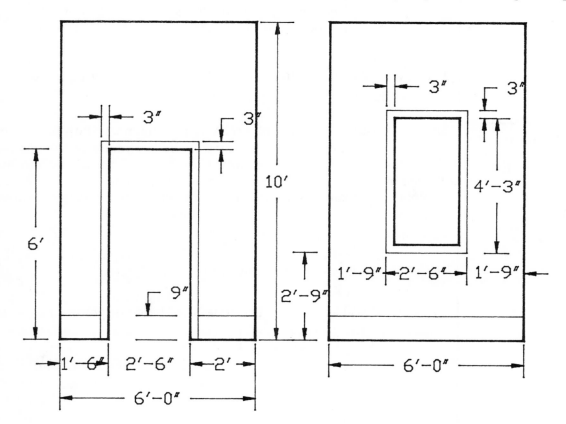

18 AutoCAD'S PRECISION DRAWING TOOLS

FUNCTION: Object snap overrides are what give CAD drawings their extraordinary precision. You will be using these overrides whenever you draw from now on. They will seem extremely awkward and cumbersome at first. But after a short time, using these tools will become second nature. You may as well not be using a CAD system if you don't use object snap. These tools bring perfection and lightning fast speed to your drawing sessions. For example, object snap can find the middle of a line in an instant. Manual drafting takes some measuring and a little math to achieve the same result.

OSNAP Overrides

The OSNAP overrides give you the power to make exact connections — lots of different types of connections. Ends of lines to ends of lines, ends of lines to centers of circles, ends of lines to the middle of other lines, and so on. You have always made these connections in pencil and paper drafting by using "eyeballing" to find the end of a line, "help-lines" to find the center of a circle, and measuring and math to find the middle of a line.

These methods of connection may have suited your purpose in pencil and paper drawings, but they fall far short of being adequate in a CAD drawing. If we could place a pencil-and-paper line-to-line connection under a microscope, we would most likely see a "large" gap between the end points and/or one or both of the lines overlapping well past the connection point.

In a CAD drawing this lack of precision is unacceptable. Here are a few reasons. CAD dimensioning is automatic. You can't look at the line, know that it's supposed to be 10' long (even though it actually measures out to 9'-11 ¾") and draw that 10' dimension — as you do all the time in manual drafting. The automatic dimensioning feature will produce a dimension that will drive you haywire. The line is not exactly the right length that you want it to be because it's not connected. The computer will examine the line and write the true 9'-11 ¾" dimension; it refuses to fudge.

Suppose that you have drawn a flat (without using the OSNAP Overrides) and then want the computer to tell you the surface area of the flat so that you can figure out how much muslin to order. If the corners of the flats are drawn with these little gaps, the computer will never be able to come up with an area figure since the shape of the flat has been compromised.

It is important for you to know that, as ungainly as they seem, and no matter how bad your mood gets while you are trying to use them at first, stick with the overrides. Using the overrides will seem as second nature as breathing in a short time, and they will bring exceptional perfection to your drawings.

Locating the OSNAP overrides
- the Root Menu under * * * *
- the Pull Down Menu under ASSIST (under TOOLS in Release 10)
- the Tablet Menu

Each of the OSNAP overrides will **snap** a line to a specified point on an **object** (a different point and/or object for each option). What follows is an examination of each of the OSNAP overrides.

Let's start with the overrides that you are most likely to use. Try each of them out on your drawing as you learn about them.

CENter
Snaps a line to or from the center of a circle. To get your line to snap to the center of a circle, place any part of the circle line inside the target.

ENDpoint
Snaps a line to or from the end of an existing line.

INTersec(tion)
Snaps a line to or from the intersection of two lines.

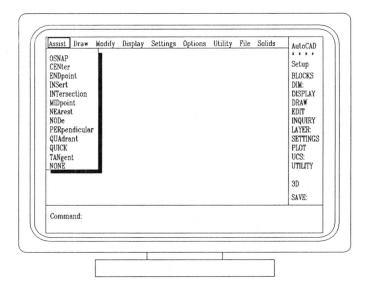

MIDpoint
Snaps a line to or from the point halfway in between the two ends of a line.

NEArest
Snaps a line to or from a line wherever that line is in the target box.

NODe
Snaps a line to or from a node. (More about nodes later on.)

PERpen(dicular)
Draws a line perpendicular (90°) to a line chosen in the target box. You can't draw a line perpendicular from a line. In Interrupt mode, choose **PERpen** only after you have picked the beginning of the line and before picking the end of the line.

QUAdrant
Snaps a line to the edge of a circle at the 12:00, 3:00, 6:00, or 9:00 (quadrant) positions of a circle.

TANgent
Snaps a line tangent to a circle closest to the point of the circle picked in the target.

NONE
Cancels OSNAP running mode. Hit **ENTER** after selecting NONE.

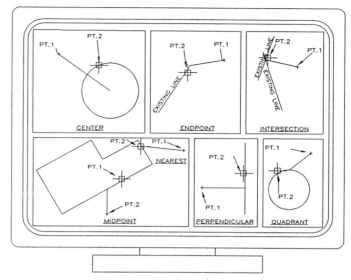

Here is how a typical OSNAP override (ENDpoint) works:

Interrupt Mode

1. Draw a couple of circles, some triangles, and a few lines on a blank screen.

2. Select LINE. AutoCAD says:

    Line from point:

3. Select ENDpoint.

    If you're not using a Tablet Menu you will first need to bring up the OSNAP options in order to select ENDpoint (see Locating the OSNAP overrides).

4. AutoCAD says: Line from point: ENDpoint of:

    This is your prompt to pick the end point of the line from which your new line will originate. As you move your pointing device you will notice that the intersection of your cross hairs has a box around it. This is called the target. You don't need to get the intersection of the crosshairs lined up with the end point of the existing line, only get the end point within the target zone.

    Place the target zone over the end point of the existing line from which your new line will originate and pick it.

5. AutoCAD says: to point:

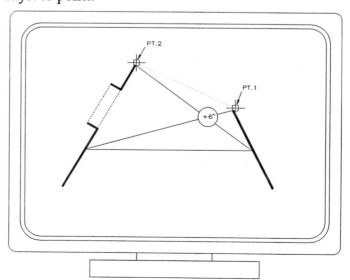

6. Select ENDpoint.

Place the target zone over the end point of another existing line at which your new line will end; pick it.

Your line is now drawn.

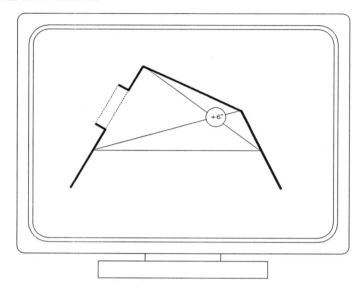

This method of using the OSNAP overrides is called Interrupt mode because you insert the override command by *interrupting* the drawing command, as we did in Steps #3 and #6 above. Instead of picking a point to draw the line, we *interrupted* the command by introducing ENDpoint. Interrupt mode is fine when you are using certain OSNAP features occasionally. However, it can be time consuming if you use it when you are doing a lot of OSNAP work (which will be all the time from now on). There is another way of using OSNAP that is more convenient if you are doing this kind of work.

The OSNAP Command

The OSNAP command (not to be confused with the OSNAP overrides) allows you to use the overrides in *Running Mode*. Running mode eliminates command interruption. This technique involves "loading up" your target box with the overrides you will be needing. After they are in place, the target box will automatically appear and you never have to call them up.

Locating the OSNAP command
- the Root Menu under SETTINGS
- the Pull Down Menu under ASSIST (under TOOLS in Release 10)
- the Tablet Menu

Loading up the overrides for running mode

1. To select the overrides that you will need:

   Select OSNAP (from the Root Menu or the Tablet only).

2. The overrides will appear in the Screen Menu Area.

   Select the overrides that you want to use for your next drawing task.
   Do this by highlighting and picking each override. Separate each override with a comma.
   (Use Endpoint and INTersection whenever you are dimensioning.)

3. Hit **ENTER**.

Using running mode

1. Select LINE.

2. Draw a line from an existing end point of an object to another existing end point of another object.

    The target will automatically appear. You will continue to have the target loaded with your OSNAP overrides until you "unload" them. To unload, simply go back to the OSNAP command and highlight NONE.

3. Hit **ENTER**.

    You can work with as many overrides as you wish in running mode. To do so, just separate each option with a comma as you "load them up." Don't load in conflicting overrides such as CENter and QUAdrant.

APERTURE and PICKBOX

At times you may find that the target zone box is either too big to do precision work in some of the more complicated parts of your drawing or too small and therefore slowing you down as you carefully place the object in the "teeny-tiny" box. You can change the size of this box (aperture) with the APERTURE command.

You may also find that the pick box — the box that appears during an ERASE — is too big or too small.

Locating the APERTURE and PICKBOX commands
*   the Root Menu under SETTINGS
*   the Tablet Menu

You can set both the APERTURE and PICKBOX between 1 and 50 pixels (picture elements). Set the aperture size with the APERTURE command and the pick box size with the PICKBOX command. Once you set the pick box and the aperture size they will remain at those settings until you change them once again.

PROJECT 14

OSNAP

1. Create a PROJ14 drawing from your ½" scale prototype.

2. Turn OFF Grid and Snap.

3. Turn ON Ortho (turn it OFF when appropriate).

4. Draw the platforms in this <u>PLATFORM PLAN</u> drawing using OSNAP.

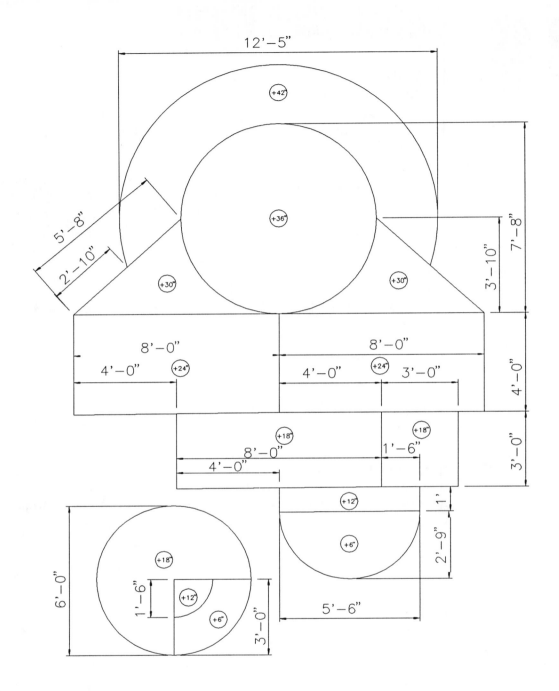

19 EDITING YOUR WORK PART II

> **FUNCTION**: EDITING YOUR WORK PART II examines some of the advanced editing commands. MOVE, COPY, MIRROR, and ROTATE are crucial functions in unlocking the power and speed of CAD drafting. With these commands you will be able to manipulate objects that have been drawn. You will also be able to reposition, turn, duplicate, and make reverse images of your drawings.

MOVE

The MOVE command manipulates the objects in your drawing by moving them from one place to another.

Locating the MOVE command
- the Root Menu under EDIT
- the Pull Down Menu under MODIFY
- the Tablet Menu

Here's how the MOVE command works

Draw an object in the upper left hand corner of a blank screen.

1. Select MOVE.

2. AutoCAD says: Select Objects.

   Select what you want to move on your drawing by enclosing it within a window or picking the individual entities.

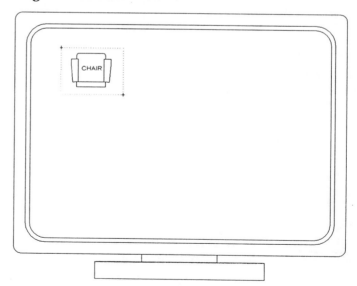

3. AutoCAD says: Select Objects.

   You are in the Select Objects loop. Select more objects to move if you need to, if not:

   Hit **ENTER**.

4. AutoCAD says: <Base point or displacement>/Multiple:

Think of the base point as a carrying handle. I usually use OSNAP overrides to pick the lower left or lower right hand corner of the object.

Pick that point.

5. AutoCAD says: Second point of displacement.

This is where you want the object to move to in reference to the handle. Move the object until it is where you want it to be.

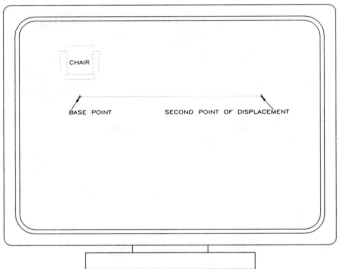

Pick that point. You have moved your object.

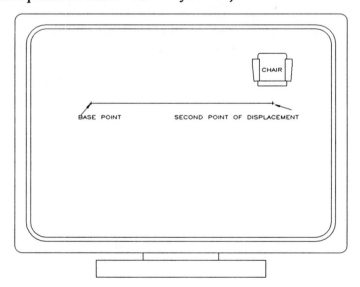

COPY The COPY command copies any object or any group of objects on your drawing and produces one or more duplicates.

Locating the COPY command
- the Root Menu under EDIT
- the Pull Down Menu under MODIFY
- the Tablet Menu

Here's how COPY works

1. Select COPY.

2. AutoCAD says: Select Objects.

    Select what you want to COPY on your drawing by making a window or by picking individual entities.

    > Hit **ENTER**.

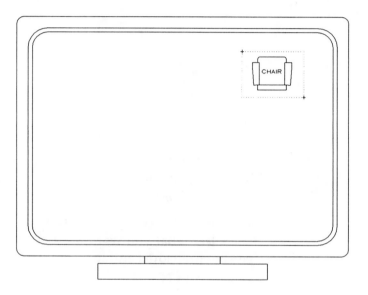

3. AutoCAD says: Base point or displacement.

    Think of this as a carrying handle. Use OSNAP overrides to pick the center, lower left, or lower right hand corner of the object.

4. AutoCAD says: Second point of displacement.

    You can now move your copy to an empty spot on your drawing. Pick that point. You now have a copy.

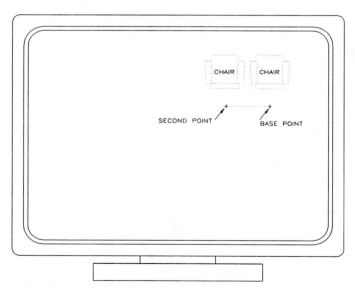

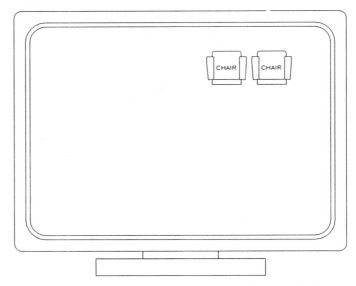

You can make a number of copies by choosing the **Multiple** option during the COPY commands. Let's test drive **Multiple**.

1. Select COPY.

2. AutoCAD says: Select Objects.

    Select what you want to COPY on your drawing by making a window or picking individual entities.

    Hit **ENTER**.

3. AutoCAD says: <Base point or displacement>/Multiple:

    Select **Multiple** from the Screen Menu Area.

4. AutoCAD says: Multiple base point.

    AutoCAD is asking for your carrying handle position again.

    Pick that point.

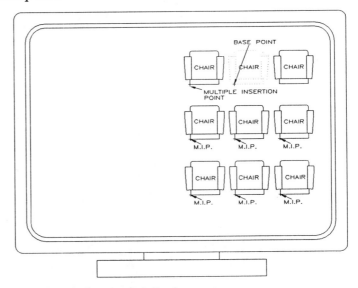

5. AutoCAD says: Second point of displacement.

    You can now move your copy to an empty spot on your drawing. Pick that point. You now have a copy.

6. Continue to move your object in order to make multiple copies of it on your drawing.

7. Hit **ENTER** when you are done.

MIRROR

With MIRROR you can make reverse image drawings of your objects or you can draw half of a symmetrical object and mirror the other half.

Locating the MIRROR command
- the Root Menu under EDIT
- the Pull Down Menu under MODIFY
- the Tablet Menu

Here's how MIRROR works

1. Select MIRROR.

2. AutoCAD says: Select objects.

   Use window to select your half object.

3. AutoCAD says: First point of mirror line.

   Pick a point that will act as the end of the line of reflection. This line can be an imaginary line or you can actually draw a line and erase it later on. It is sometimes helpful to have Ortho on for MIRROR operations.

4. AutoCAD says: Second point of mirror line.

   Pick the other end of the imaginary reflecting line.

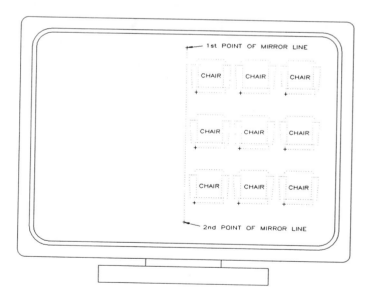

5. AutoCAD says: Delete old objects?

6. Select NO.

   You now have your mirrored copy.

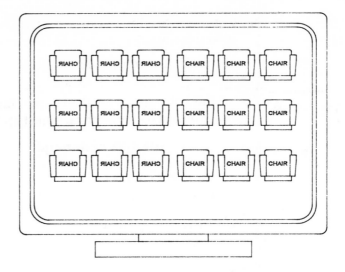

ROTATE

ROTATE manipulates an object by turning it in your drawing.

Locating the ROTATE command
- the Root Menu under EDIT
- the Pull Down Menu under MODIFY (Release 11 and beyond)
- the Tablet Menu under EDIT

Here's how you might use ROTATE

On a blank screen, draw a line from just to the right of the center of the screen to almost the edge of the screen. Draw it at 0°, use Ortho.

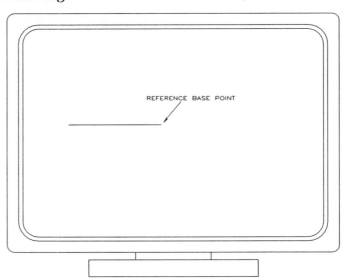

REFERENCE BASE POINT

1. Select ROTATE. Turn Ortho off.

2. AutoCAD says: Select objects:

   Pick the object to be rotated.

3. AutoCAD says: Select objects:

   Hit **ENTER** to get out of the loop.

4. AutoCAD says: Base point:

    Pick the point about which the object will rotate. In this example, pick the right end point of the line.

5. AutoCAD says: <Rotation angle>/Reference:

    You are presented here with two methods for rotating your object. The rotation angle method is a relative method. Using it will rotate the object counterclockwise by the number of degrees that you specify from the current angle. The reference method is an absolute method. Using it will rotate the object to a specific absolute angle. Let's start with the rotation angle method.

Rotation angle method

6. Type 90 (referring to 90° from the current position counterclockwise). The line should have rotated 90° counterclockwise, as in the example below.

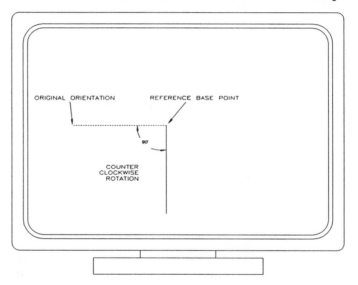

Reference method

Restore the line to its original orientation (Select U).

1. Select rotate.

2. AutoCAD says: Select objects:

    Pick the object to be rotated.

3. AutoCAD says: Select objects:

    Hit **ENTER** to get out of the loop.

4. AutoCAD says: Base point:

    Pick the same base point as before.

5. AutoCAD says: <Rotation angle>/Reference:

    Type R

6. AutoCAD says: Reference angle <0>:

    Type 180

    This is the angle at which our line lies in reference to the base point.

7. AutoCAD says: New angle:

Type 90 (referring to AutoCAD's absolute angle 90°).

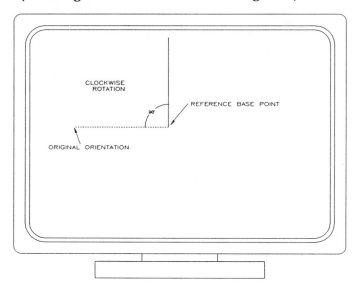

This time typing 90 gives you an entirely different result.

PROJECT 15

MOVE, COPY, MIRROR, ROTATE

1. Create a PROJ15 drawing from your ½" scale prototype.

2. In the upper left hand corner of the sheet, use your LAYOUT layer to draw a vertical line. Use Ortho to draw your line.

3. On your OUTLINES layer, draw one-half of this simple fireplace. Make sure that the fireplace touches the vertical guideline at what would be the center.

4. Make a complete fireplace by using the MIRROR command.

5. Move the fireplace from the upper left hand corner of the page.

6. Make a row of five fireplaces.

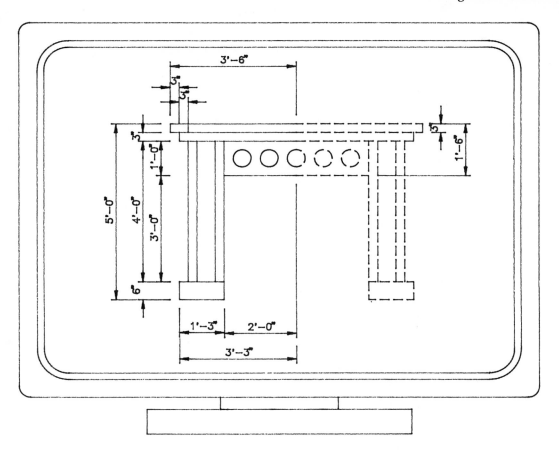

20 EDITING YOUR WORK PART III

FUNCTION: These editing commands give you the power for the first time to erase part of an entity. You will now be able to erase just a part of a line. This skill comes in handy for "erasing" the batten out of lighting instruments in a <u>LIGHT PLOT</u>. Or placing chairs around a table in a <u>FLOOR PLAN</u> and "erasing" the part of the chair below the table top.

BREAK

This command allows you to "erase" part of a line, circle, arc, or polyline by breaking it into two or three entities. BREAK then erases the portion of the entity that you want to get rid of.

Locating the BREAK command
- the Root Menu under EDIT
- the Pull Down Menu under MODIFY
- the Tablet Menu

Using the BREAK command

Draw a line on your screen.

1. Select BREAK.

2. AutoCAD says: Select object:

    Pick a point on the line.

3. AutoCAD says: Enter second point (or F for first point):

    To break a line you have to indicate the first point of the break and the second point of the break. You are presented with two methods for indicating those breaks:
    One step method — (enter second point) combines the object pick with the first point of break pick
    Two step method — (or F for first point) separates the object and the first point of break pick into two steps

One step method (enter second point)

4. With this method, where you pick your object becomes the first point of the break.

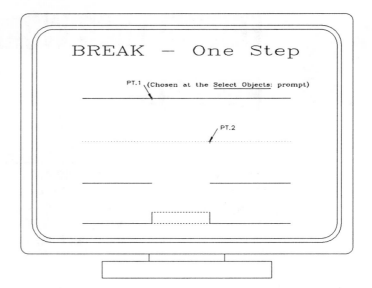

Pick the second break point. Your line should now be broken. Let's try the two step method.

Two step method (or F for first point)
(Available on the Tablet Menu as a separate command)

1. Select BREAK.

2. AutoCAD says: Select object:

   Pick the line.

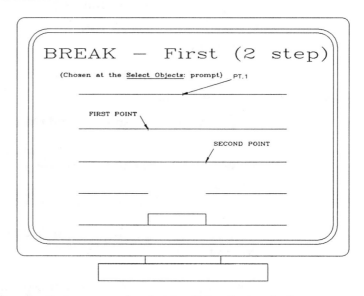

3. AutoCAD says: Enter second point (or F for first point):

   Type F

4. AutoCAD says: Enter first point:

   Pick the first point of your break.

5. AutoCAD says: Enter second point:

   Pick the second point of your break.

You have now broken your line. Notice that with both methods the unwanted part of the line is automatically removed.

BREAK @

BREAK @ works almost like the other BREAK command options. However, you can make only one break point (not two as before) and no part of the line will be erased. The entire line (or circle, arc, or polyline) will remain intact. What was formerly one entity is now two. Many AutoCAD novices are puzzled as to why the command didn't seem to work! It does work! It's just that you can't see anything happen. However, what was formerly one line is now two shorter ones.

This command is good for dividing a line up into smaller measurable units. It is also a way of placing snapable end points within a longer line.

Locating the BREAK @ command
- the Root Menu under EDIT, BREAK
- the Tablet Menu

Here's how the command works

1. Select BREAK @.

2. AutoCAD says: Select object:

   Pick the line you want to BREAK @.

3. AutoCAD says: Enter second point (or F for first point):

   Type F (it may have been done for you automatically)

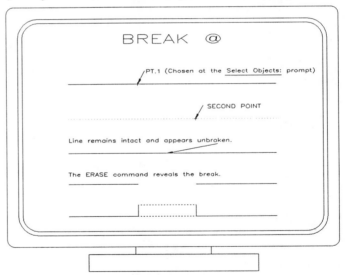

4. AutoCAD says: Enter first point:

   Pick the point where you want the break to occur.

5. AutoCAD says: Enter second point:

   You don't enter a second point. The break has already happened. Try it out by drawing a line from the break using OSNAP ENDpoint.

TRIM

This command is used to cut off, or trim, lines, arcs, circles, or polylines that cross other lines, arcs, circles, or polylines. This makes the trimmed entity end exactly at another entity.

Locating the TRIM command
- the Root Menu under EDIT
- the Pull Down Menu under MODIFY
- the Tablet Menu

Let's try the TRIM command

In the following example, you will be trimming a line to make the opening for a door (in <u>PLAN</u>). Draw a straight line and two short lines representing the reveals.

1. Select TRIM.

2. AutoCAD says: Select cutting edge(s) . . .

A cutting edge is the entity that you want to trim to — the entity that you want to trim crosses the cutting edge.

> Pick one of your lines.

3. AutoCAD says: Select objects:

> Hit **ENTER**.

4. AutoCAD says: Select object to trim:

Pick the part of the line that you want to get rid of. Your line should now be trimmed. You can sometimes select large groups of cutting edges with **Crossing**.

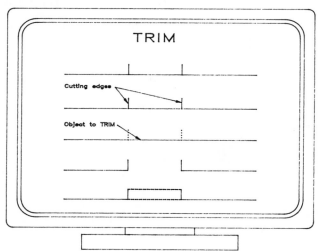

PROJECT 16

BREAK, BREAK @, TRIM

1. Create a PROJ 16 drawing from your ½" scale prototype.

2. Make your OUTLINE layer current.

3. Change Snap to 1".

4. Turn on Snap, Ortho, and Grid.

5. Draw the eight light window and its molding by following these steps:

a. Draw the rectangle.

b1. Draw the 2" window frame inside the rectangle.

b2. Divide the window up into four sections by drawing three vertical lines.

b3. Draw the other two verticals by referring to the measurements.

c1. Center the 2" mullions on the vertical and horizontal guidelines.

c2. Erase the vertical and horizontal guidelines.

d. Draw one of the three panes in. Use COPY, MULTIPLE, and ORTHO to build all of the panes.

e. Draw the sill and trim moldings as indicated.

f. Trim the overlapping lines (use the TRIM **Crossing** option to select many of the cutting edges at one time).

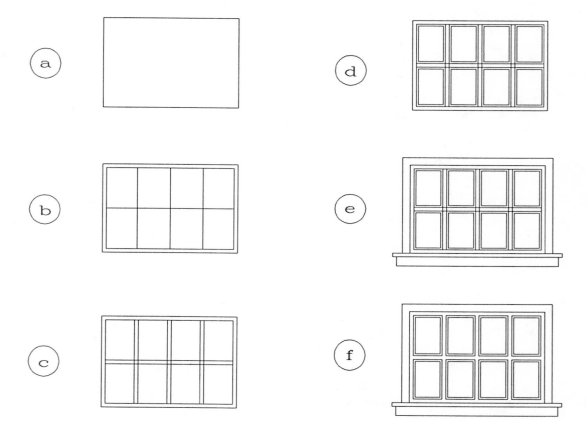

21 EDITING YOUR WORK PART IV

> **FUNCTION**: In the previous chapter you altered an entity for the first time. Here are some more commands that alter entities in other ways.

CHAMFER

There is a term in construction called "chamfer." It means to take the edge off of a 90° corner by angling it with a 45° router blade. You might chamfer the edge of the trim around a window or door for instance. AutoCAD's CHAMFER command also takes the sharp point off of a corner and replaces it with a bevel.

Locating the CHAMFER command
- the Root Menu under EDIT
- the Pull Down Menu under MODIFY (Release 11 and beyond)
- the Tablet Menu under EDIT

Here's how the CHAMFER command works

Draw two lines 15'-0" long meeting at 90°. Before you can chamfer an object, you must set up chamfer distances. These distances are the distance from the corner to the beginning of the chamfer. You aren't restricted to 45°; you can chamfer to any angle you want. But you don't specify an *angle* with the CHAMFER command! Instead, you specify how far away from the old corner the new cut edge will be.

1. Select CHAMFER.

2. AutoCAD says: Polyline/Distances/<select first line>

    Select distance by typing D

3. AutoCAD says: First chamfer distance

    Type 5'

4. AutoCAD says: Second chamfer distance

    Type 5' (Equal distances will make a 45° angle)

Now that you have set up the chamfer distances you can begin chamfering your object.

1. Select CHAMFER.

2. AutoCAD says: Polyline/Distances/<select first line>

    You are now ready to select your first line of the two to be chamfered. Since this choice is the default:

    pick your line with the pick box.

3. AutoCAD says: Select second line

    Pick the other line.

The lines should now be chamfered.

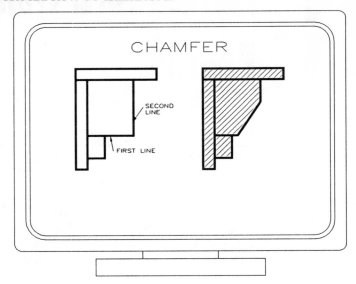

FILLET

FILLET connects two lines with an arc. The lines do not need to be connected in order for the command to work. If they are connected, the command has the effect of rounding off a squared corner. It is a terrific way to make furniture symbols for a <u>FLOOR PLAN</u>. A curved corner dining room table can be made by drawing a rectangle and then FILLETing the corners. This command is also quite handy for full scale details of set moldings.

Locating the FILLET command
- the Root Menu under EDIT
- the Pull Down Menu under MODIFY
- the Tablet Menu under EDIT

Here's how FILLET works

Before getting started, draw a number of line pairs meeting at 90° angles on a blank ½" scale framework drawing.

Before you can FILLET an object, you must set up a FILLET radius.

1. Select FILLET.

2. AutoCAD says: Polyline/Radius/<select two objects>:

   Select Radius by typing R

3. AutoCAD says: Enter fillet radius

   Type 2′

Now that you have set up the radius you can begin FILLETing your object.

1. Select FILLET.

2. AutoCAD says: Polyline/Radius/<select two objects>:

   You are now ready to actually FILLET your two objects. Since this choice is the default:

   Pick the two lines of one of the line pairs with the pick box.

The lines should now be FILLETed.

Practice with different radii on other line pairs.

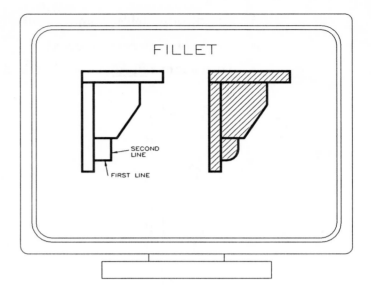

FILLET 0 and CHAMFER 0

These commands *don't* chamfer or fillet. Instead both FILLET 0 and CHAMFER 0 connect any two lines that would otherwise meet if they were to be extended. The 0 refers to a radius of zero (in the case of FILLET) or a distance of zero (as in the case of CHAMFER).

Both commands can be found as an option with their respective primary commands on the Screen Menu. In addition, FILLET 0 can be found on the Tablet Menu next to FILLET.

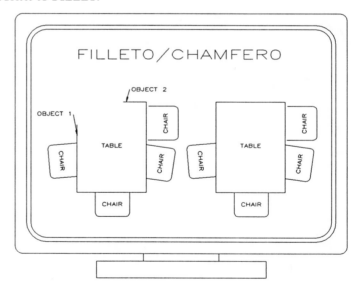

PROJECT 17

CHAMFER, FILLET, CHAMFER 0, FILLET 0

1. Create a PROJ17 drawing from your ½" scale prototype.

2. Draw a 4' x 8' rectangular dining room table.

3. Make a copy of the table.

4. On one of the tables, fillet each corner with a radius of 1'-11".

5. On the other table, chamfer with a 1' distance.

6. Draw the dimensioned object.

7. Turn it into a <u>PLAN</u> view of a grand piano.

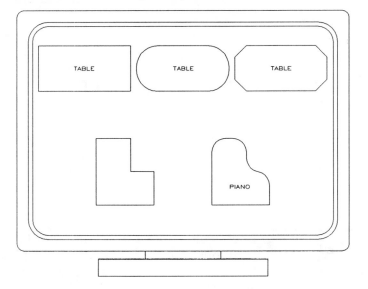

22 EDITING YOUR WORK
PART V

> **FUNCTION**: These editing commands allow you to place copies of drawn objects in highly exact positions or patterns. In a <u>PLAN</u>, a line could be offset from an existing line with an exact measurement in order to represent a thick wall for example. ARRAY can instantly fill an entire exterior wall with windows in a pattern that you specify. These commands make quick and accurate work out of repetitive duplication.

OFFSET

Locating the OFFSET command
- the Root Menu under EDIT
- the Pull Down Menu under MODIFY (Release 11 and beyond)
- the Tablet Menu

Here's how OFFSET works
Before you begin, call up your ½" scale prototype. Draw two rectangles on the screen.

1. Select OFFSET.

2. AutoCAD says: Offset distance or Through:

    You are being presented with two options — the distance method and the through method — for offsetting objects. Let's try the through method first.

Through method
Select Through.

3. AutoCAD says: Select object to offset:

    Pick one side of the rectangle that you drew earlier.

4. AutoCAD says: Through point:

    AutoCAD is now ready to draw your offset line through a point that you pick. Pick a point near your original line. Your new offset line appears. Repeat for all four sides.

Distance method
1. Select OFFSET.

2. AutoCAD says: Offset distance or Through:

    Type 1'

3. AutoCAD says: Select object to offset:

    Pick one side of the rectangle.

4. AutoCAD says: Side to offset?

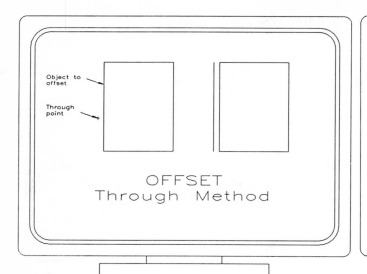

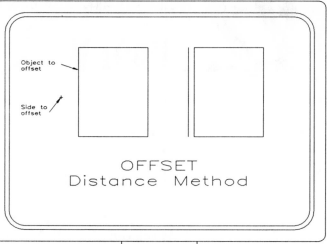

Here you make a choice as to which side of your original line you want your new offset line to appear on.

Pick a point outside of the rectangle by moving your cross hairs to that area and picking.

5. Your new offset line appears. AutoCAD always remembers the offset distance that you last typed in and will give it to you in the default brackets every time you call up this option.

AutoCAD says:

Select object to offset?

Repeat Steps #3 and #4 until all sides of the rectangle have been offset.

6. Now that all four sides have been offset, let's close up the open corners and turn these offset lines into a rectangle. This might be helpful for trimming molding around a window or similar tasks.

Select CHAMFER 0 (dis = 0 if you are using the Screen Menu).

7. Select pairs of lines at corners. CHAMFER 0 (or FILLET 0) will instantly "heal" these corners and make your new rectangle.

This OFFSET/CHAMFER 0 method is the method that you will use for drawing an object around a smaller twin. This could be a section detail of a cornice molding showing lumber thickness, a costume pattern showing seam allowance, or even batten thickness on a LIGHT PLOT.

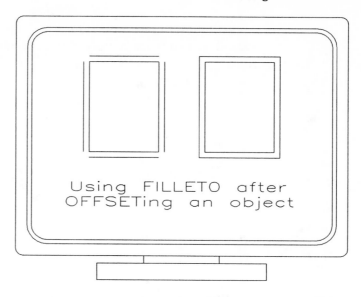

ARRAY

ARRAY is an editing command that will make an instant pattern out of any object. It could be a pattern of multiple windows on a building, or in a <u>FLOOR PLAN</u> you could create an instant seating pattern for a setting that requires rectangular lecture hall style seating. You could also ARRAY a group of chairs around a circular conference table.

Locating the ARRAY command
- the Root Menu under EDIT
- the Pull Down Menu under MODIFY (Release 11 and beyond)
- the Tablet Menu

Here's how to use ARRAY
Before we try ARRAY, call up your ½" scale prototype. Draw a chair at a round table as in the illustration.

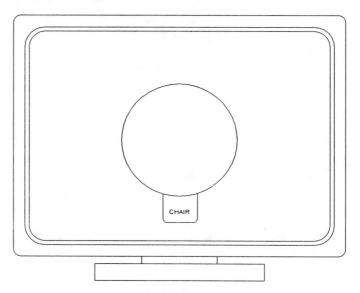

1. Select ARRAY AutoCAD says: Select objects:

   Pick the chair.

2. AutoCAD says: Rectangular or Polar Array (R/P):

AutoCAD gives you two array variations — Polar and Rectangular. Each variation produces a very different result. We'll survey the Polar variation first.

Select **Polar**.

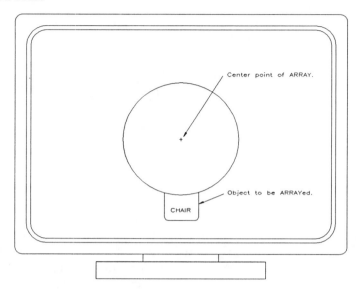

Polar variation

3. AutoCAD says: Center point of array:

    For our example, pick the center of the circle (use OSNAP **CENter**).

4. AutoCAD says: Number of items:

    Try 7.

5. AutoCAD says: Angle to fill (+=ccw, -=cw) <360>:

    This is where you specify the amount of an imaginary arc that would be filled by your array.

    A positive number will draw the array counterclockwise from 0°. A negative number will draw the array clockwise. Let's get a full circle array by typing 360 (or simply hitting **ENTER** since 360 is shown as the default in brackets).

6. AutoCAD says: Rotate objects as they are copied?<Y>

    Selecting NO would maintain the current vertical orientation of your object as it is arrayed in a 360° circle. Selecting the default, YES, rotates the object so that the part of the object currently closest to the picked center point remains so as the object is arrayed.

    Hit **ENTER**.

7. AutoCAD will now array your object. Here again AutoCAD makes quick work of a deceptively complex drafting issue. Now let's try a rectangular array.

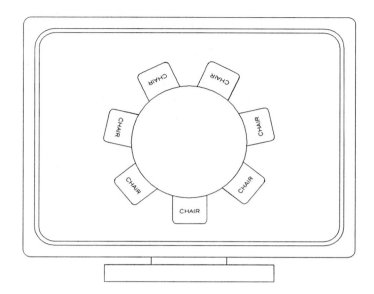

Rectangular variation

Erase your screen. Draw a 2′ x 2′ square (representing a large chair perhaps) near the lower left corner.

1. Select ARRAY. AutoCAD says: Select objects

    Select your rectangle.

2. AutoCAD says: **Rectangular** or **Polar** (R/P):

    Select **Rectangular**.

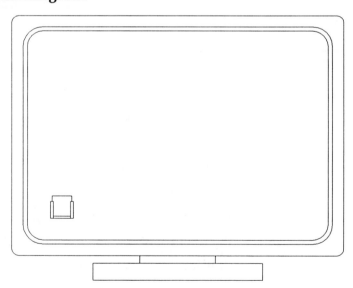

3. AutoCAD says: Number of rows (---) <1>:

AutoCAD is showing you 1 row.

    Type 4

4. AutoCAD says: Number of columns (|||) <1>: AutoCAD is showing you 3 columns.

    Type 7

5.   AutoCAD says: Unit cell or distance between rows (---):

With our 2′x 2′ square chair in mind:

Type in 4′

This will eventually result in a 2′ space between rows of chairs.

6.   AutoCAD says: Distance between columns (---):

Type in 2′

The result should now appear on the screen — all chairs should be touching each other side to side and 2′ apart front to back.

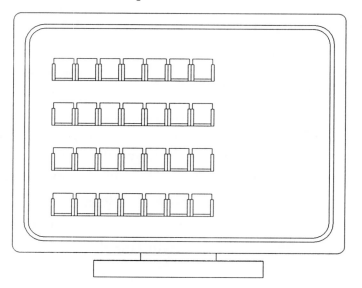

PROJECT 18

OFFSET, ARRAY

1.   Create a PROJ18 drawing from your HALFPROT drawing.

2.   Draw the window.

3.   Use OFFSET to develop the majority of the detail.

   a.   Draw the rectangle.

   b.   OFFSET to develop the trim moldings.

   c.   Connect the corners with FILLET 0.

   d.   Use OSNAP **MIDpoint** to draw the guidelines for the mullions.

   e.   Use OFFSET .5" to draw the mullion outlines.

   f 1. Erase the center mullion guidelines.

   f 2. Use OFFSET to draw one of the window panes.

   f 3. Use TRIM **Crossing** to trim the corners.

   f 4. COPY the pane to the other three positions.

4.   Draw a 15′ wide by 24′ high rectangle representing a wall <u>ELEVATION</u>.

5. MOVE the window to the lower left corner position of the wall as indicated. Use helper lines in the LAYOUT layer.

6. Use ARRAY to complete the <u>ELEVATION</u> as shown.

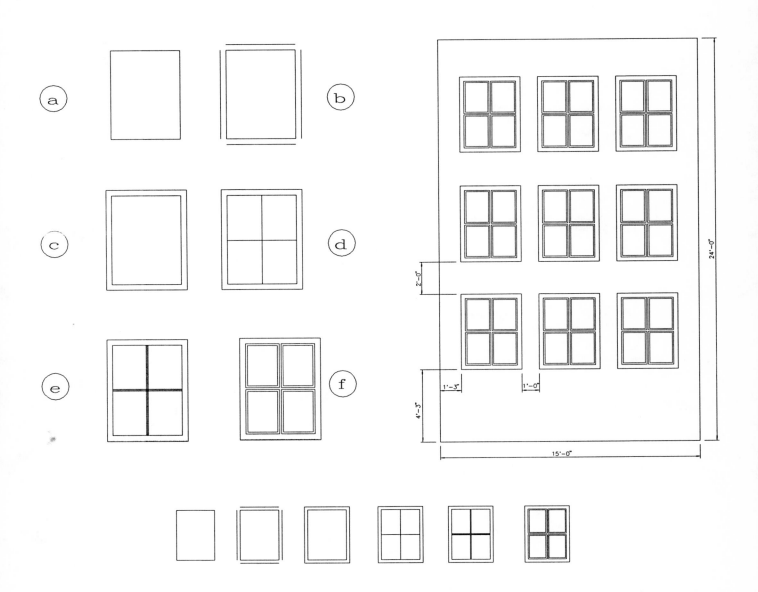

23 EDITING YOUR WORK PART VI

> **FUNCTION**: This group of editing commands allows you to treat your objects as if they were rubber. After mastering STRETCH, SCALE, and EXTEND you will be able to stretch them, squeeze them, and make them larger or smaller.

STRETCH

With the STRETCH command you can literally stretch an object in one direction. It does this by moving parts of your object while staying connected to the rest of it. Not all of the object will be stretched proportionally. It will stretch in only its X or Y direction. If, for instance, you have already drawn a door but now need a second, taller version of it, you can use the STRETCH command to do the job. It will make the door taller but not wider. With STRETCH you could also take a chair symbol in a <u>FLOOR PLAN</u> and turn it into a sofa. If the shorter version has been dimensioned, the dimensions will automatically stretch and change along with the object.

Locating the STRETCH command
- the Root Menu under EDIT
- the Pull Down Menu under MODIFY
- the Tablet Menu

Let's try STRETCH
Before you begin, draw a medium size rectangle on the screen.

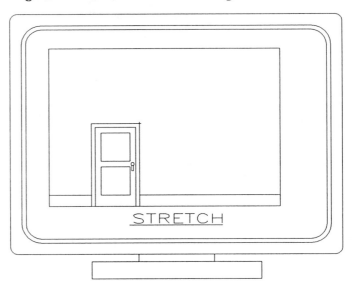

1. Select STRETCH.
2. AutoCAD says: Select objects to stretch by window . . .

You can use either a standard window or a crossing window.

Type C (you may be forced to use the **Crossing** option only).

3. AutoCAD says: First corner:

Keep the left side of your rectangle out of the crossing window by placing the first corner of your crossing window below and to the right of the left side of your rectangle.

4. AutoCAD says: Second corner:

Make your window and pick your second point above and to the right of your rectangle.

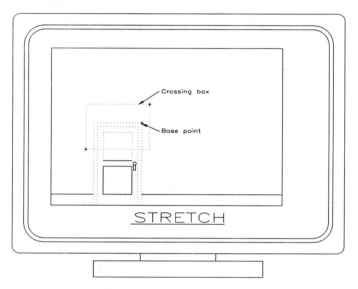

AutoCAD is going to stretch and/or move everything that is dashed. It will leave everything that is not dashed. Select **Add** or **Remove** in order to alter what entities will or will not be stretched.

5. AutoCAD says: Select objects:

Hit **ENTER**.

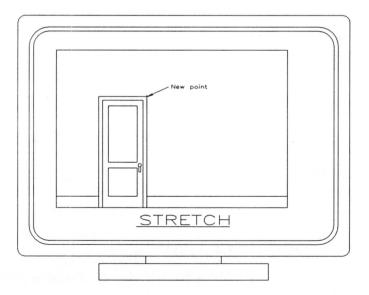

6. AutoCAD says: Base point:

> Pick the base point.

The base point is the carrying handle for the stretch.

7. AutoCAD says: New point:

> Pick the new point.

This is the new position of the carrying handle.
Your object should now be stretched.

SCALE

SCALE changes the sizes of objects proportionally — in both the X and Y directions. A better name for this command might be SIZE, or ENLARGE AND REDUCE. It has nothing to do with drawing scales (½"=1'-0", etc.) as the command name implies. Use this command when you want to make objects smaller or larger. A big door can become a small door, not just a shorter door.

Locating the SCALE command
- the Root Menu under EDIT
- the Pull Down Menu under MODIFY (Release 11 and beyond)
- the Tablet Menu

Here's how the SCALE command works
To get started, bring up your ½" scale prototype drawing. Draw a 3' X 5' rectangle on the screen.

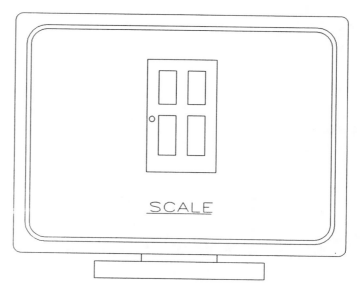

1. Select SCALE.

2. AutoCAD says: Select objects:

> Select your rectangle with a window.

3. AutoCAD says: Select objects:

> **ENTER** to get out of the loop.

4. AutoCAD says: Base point:

> This point that you are about to pick is the one point of the drawing that

will not move while the rest of the object is enlarging or shrinking. This is where you control the movement of the object as it scales larger or smaller.

Pick a point on or off of the object.

5. AutoCAD says: <Scale factor>/Reference:

Like so many other AutoCAD commands, you are given two methods to chose from in scaling an object. The scale factor method scales an object by the number you type in. 2 will double the size. .5 will make it half the size. The reference method scales the object to a specific dimension.

Scale factor method

6. Try the scale factor method first.

Since Scale factor is in brackets, it is the default. You don't need to select S at this time.

Type .5

The rectangle should now be half its original size. Get the rectangle back to its original size and let's look at the reference method.

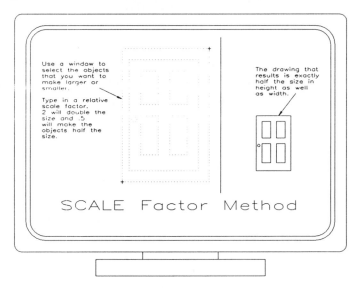

Use a window to select the objects that you want to make larger or smaller.

Type in a relative scale factor. 2 will double the size and .5 will make the objects half the size.

The drawing that results is exactly half the size in height as well as width.

SCALE Factor Method

Reference method

1. Select SCALE.

2. AutoCAD says: Select objects:

    Select your rectangle with a window.

3. AutoCAD says: Select objects:

    ENTER to get out of the loop.

4. AutoCAD says: Base point:

    Pick your base point.

5. AutoCAD says: <Scale factor>/Reference:

    Select Reference.

6. AutoCAD says: Reference length:

Type 5' (the current length of the rectangle)

7. AutoCAD says: New length:

Type 7'

The rectangle is now 7' long. If the width was the important measurement that you needed to make longer, you would have typed that measurement in as the reference length. Use the Reference method when you have a specific size in mind.

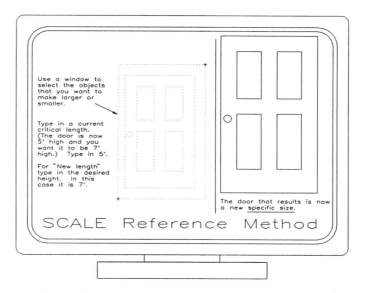

EXTEND

EXTEND will extend existing lines, arcs, and polylines to an existing boundary. The boundary could be a line, arc, circle, or polyline.

Locating the EXTEND command
- the Root Menu under EDIT
- the Pull Down Menu under MODIFY
- the Tablet Menu

Let's explore the EXTEND command
Before you go any further, draw a line that would touch the rectangle that we used in the previous command but stops short by a couple of feet.

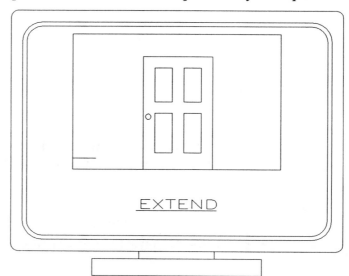

1. Select EXTEND.

2. AutoCAD says: Select boundary edge(s) . . .

   Select objects:

The boundary edge is the entity that you will be extending your line to. Pick the side of the rectangle nearest the line to be extended.

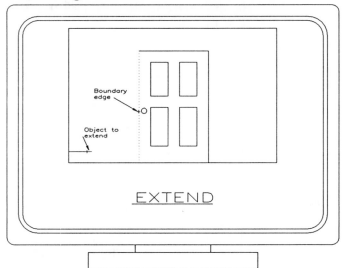

EXTEND

3. AutoCAD says: Select objects:

   Hit **ENTER.**

4. AutoCAD says: Select object to extend:

   Pick the line that you want to extend.

EXTEND

Your line should now meet the rectangle.
This is an important and powerful command that you will use quite often.

PROJECT 19

STRETCH, SCALE, EXTEND

1. Create a PROJ19 drawing from your HALFPROT drawing.

2. Draw the table and chair to the dimensions specified.

3. Place the furniture as indicated.

4. Stretch the chair to make the sofa.

5. Stretch a table to make the coffee table.

6. Scale up the table to make the end tables.

7. Draw the large rug on the left as shown.

8. Rotate the rug.

9. Add another smaller rug. Make this rug by offsetting the outside edge of the rug. Complete the new rug by extending the long sides of the larger rug and then trimming the excess.

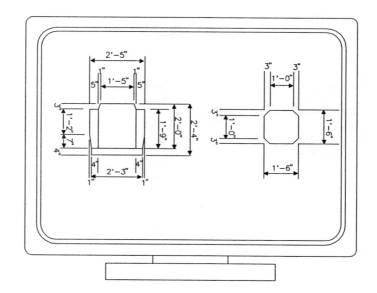

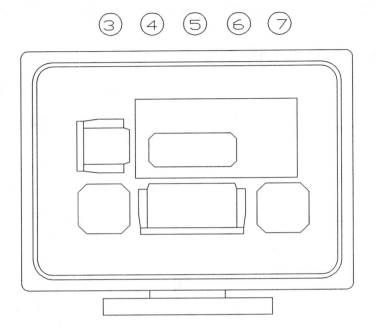

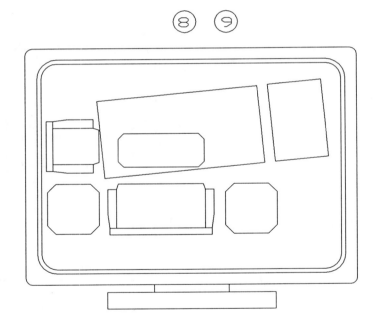

24 EDITING YOUR WORK PART VII

> **FUNCTION**: These are the "I've changed my mind" commands. They are powerful and far-reaching commands that allow you to change a great number of things. Earlier you CHANGEd your mind about text. That's just a sample of what these commands can do for you.

CHANGE

The CHANGE command has two options. Each of these options has many sub-options. Here is a brief description of the options and sub-options that change affects. Experiment with each of the options as you learn about them.

Change point
- relocate the end points of lines
- alter the circumference of a circle
- relocate a Block
- relocate text
- change a text style
- change text height
- change text angle
- change text string (change what it says)
- redefine an Attribute (in the same way that you can redefine text, with the addition of the ability to change the tag)

Properties
- move an object from one layer to another
- change the color of an object
- change the linetype of an object
- change the elevation of a 3D object (not valid after Release 10)
- change the thickness of a 3D object (not valid after Release 10)

Locating the CHANGE command
- the Root Menu under EDIT
- the Tablet Menu under EDIT

Here are a few examples of how the CHANGE command works

Bring up an existing drawing that you can experiment on.

Change point option

1. Let's change the end point of a line.

    Select CHANGE.

2. AutoCAD says: Select objects:

    Select any line on your drawing.

    Hit **ENTER** to get out of the Select objects loop.

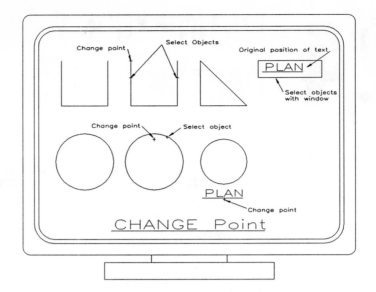

3. AutoCAD says: Properties/<Change point>:

Change point is the default, therefore you don't need to type C. Pick the point on your drawing (near the end point of the line you selected) where you want the line to now end up. Make sure that Ortho is OFF. It can produce some strange results in this command option.

4. Your line is now repositioned. Try Change point with a circle and with text.

Properties option

1. Let's change the color of an object.

   Select CHANGE.

2. AutoCAD says: Select objects:

   Select any object on your drawing.

   Hit **ENTER** to get out of the Select objects loop.

3. AutoCAD says: Properties/<Change point>:

   Change point is the default.

   Type P in order to operate in the Properties option.

4. AutoCAD says: Change what property (Color/ Elev/ LAyer/ LType/ Thickness)?

   Select **Color**.

5. AutoCAD says: New color <BYLAYER>:

   Type red

MEMO

Whenever you attempt to change the color of an object, AutoCAD threatens you with <BYLAYER>. This is a note reminding you that you have decided to keep colors separated by layer. AutoCAD has noticed that you are about to "screw things up." By changing the color of that object you will now contaminate your beautiful layer system. AutoCAD is right! Try to avoid mixing colors in a layer. It will only confuse things later on. The same warning will appear when you try this with linetype.

---

6. AutoCAD says: Change what property (Color/ Elev/ LAyer/ LType/ Thickness)?

    This is the Change loop, which acts similarly to the Select Objects loop.

    Hit **ENTER** one more time.

7. Your object now has a new color. Now, try changing the layer and linetype of an object.

CHPROP This command changes only the properties of objects. It works identically to the properties sub-option of CHANGE.

PROJECT 20

CHANGE, CHPROP

1. Create a new PROJ20 drawing from your PROJ19 drawing (PROJ19=PROJ20).

2. Add text in the OUTLINE layer to identify each of the pieces of furniture. Copy the text in the example drawing.

3. Change the coffee table text to read COFFEE TABLE.

4. Change the text so that it is in the TEXT layer.

5. Change the layer that the rug is in to DETAIL1.

6. Use CHANGE **Point** to change the shape of the rug as drawn in the example.

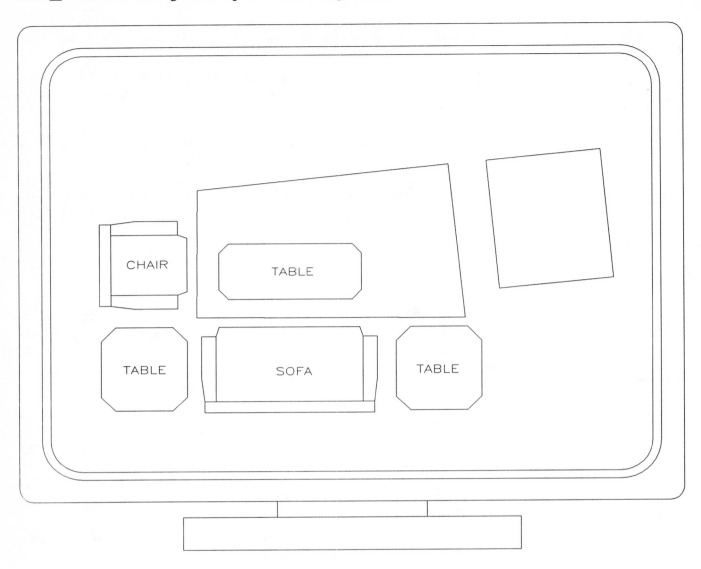

25 DIMENSIONING TECHNIQUES PART I

> **FUNCTION**: AutoCAD dimensions automatically for you. When the drawing phase is over, you don't need to begin measuring between points on your drawing as you would with manual drafting. AutoCAD already "knows" the dimensions of everything! These next three chapters will introduce you to AutoCAD's impressive, powerful, and unerring dimensioning features.

All of your hard work spent practicing CAD precision drawing techniques is about to pay off. You are going to be rewarded for your dozens of late nights spent with OSNAP, Ortho, Grid, and Snap. As a result of your struggles, dimensioning — formerly one of the more excruciating operations at the end of any drafting session — will be a waltz.

Locating the DIM: commands
- the Root Menu under DIM:
- the Tablet Menu

The DIMension Options

AutoCAD provides several options to assist you in dimensioning. Here are the ones that are the most important for you to master for your type of drawing:

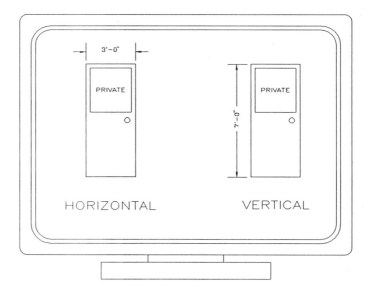

horiz
For dimensioning horizontal lines.

vert
For dimensioning vertical lines.

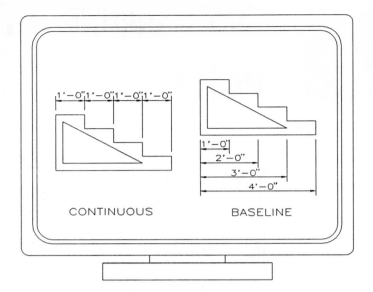

continuous
For side by side dimensioning.

baseline
For dimensions that refer to a common base point.

leader
Places a leader line including the leader text on the drawing.

DIM1:
Choosing this option allows you to perform one dimensioning task before AutoCAD automatically returns to the command prompt.

center
Places a double crossed center line or mark at the center of a circle.

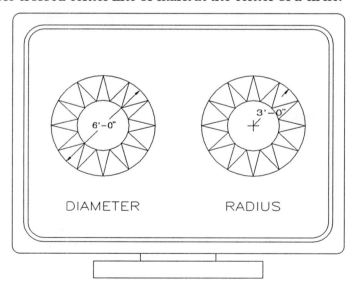

radius
Determines the center of a circle or an arc and places a dimension.

diameter
Dimensions the diameter of a circle.

angular
Dimensions angles in degrees.

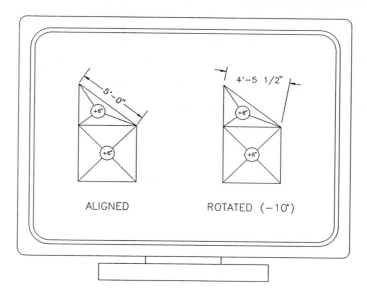

rotated
Measures an angled dimension between two points. You specify the angle.

aligned
Dimensions the length of angled lines.

MEMO

Always *dimension* your drawing as a *next to last* step (the final step should be notes, including any leader notes). This way you will only need to make the DIMENSION layer current once, and you are therefore less likely to place your dimensions in the wrong layer. If you do accidentally place a dimension on another layer, don't ERASE and redimension, simply CHANGE the layer property.

Dimension in OSNAP Running Mode. Before any dimensioning assignment, you should "load up" your OSNAP cross hair target box with the **ENDpoint** and **INTersec(tion)** options. While you are dimensioning, AutoCAD is constantly asking you for the end points of lines that need to be dimensioned. Interrupting each dimensioning command would be quite time consuming and aggravating. Use OSNAP running mode to make your dimensioning task near effortless.

Make the dimension layer current. All dimensions should be on the same layer — I suggest you call it DIMENSIONS and use a blue continuous line. By having all dimensions on the same layer you will be assured that they will all eventually be plotted with a thinner pen.

Dimension Techniques

The following is a rundown on how some of AutoCAD's dimension commands and options work. The **vertical** option is described in detail. It'll give you a good sense of the type of communication involved with all of the dimension options. The functions of the other options are summarized.

vertical

1. Make your DIMENSION layer current.

    Make TEXT the current style.

2. Select DIM: from the Root Menu. If you are using a Tablet Menu, select VERT and skip to Step 5.

    The command prompt has now been replaced by the Dim prompt. You can only do dimensioning work when the Dim prompt is present. To get the command prompt back, you must type EXIT first. (Had you selected DIM1, you would have been allowed to perform one dimensioning task and then AutoCAD would automatically return you to the Command prompt.)

3. AutoCAD says: Dim:

    Select **vertical**.

4. Now select **linear** and **vertical**.

5. AutoCAD says: First extension line origin or RETURN to select:

    With many of AutoCAD's dimensioning features you are presented with two methods: you can either select the origin of each extension line or simply hit **ENTER** and it will ask you for the line that you want to dimension. AutoCAD figures out where the extension line origins are. Let's try both options starting with first extension line origin method.

First extension line origin method

Put one end of the *vertical* line you want to dimension in the target box.

Pick that point.

4. AutoCAD says: Second extension line origin:

    Put the other end of the *vertical* line you want to dimension in the target box.

    Pick that point.

5. AutoCAD says: Dimension line location:

    Pick where you want the dimension line to appear (1' away in a ½" scale drawing; 2' away in a ¼" scale drawing). When you are dimensioning drawings that originate from your ½" scale prototype, and you have set up your Grid according to the suggestions in Chapter 9, pick the dimension line location point 1' (or one Grid square) away from the object.

6. AutoCAD then shows you the dimension text that it is about to place on your drawing. If you want to change it, just type the new text and then hit **ENTER**. If not, simply hit **ENTER**. The dimension will appear automatically.

Return to select method

1. Select DIM: from the Root Menu. If you are using a Tablet Menu select VERT and then skip ahead to Step 4.

2. AutoCAD says: Dim:

    Select **linear**.

3. Select **vertical**.

4. AutoCAD says: First extension line origin or RETURN to select:

   Hit **ENTER**.

5. AutoCAD says: Select line, arc, or circle:

   Pick the *vertical* line you want to dimension.

   Hit **ENTER**.

6. AutoCAD says: Dimension line location:

   Pick where you want the dimension line to appear.

7. AutoCAD then shows you the text that it is going to place in the dimension. If you want to change it, just type the new text and then hit **ENTER**. If not, simply hit **ENTER**. The dimension will appear automatically.

horiz

Functions identically to the vertical option.

continuous

To dimension a string of side by side connecting dimensions:

1. Dimension the object farthest to one side or the other of your object using the **vertical** or **horizontal** option.

2. Use the first extension line origin method to pick the extreme outside extension line first.

3. After the first distance has been dimensioned select **continuous**.

4. AutoCAD will ask you for the origin point of the second extension line. It will automatically place the new dimension line in line with the first dimension line whenever possible.

baseline

The command structure for doing common base point dimensions is similar to that for the **cont** option.

1. Dimension the distance that contains the common base point first. Use the **vertical** or **horizontal** option.

2. Use the first extension line origin method to pick the common base point extension line first.

3. After the first distance has been dimensioned select **baseline**.

4. AutoCAD will ask you for the origin point of the second extension line. It will automatically "stair-step" the new dimension line.

leader

To place a leader line including the leader text on the drawing:

1. **leader** is a dimensioning option but you will really use it for text. Change to the TEXT layer when you use **leader**.

2. Select **leader**. When AutoCAD asks you for the Leader start, pick the point where you want the tip of the arrowhead of your leader to be (use an OSNAP option).

3. AutoCAD puts you into a "To point:" loop. Each point that you pick places an "elbow" in your leader line.

4. When you have finished bending your leader, hit **ENTER**.

5. You will next be asked for dimension text. You can type in short text at this point. I suggest that you select CANCEL twice (**CTRL C**) to get out of the **leader** option and use DTEXT to place text consisting of long notes.

DIM1:

To perform a single dimension option function and then automatically return to the Command prompt select DIM1: followed by the dimension option.

center

To automatically draw a double crossed center line or + mark at the center of a circle, simply select center and pick the circle by touching the actual circle line (not the center).

radius

To automatically locate the center of a circle or an arc and place a radius dimension, select the circle or arc. You will then be shown the text that is about to be printed. Hit **ENTER** to complete the command or type a new dimension text followed by **ENTER**.

diameter

Performs identically to the **Radius** option.

angular

When dimensioning angles using this option you will be asked for the two angled lines, the place where you want the dimension arc to be drawn, and then you will be given the chance to approve the dimension text.

rotated

Works identically to the **horizontal** or **vertical** options except that you are going to tell AutoCAD to dimension a horizontal or vertical distance between the beginning and ending points of an angled line.

aligned

Works identically to the **horizontal** or **vertical** options except that you are going to dimension the length of an angled line.

PROJECT 21

DIMension Options

1. Create a new drawing called PROJ21 from AutoCAD's default drawing screen.

2. Change AutoCAD's default drawing screen units. Go to the UNITS command and set up architectural units. Leave all other defaults preset.

3. Make an OUTLINES layer (white) and a DIMENSIONS layer (blue).

4. Copy this dimension sample drawing onto your screen. Draw all of the shapes according to the dimensions specified. Don't forget to draw the objects in the OUTLINES layer.

5. Make the DIMENSION layer current.

6. Load up OSNAP running mode with **ENDpoint** and **INTersec(tion)**.

7. Dimension the sample as shown.

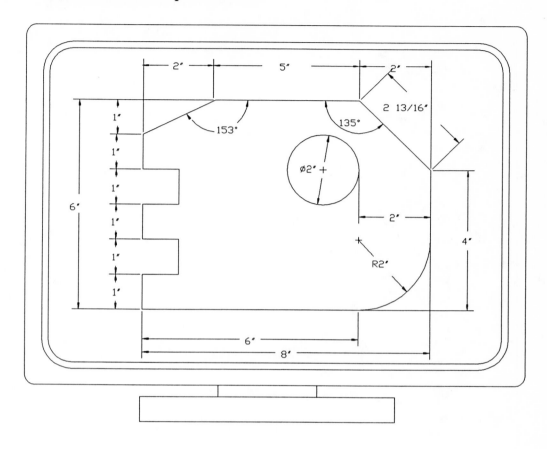

26 DIMENSIONING TECHNIQUES PART II

> **FUNCTION**: AutoCAD's many editing commands make an almost limitless variety of changes to your drawings possible. The important associative dimension properties investigated in this chapter make it possible to avoid redimensioning those drawings that you edit.

Associative Dimensioning

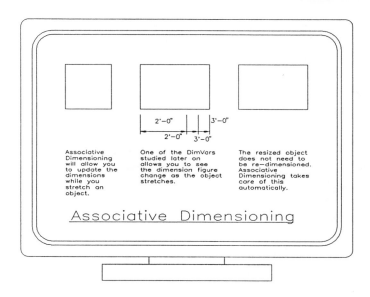

When associative dimensioning is in effect you can stretch a dimensioned object and have the measurement automatically update itself. Experiment with associative dimensioning. Draw a simple object on your blank default Auto-CAD screen, dimension it, and then stretch it. Be sure to note the dimension figure before and after the stretch.

Associative dimensioning can be a real timesaver. However, altering certain parts of the dimension later on can be a hassle. You see, an associative dimension causes all of the parts of the dimension — figures, extension lines, dimension line, arrow tips — to be combined into one entity. If you attempt to erase an unwanted extension line, you will erase all of the parts that make up a dimension. You can erase that one extension line, but in order to do so you must first "explode" the dimension.

EXPLODE

EXPLODE is not an associative dimensioning command, but it's important that you understand something about it before you go any further. EXPLODE is an editing command that you will primarily use to explode blocks. What is EXPLODE? And what's a block? We're getting a little ahead of ourselves here. Take a look at EXPLODE now, and I promise that you'll get to find out about blocks a little later. Yes, EXPLODE is primarily used with blocks but it is also the only way to edit associative dimensioning entities.

EXPLODEing an entity breaks it up into two or more entities. For instance, you remember that a polygon created with the POLYGON command is a single entity. A five-sided pentagon is not made up of five individual line entities but is instead a single object. You can only edit one of the sides by using EXPLODE to break the pentagon into five separate line entities.

Locating the EXPLODE command
- the Root Menu under EDIT
- the Tablet Menu

How the EXPLODE command works
Before trying EXPLODE, create a pentagon using the POLYGON command.

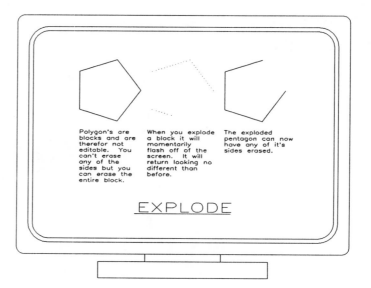

1. Try to erase one side of the polygon. It's impossible. Because it is a single entity, you can only edit the entire object. Here's how EXPLODE makes editing your polygon possible.

2. Select EXPLODE.

3. AutoCAD says: Select block reference, polyline, dimension, or mesh:

Pick your block or dimension.

4. The Command prompt will return and the object or dimension looks no different. However, it is now completely possible to erase one of the sides.

Here's a way to retain this concept. Entities such as the pentagon are made up of lines that are "super-glued" together. Using the EXPLODE command "unglues" them.

DIMASO Associative dimensioning can be turned on or off. You've seen the advantages to having it on. An advantage to having it off, of course, is that it is simple to go back later and edit any part of the dimension structure of a non-associative dimension. DIMASO (dimension associative) is the key to turning associative dimensioning on or off.

Locating DIMASO
- the Root Menu under DIM:, DIM VARS
- the Tablet Menu under DIM VARS

DIMASO is just one of more than thirty DIM VARS (dimension variables). DIM VARS are options for customizing AutoCAD's dimension features. DIMASO is the name of the associative dimensioning DIM VARS. To turn it on or off, select it from the DIM VARS menu. Highlight and pick it to toggle it on or off.

HOMETEXT, NEWTEXT, UPDATE

These three commands provide ways for you to manipulate, alter, or change dimension text, DIM VARS, or UNITS on a completed drawing, without having to start the dimension process all over again.

Locating these three commands
- the Root Menu under DIM
- the Tablet Menu (Release 11)

Here's a brief description of each of these commands. Try them out on a completed drawing of yours. See which ones will be helpful to you.

HOMETEXT
If you have moved the position of text created associatively, HOMETEXT will return the text to its original, or home, position. You may have noticed that when you stretch a dimensioned object, the dimension text is often no longer centered. HOMETEXT returns the text to its *home* in the center.

NEWTEXT
This command provides a way to change the dimension text of associatively created dimensions. After calling up the command you will be asked for a new dimension text. Type the text in and then pick the old text on the drawing that you want to change.

UPDATE
UPDATE is the command to use when you have changed one, two, or more DIM VARS settings *after* the drawing has been completed.

After changing any of your UNIT settings or DIM VARS settings, go back to your drawing editor. Call up the command and window select the drawing you want updated. Your associatively created dimensions now reflect all changes.

PROJECT 22

ASSOCIATIVE DIMENSIONS, HOMETEXT, NEWTEXT

1. Create a PROJ22 drawing from AutoCAD's default drawing screen. (Do not draw from a prototype.)

2. Create OUTLINE (white) and DIMENSION (blue) layers. Do not change the units to architectural.

3. Draw the wall.

4. Dimension the door width and the window height as indicated.

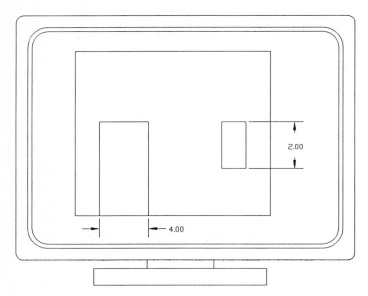

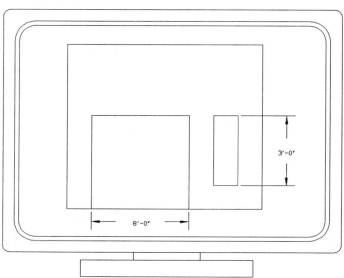

5. Stretch the door to twice the width.

6. Stretch the window height from 2 to 3.

7. Use NEWTEXT to change the text to feet and inches (for example you would change the dimension of 3 to 3′-0″).

8. Use HOMETEXT to center the text after the stretch if necessary.

27 DIMENSIONING TECHNIQUES PART III

> **FUNCTION**: Dimension variables (DIM VARS) give you the freedom to customize AutoCAD's dimension features. Being able to toggle important associative dimensioning properties is just one of the many variables that can fashion dimensioning to your tastes and project needs.

DIM VARS Settings

What follows is an explanation of each of the dimension variables. These variables do a variety of things including setting decimal places, altering the arrow size and style, changing the text size, and letting you decide where you want the dimension text in relation to the dimension arrow.

In the next and final chapter on creating your prototype drawing, you will alter many of AutoCAD's default DIM VARS settings in your own prototype drawings in order to make drawings that are appropriate for theater or film/television work.

Locating the DIM VARS settings
- the Root Menu Area under DIM:
- the Tablet Menu

Alternate Units DIM VARS

DIMALT (dimensions alternate)
- Toggle on or off.
- Allows you to use an alternate dimensioning system at the same time that you are using feet and inches. This would be a way of notating the dimensions in feet and inches and the metric system simultaneously.

DIMALTD (dimensions alternate decimal)
- Set number of places.
- For setting the number of decimal places in your alternate units.

DIMALTF (dimensions alternate factor)
- Set scale factor.
- For setting the alternate unit intended plot scale factor.

DIMAPOST (dimensions alternate post)
- For setting an alternate text suffix.

Associative Dimension DIM VARS

DIMASO (dimension associative)
- Toggle on or off.
- For turning associative dimensioning on or off.

DIMSHO (dimension show)
- Toggle on or off.
- Shows the dimension figure in an associative dimension changing as the object is being stretched.

Arrow/Tick DIM VARS

DIMASZ (dimension arrow size)
- Size in inches.
- Sets the size of the dimension arrow.
- Set at 0" if you want to use ticks.

DIMBLK (dimension block)
- Sets the name of a custom arrow that you design.

DIMBLK1 (dimension block 1)
- Sets the name of a custom arrow that you design.

DIMBLK2 (dimension block 2)
- Sets the name of a custom arrow that you design.

DIMSAH (dimension separate arrowheads)
- Toggle on or off.
- Toggle on to use the custom arrowheads available in DIMBLK1 or DIMBLK2.

DIMTSZ (dimension tick size)
- Set a tick size in inches.
- Allows you to use ticks (slashes) instead of arrows.
- Set at 0" if you want to use arrows.

Dimension, extension, and center line DIM VARS

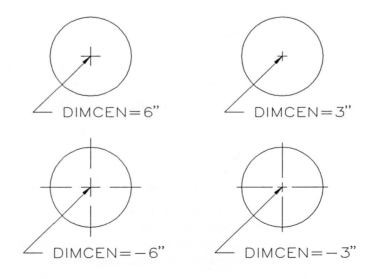

DIMCEN (dimension center)
- Set size in inches.
- Sets the size of a circle or an arc center mark as drawn by the **Circle**, **Diameter**, or **Radius** command options.

DIMCLRD (dimension line color)
- Set a color for dimension lines, arrowheads, and leaders.

DIMCLRE (extension line color)
- Set a color for extension lines.

DIMCLRT (dimension text color)
- Set a color for dimension text.

DIMDLE (dimension dimension line extension)
- Set in inches.
- Sets the extension length of the dimension line beyond the extension line.

DIMDLI (dimension line increment)
- Set in inches.
- Sets the dimension line offset placement increment if dimension text would ordinarily be placed over other dimension text in the baseline or continuous dimension commands.

DIMEXE (dimension extension)
- Set in inches.
- Sets the extension line length beyond the dimension line.

DIMEXO=2.5"   DIMEXO=1"

DIMEXO (dimension extension offset)
- Set in inches.
- Sets the extension line origin offset (spacing) from the object.

DIMGAP (dimension line gap)
- Sets the gap size around the text.

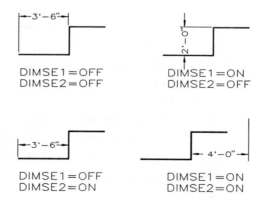

DIMSE1 (dimension suppression extension 1)
- Toggle on or off.
- Keeps the first extension line from appearing and plotting.

- Extension lines that overlap on your drawing will be drawn twice by your plotter and will look darker than a normal extension line. Suppressing one of the lines will prevent this.

DIMSE2 (dimension suppression extension 2)
- Toggle on or off.
- Keeps the second extension line from appearing and plotting.

DIMSOXD=OFF   DIMSOXD=ON

DIMSOXD (dimension suppression outside extension dimension)
- Toggle on or off.
- Setting this variable determines whether or not dimension lines in a tight space will be drawn outside the extension lines. If set to ON, no dimension lines will be drawn in these situations.

DIMTOFL=OFF   DIMTOFL=ON

DIMTOFL (dimension text outside force line)
- Toggle on or off.
- Draws a dimension line between the extension lines, even if the space is so tight that the dimension text itself has been forced outside the lines.

Dimension Determining DIM VARS

DIMLFAC (dimension length factor)
- Set a relative scale factor.
- Allows you to draw, on a drawing of one scale, a detail in a different scale.

DIMRND (dimension rounding)
- Set a value.
- Sets a rounding off value for dimensions.

DIMSCALE (dimension scale)
- Set a scale factor (see Chapter 28 for determining this scale factor).
- Determines the eventual plotted scale of your drawing.

Dimension Text DIM VARS:

DIMAPOST (dimension alternate post)
- Places an alternate dimension text, such as the metric equivalent, after your standard feet and inches text.

DIMPOST (dimension post)
- Sets a default suffix for the dimension text (such as mm or cm).

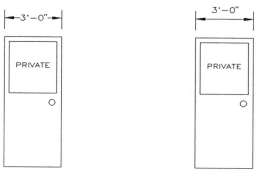

DIMTAD (dimension text above dimension)
- Toggle on or off.
- Places the dimension text above the dimension line.

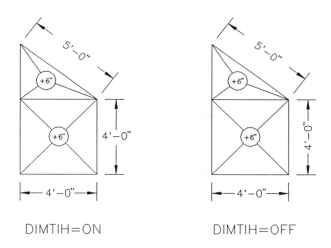

DIMTIH (dimension text inside is horizontal)
- Toggle on or off.
- Makes the dimension text inside the extension lines horizontal, even if the dimension is vertical or angled.

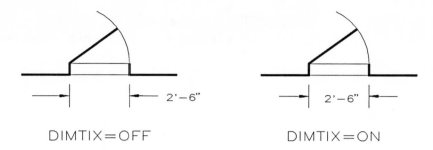

DIMTIX=OFF   DIMTIX=ON

DIMTIX (dimension text is inside extension)
- Toggle on or off.
- Places the dimension text inside the extension lines if the space is so tight that AutoCAD would normally force them outside.

DIMTOH=ON   DIMTOH=OFF

DIMTOH (dimension text outside is horizontal)
- Toggle on or off.
- Makes all dimension text forced outside the extension lines horizontal.

DIMTVP (dimension text vertical position)
- Set a position.
- Sets the dimension text position relative to the dimension line.
- DIMTAD must be OFF for DIMTVP to function.

DIMTXT (dimension text)
- Set a height in actual (not scale) inches.
- Sets the height of the dimension text.

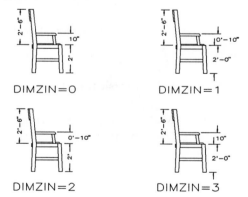

DIMZIN=0   DIMZIN=1

DIMZIN=2   DIMZIN=3

DIMZIN (dimension zero included)
- Set one of four options (0-3).
- Determines the status of 0′ and 0″ in the dimension text.

    0. = Does not write 0′ or 0″.

Example: 8" or 5'.

1. = Writes 0' and 0".

Example: 0'-8" or 5'-0".

2. = Writes 0' but not 0".

Example: 0'-8" or 5'.

3. = Does not write 0' but does write 0".

Example: 8" or 5'-0"

Tolerance DIM VARS

DIMLIM (dimension limits)
- Toggle on or off.
- Allows the dimension tolerance limits text, set by the other tolerance DIM VARS, to be drawn.

DIMTFAC (dimension tolerance scale factor)
- Sets the scale factor for tolerance dimensions.

DIMTM (dimension tolerance minus)
- Set a tolerance in inches.
- Sets the minus tolerance.

DIMTOL (dimension tolerance)
- Toggle on or off.
- Generates dimension tolerances in your dimensions.

DIMTP (dimension tolerance plus)
- Set a tolerance in inches.
- Sets the plus tolerance.

28 CREATING A PROTOTYPE PART IV

> **FUNCTION**: Your prototypes will almost be complete once you have gone through this chapter and have set your DIM VARS. Each DIM VARS possibility will be accompanied by a setting recommendation. These are DIM VARS settings that work well for theater as well as film/television drawings.

Each of the following recommendations is based on:

- The choice that makes the most sense for theater, film, and television drawing.
- The style that comes closest to being the standard in the standardless world of theatrical drafting.
- The clearest to read and easiest to understand of the options.

I suggest that you start out with the suggested settings and then change the selections that bother you or aren't quite right for your particular project. The DIM VARS settings can be changed at any time. Don't forget to save all of your prototypes after setting your DIM VARS.

Setting the DIM VARS

1. Set each DIM VARS by selecting it from the DIM VARS menu in the Screen Menu Area. In each case, select or type in your new setting.
2. Leave all DIM VARS at their default values and settings except for the following:

DIM VARS Option	½" proto	¼" proto
DIMASZ	⅛"	⅛"
DIMCEN	-⅛"	-⅛"
DIMDLI	⅜"	⅜"
DIMEXE	¹⁄₁₆"	¹⁄₁₆"
DIMEXO	⅛"	⅛"
DIMRND	1"	1"
DIMSCALE	24	48

The DIMSCALE setting is the reciprocal of the intended plot scale. Remember that in Chapter 11 you found out that a ½" scale drawing is a ¹⁄₂₄" scale drawing. A ¼" scale drawing is a ¹⁄₄₈" scale drawing. This variable automatically makes the height of all dimension-related DIM VARS (text height, arrow size, etc.) consistent if you change plotting scale. If you decide to plot a drawing done on your ½" scale prototype in ¼" scale, your text size will stay at ³⁄₃₂" as long as you change your DIMSCALE prior to plotting. This is also true of other size-related DIM VARS such as arrow size.

DIMSOXD	ON	ON
DIMTAD	ON	ON
DIMTIH	OFF	OFF
DIMTIX	ON	ON
DIMTOH	OFF	OFF
DIMTXT	3/32"	3/32"

If you have a separate DTEXT style called DIMENSIONS, set the text height in the STYLE command at 0". That way DIMTXT will control the height.

DIMZIN	3	3

3. Save your prototype.

4. Repeat Steps 1-4 for each of your prototype drawings.

PROJECT 23

SETTING DIMension VARIABLES

1. Call up one of your prototype drawings.

2. Set your DIM VARS according to Steps 1-4 in this chapter.

3. Repeat for each of your prototype drawings.

4. Create a new PROJ23 drawing from your PROJ18 drawing.

5. Set the DIM VARS for this drawing according to Steps 1-6 in this chapter.

6. Erase all but the window filled building ELEVATION drawing.

7. Copy the building three times on the sheet.

8. Dimension each of the buildings fully (read the next step first).

9. Change the DIMZIN setting to a different setting prior to dimensioning each of the examples. Set it to 0 for the first ELEVATION, 1 for the 2nd, and 2 for the third.

10. Copy one of the windows to a blank area on your drawing.

11. Scale it up to twice the size in order to make a 1" scale drawing.

12. Change the DIMLFAC in order to dimension the window in the new correct scale.

13. Dimension the window with DIMZIN set to 3.

14. Set the DIMLFAC back to its original setting.

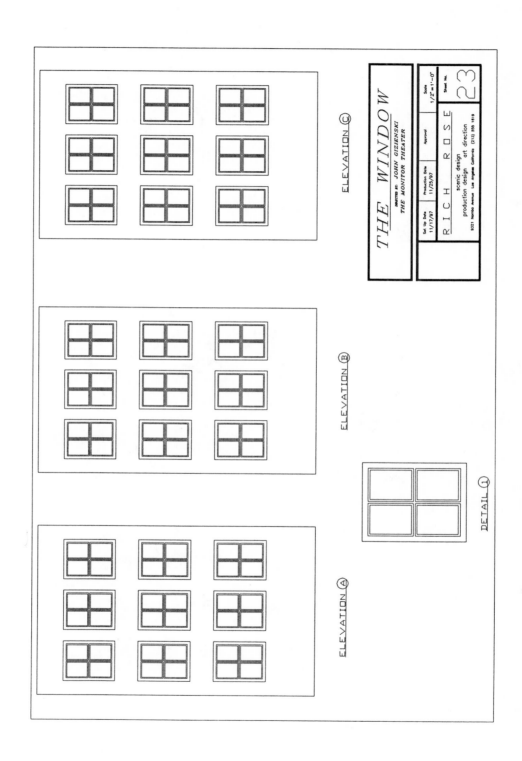

29 DRAWING WIDE LINES, SOLIDS, AND PATTERNS

> **FUNCTION**: With this group of commands you will have the ability to draw lines wider or thicker than you have been drawing up to this point. You will also be able to fill in areas completely solid or with a pattern. These commands are most helpful for representing objects that have been cut away in <u>SECTIONS</u>, <u>SECTION VIEWS</u>, and <u>PLANS</u>, and for filling in large areas of texture such as tile or brick in a floor or a wall.

PLINE (Polyline)

PLINE is the "thick-line" drawing command. A PLINE can have the same thickness as a line drawn with the LINE command (set width at 0") or it can be several inches or feet wide.

When you drew a series of connected lines or arcs, each was a separate entity. A series of connected lines or arcs drawn with PLINE will be a single entity. You may want to draw a particular object using a 0" pline in order to make it easier to edit. You might find that you need a chair in a <u>FLOOR PLAN</u> but aren't quite sure about its position. Drawn with PLINE the chair is "pickable." Without PLINE, each of the several lines that make up the chair must be picked or the entire object must be windowed in order to move it.

Use PLINE to draw the parts of any scenery that have intersected the cutting plane line. When you go to plot out your drawing, the plotter will give you a nice bold, heavy weight section line.

Locating the PLINE command
- the Root Menu under DRAW
- the Pull Down Menu under DRAW
- the Tablet Menu

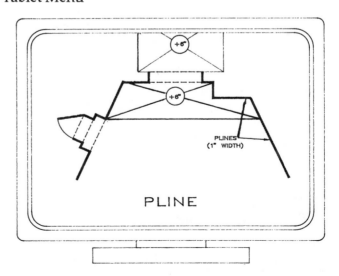

PLINE

Here's how PLINE works
Use your blank ½" prototype to experiment with these commands.

1. Select PLINE.

2. AutoCAD says: From point:

    Pick the start point.

3. AutoCAD says: Current line width is 0'-0"

    Arc/Close/Halfwidth/Length/Undo/Width/<Endpoint of line>:

    To set a new line width, select **Width**.

4. AutoCAD says: Starting width <0'-0">:

    Type 4"

5. AutoCAD says: Ending width <0'-2">:

    Hit **ENTER**.

6. AutoCAD says: Arc/Close . . . /<Endpoint of line>:

    Pick the end point.

7. AutoCAD says: Arc/Close . . . /<Endpoint of line>:

    Pick the next point.

8. AutoCAD says: Arc/Close . . . /<Endpoint of line>:

Continue picking points. When you have finished drawing your lines, hit **ENTER**.

That's all there is to it! Let's look at the other PLINE options that you were presented with.

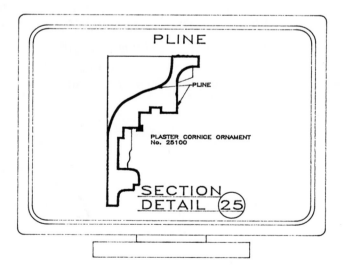

PLINE Options

Arc

Draws a PLINE arc or polyarc. Choosing this option brings up a set of **Arc** sub-options:

Angle/ CEnter/ Close/ Direction/ Halfwidth/
Line/ Radius/ Second pt/ Undo/ Width

Close
Draws a line from the last end point that you picked to the first end point.

Halfwidth
Specify here half the width of the line that you want. You would type 2" to get a 4" line.

Length
You can specify a PLINE's length and AutoCAD will draw it for you automatically.

Undo
Undoes the last PLINE segment while you are still in the PLINE command.

Width
Specifies the width of the line that you want to draw.

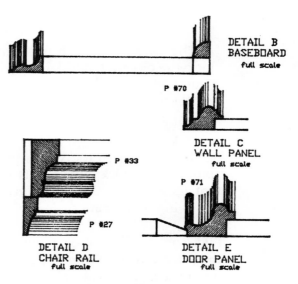

SOLID
Use the SOLID command to completely fill areas in. This command works well in <u>FLOOR PLANS</u> to represent posts and other vertical supports. It can also help you out when filling in "cut" areas of a <u>SECTION</u> view. You can make shapes other than rectangles or triangles by "building" the area to be filled with solid triangles.

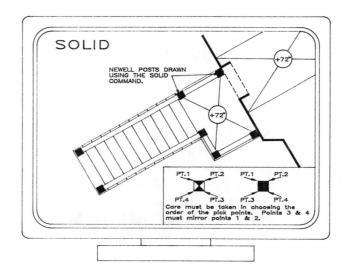

Locating the SOLID command
- the Root Menu under DRAW

Take a look at how SOLID works

1. Select SOLID.

2. You are going to make a solid rectangle shape without drawing any lines. Turn on Ortho, Grid, and Snap.

3. AutoCAD says: First point:

   Pick the upper left corner of your rectangle to be.

4. AutoCAD says: Second point:

   Pick the upper right corner of your rectangle.

5. AutoCAD says: Third point:

   Pick the lower left corner of your rectangle.

   The third and fourth picks must mirror the first and second — don't go clockwise or counterclockwise, but make a "Z" pattern with your pick points. If you had picked the lower right corner as your third point, the result would have been a bowtie or an hourglass.

6. AutoCAD says: Fourth point:

   Pick the lower right corner of your rectangle. Your rectangle should now be filled in solid. AutoCAD continues to say third point and fourth point. This allows you to pick more points when drawing odd shaped solids. Make sure that these extra third and fourth points always relate to the previous two points in the "Z" pattern.

FILL

FILL controls the fill of a solid or a polyline wider than 0". This command toggles on or off. When FILL is off the solid will be unfilled leaving only an outline. Filled in solids take up valuable drawing time each time your drawing regenerates. Keeping FILL off until you are ready to plot will save you a lot of regeneration time.

Locating the FILL command
- the Root Menu under DRAW, SOLID

How FILL works

1. Select FILL.

2. Turn FILL off.

3. Type REGEN and take a look at the effect on your solid rectangle.

   You can also draw solids with FILL off.

HATCH

With this command you can choose from a large assortment of patterns with which to fill areas in your drawings. These patterns might be floors of tile or of a geometric pattern, walls of brick or another material, or the diagonally lined hatched "cutaway" areas of a section detail.

Type ? after selecting the command to see a list of patterns available or, better yet, use the Pull Down Menu to see each pattern. Here are just some of the patterns available:

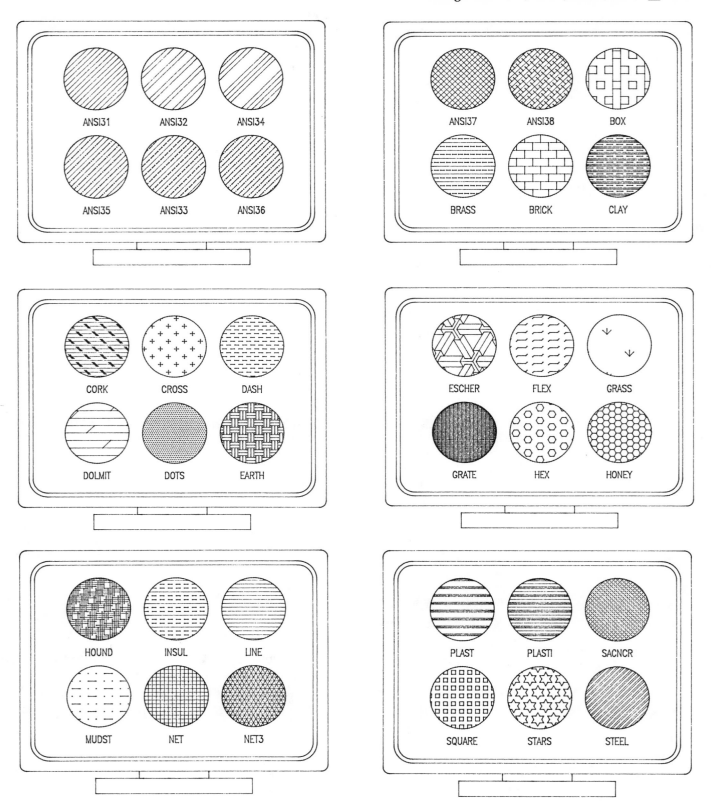

Locating the HATCH command
- the Root Menu under DRAW
- the Pull Down Menu under DRAW

How the HATCH command works from the Root Menu

From your ½" scale prototype, draw a rectangle that you can hatch.

1. Select HATCH.

2. AutoCAD says: Pattern(? or name/U,style):

    Type Brick

3. AutoCAD says: Scale for pattern <1>:

    Type in your DIMSCALE setting (24 for ½" or 48 for ¼").

This sets the pattern size to ANSI standards.

4. AutoCAD says: Angle for pattern <0>:

    Hit **ENTER**.

5. AutoCAD says: Select objects:

    Window the object to be hatched.

    Your rectangle should now be hatched.

How the HATCH command works from the Pull Down Menu

Erase your hatch pattern by picking it inside your rectangle.

1. Select the DRAW Pull Down Menu.

2. Select HATCH.

    You will be shown all of AutoCAD's hatch patterns. Pick the brick pattern.

3. AutoCAD says: Pattern(? or name/U,style): brick
    Scale for pattern <1>:

    Type in your DIMSCALE number (24).

4. AutoCAD says: Angle for pattern <0>:

    Hit **ENTER**.

5. AutoCAD says: Select objects:

    Window the object to be hatched.

    Your rectangle should now be hatched.

HATCH U

AutoCAD provides another pattern option called U. This option is designed to let *yoU* design a simple pattern very quickly. You will find that the most convenient use for this option is to draw the universal section line pattern of parallel diagonal lines. Selecting this option from the Screen Menu Area gives you the ability to quickly fill in the "cut" areas of solid objects in <u>SECTION</u>.

Choose 45° and say no to double hatch.

Style Codes

If you experiment with HATCH you will notice that the command can have three different personalities when it comes to other objects that might lie within the main area that you want to hatch.

NORMAL, n

By simply typing in the pattern name followed by ,n AutoCAD will alternately hatch in every other area.

PATTERN,o

By typing in the name of the pattern followed by ,o AutoCAD will only hatch the outermost area if there are other areas within the main area.

PATTERN,i

By typing ,i after the pattern name, AutoCAD will ignore any other areas within the main windowed area and hatch right over everything.

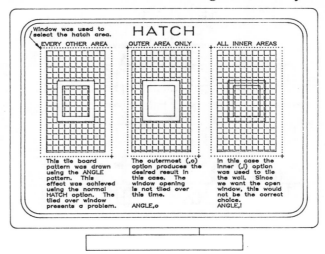

PROJECT 24

PLINE, SOLID, FILL, HATCH

1. Create a new PROJECT 24 drawing from your PROJECT 23 drawing.

2. Use the HATCH command to brick each of the buildings. Keep the BRICK hatch on one of your DETAIL layers.

3. In <u>ELEVATION A</u>, use BRICK,o. Notice that the HATCH has problems with certain parts of the wall. The example shows certain parts of the problem areas corrected. This was done by outlining the area with a continuous line in the LAYOUT layer. Each of the lines was then picked (in a clockwise direction) at the Select objects: prompt. Freeze the LAYOUT layer after you have hatched in the break.

    The identical problem in the middle of the drawing was fixed by copying that BRICK hatch block to this area.

4. In <u>ELEVATION B</u> use BRICK,i.

5. In <u>ELEVATION C</u> use normal BRICK. Zoom in and out of the windows to see the effect of this "every other object" hatch option. This problem could be corrected by turning off the OUTLINE layer, exploding the BRICK block, and then using **Window** to erase the errant "brick bits." Turn the OUTLINE layer back on in order to finish the drawing.

    This method is much easier than using the correction method in Step 3.

6. Draw a <u>SECTION</u> view of the 1" scale window. Use PLINE when appropriate.

7. Scale up the top part of your <u>SECTION</u> view to develop a <u>DETAIL</u> view of the top of the window.

8. Use PLINE to create a new drawing of this detail.

9. Use HATCH,U to make the section fill lines.

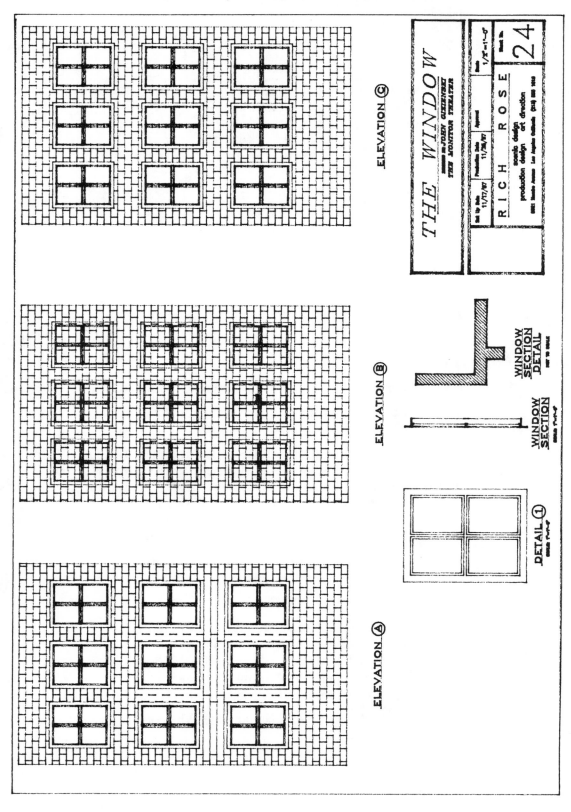

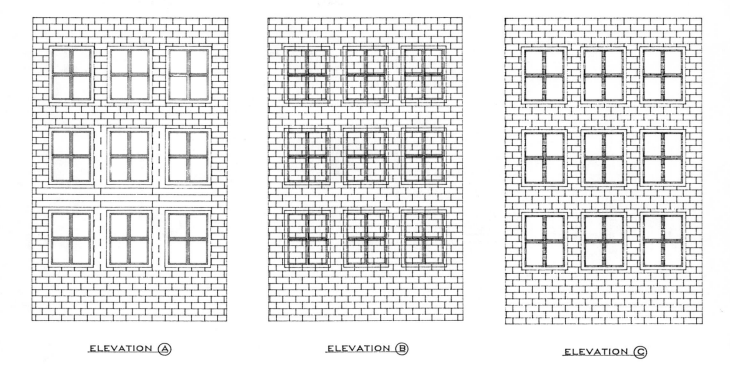

ELEVATION Ⓐ   ELEVATION Ⓑ   ELEVATION Ⓒ

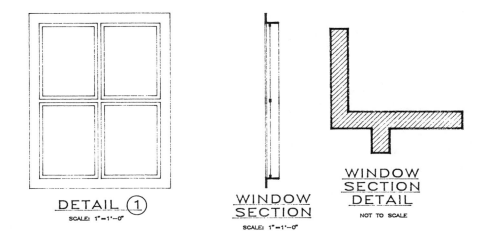

DETAIL ①
SCALE: 1"=1'—0"

WINDOW
SECTION
SCALE: 1"=1'—0"

WINDOW
SECTION
DETAIL
NOT TO SCALE

30 EDITING POLYLINES

> **FUNCTION**: Editing PLINES requires the use of this special polyline edit command. As you will see, PEDIT is more than just erasing and trimming. This command has many options that permit you to have subtle control over PLINES.

PEDIT (Polyline Edit)

In order to edit any PLINE you must use the PEDIT command (most of the time). You can use *some* of the other editing commands to do *some* PLINE editing. For example, TRIM can be made to remove part of a PLINE.

An exciting use for PEDIT is to curve lines that were previously straight. Meandering lines (difficult to draw in CAD) can be first drawn as straight PLINES and then later curved. The results are quite nice. This is easier than using the ARC command with its often unpredictable results. You can use this technique to draw tree trunks and branches in <u>ELEVATIONS</u>. Draw the outline and grain first using PLINE with a width of 0". At this point they have a stiff, mechanical, computer-drawn look. However, after editing them with **Fit curve** or **Spline**, they look quite close to hand drawn.

Locating the PEDIT command
- the Root Menu under EDIT
- the Pull Down Menu under MODIFY
- the Tablet Menu

Let's take a look at the PEDIT command

1. Draw a series of connected polylines in AutoCAD's default drawing screen. Use a width of .25.

2. Select PEDIT.

3. AutoCAD says: Select Objects:

    Pick a polyline.

4. AutoCAD says: Pedit Select polyline:
    Open/ Join/ Width/ Edit vertex/ Fit curve/
    Spline curve/ Decurve/ Undo/ eXit <X>:

    These are PEDIT's nine options. Each one affects the PLINE in a different way. We'll examine these shortly. Let's try one of them out.

    Select **Fit curve**.

    Before your eyes, the rigid angular polyline that you drew has become a fluid, graceful, flowing line.

Let's try out another option.

1. Select **Decurve**. Your angular polyline is back.

2. Select **Spline**. Your line has been curved again but with different results this time. Can you tell what happened? Examine the **Fit curve** and **Spline** options below to see what the difference is.

PEDIT Options

Open (Close)
Replaced by **Close** if the polyline is open. Opens a closed polyline (or closes an open polyline).

Join
Joins polyline pieces into one polyline.

Width
Changes the width of a polyline or segments of a polyline.

Edit vertex
Moves or inserts polyline vertices. A vertex is the place where two polyline segments meet. **Edit vertex** has its own option menu that appears when you select it.

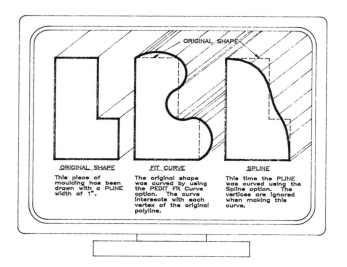

Fit curve
Changes a multi-segmented polyline into a curved line. It does this while keeping the start point and end points intact as the path of the line goes through each vertex.

Spline curve
Changes a multi-segmented polyline into a curved line. It does this by keeping the start and end points of the line intact. However, when the line is curved it is pulled tight a bit so that its path misses all of the other vertices.

Decurve
Changes a curved or splined polyline back into its original angular form.

Undo
Undoes one step at a time as long as you are in the original command.

eXit
Exits you from the command.

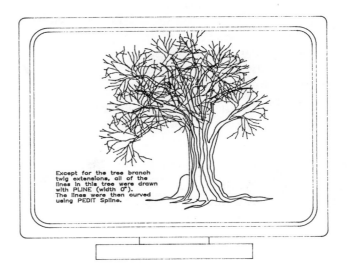

Except for the tree branch twig extensions, all of the lines in this tree were drawn with PLINE (width 0"). The lines were then curved using PEDIT Spline.

Edit Vertex Options

When you select the **Edit vertex** option, you will be presented with this list of options. An X will appear at one of the vertices. You will identify the vertices or segments that you want to edit by advancing the X from vertex to vertex in order to indicate the edit area. Here are the vertex editing options available:

Next
Advances the X to the next vertex.

Previous
Advances the X to the previous vertex.

Break
Breaks a vertex to vertex segment out of your polyline. When you type B you are marking the first vertex (beginning of your break).

Insert
Lets you insert a new vertex. It adds it after the vertex that is currently marked.

Move
Moves a vertex.

Regen
Causes a regeneration of the polyline.

Straighten
Straightens the segment between two vertices.

Tangent
Places a tangent direction to a vertex for Curve fit.

Width
Changes the width information between two polyline vertices. See the effect by using **Regen**.

eXit
Exits you from this menu and returns you to the PEDIT menu.

After you select any one of the above options, this third menu will appear:

Next
Moves the X forward one vertex.

Previous
Moves the X back.

Go
Initiates the command.

eXit
Returns you to the previous menu.

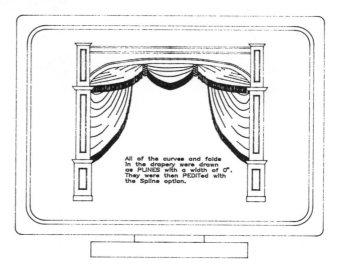

PROJECT 25

EDITING POLYLINES

1. Begin a new drawing called PROJ25 from AutoCAD's default drawing screen.

2. Use a polyline width of 0 to draw this curtained proscenium.

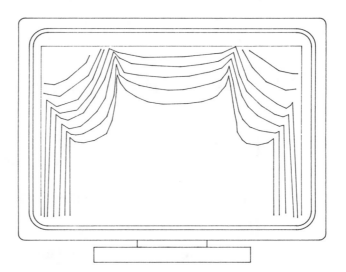

3. Use **Spline** to make the curtain lines flow like fabric.

4. Use **ENDpoint** to connect the bottom of the curtain panels.

5. Use **Fit curve** to curve these two lines.

6. Add the tiebacks with PLINE (width .10).

7. Add fringe to complete the drawing.

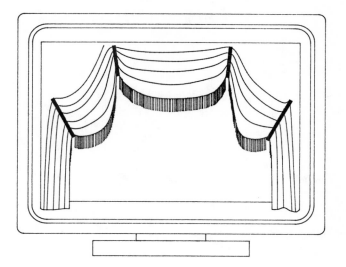

31 GATHERING INFORMATION

> **FUNCTION**: There are times when you will need to gather some information about a part of your drawing. The commands covered in this chapter can help you out. They can tell you the absolute coordinates of any point, the length of any line, and much more.

Locating ID, DIST, AREA, LIST, DBLIST
- the Root Menu under INQUIRY
- the Pull Down Menu under UTILITY (except for DBLIST) (Release 11 and beyond)
- the Tablet Menu

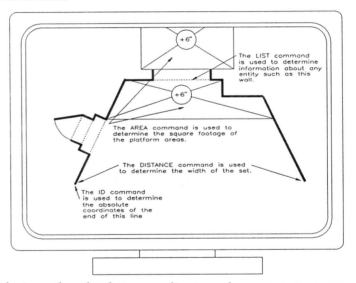

ID (Identification)

This command gives the absolute coordinates of any point on your drawing that you pick. Using this command is sometimes necessary when using keyboard coordinate entry. Use OSNAP options to locate the precise point.

```
ID Point:   X = 4'-1"     Y = 8'-4"     Z = 0'-0"
Command:
```

After you pick a point (with the help of OSNAP), AutoCAD will give you the X, Y, and Z (3D) coordinates of that point.

DIST (Distance)

DIST gives you the distance between two points that you pick. Using this command is like picking up a scale rule to check the length of something on your drawing.

— 203 —

```
DIST First point:   Second point:
Distance = 9'-11",   Angle in X-Y Plane = 1,   Angle from X-Y Plane = 0
Delta X = 9'-11",   Delta Y = 0'-1",    Delta Z = 0'-0"

Command:
```

After you pick two points (again, with the help of OSNAP) AutoCAD will give you the distance in feet and inches between those two points, the angle of the line in the XY plane, delta X (change in the X distance), delta Y, and delta Z.

AREA

AREA computes the square feet of an area that you specify on your drawing. It can keep a running total and ADD up several such areas. AREA will also tell you the length of the perimeter of that area.

```
AREA
<First point>/Entity/Add/Subtract:
Next point:
Next point:
Next point:
Next point:
Next point:
Next point:
Next point:
Area = 1460 square in. (10.14 square ft.), Perimeter = 17'-1"

Command:
```

After selecting the points that define the area, AutoCAD will tell you both the square feet and the perimeter distance.

AREA can also tell you the area of a circle. Select AREA's **Entity** option to do so. AutoCAD will then tell you both the area and the circumference of the circle.

LIST

This command gives you a list of information about an entity that you select. You can use LIST to find the length of a line, the LAYER that it is on, and more. DISTANCE will also tell you the length of a line, but LIST will do it in fewer steps and will yield more information.

```
LIST
Select objects: 1 selected, 1 found.

Select objects:
               LINE        Layer: HIDDENOUTLINES
        from point, X=    7'-6"   Y=   13'-0"   Z=     0'-0"
          to point, X=   10'-0"   Y=   13'-0"   Z=     0'-0"
     Length =    2'-6",   Angle in X-Y Plane =      0
            Delta X =    2'-6", Delta Y =      0'-0", Delta Z =     0'-0"

Command:
```

If you select LIST and pick a line (or some other entity on your drawing) AutoCAD will tell you:

- the type of entity (line, circle, etc.)

- the LAYER that the entity is on

- the absolute coordinates of the origin point

- the absolute coordinates of the end point

- the length of the line

- the angle of the line

DBLIST (Data Base List)

DBLIST gives you information about every entity in your drawing. It is the list of lists. Turning on printer echo (select PRINTER from the TOGGLE area of the Tablet Menu or type **Ctrl Q** on the keyboard) will print out your list. If the speed of the scrolling is too fast, you can stop and start the scroll with **CTRL S**.

PROJECT 26

INQUIRY COMMANDS

1. Call up your PROJ25 drawing.
2. Turn on printer echo.
3. Identify the absolute coordinates of the lower end of each of the tiebacks.
4. Determine the open distance between the curtain panels.
5. Pick one of the fringe lines and determine the entity type, layer, and length.

32 CREATING A PROTOTYPE PART V

> **FUNCTION**: With these commands and options you can customize a large assortment of AutoCAD's features (including the DIM VARS). Just as the dimension variables allowed you to customize AutoCAD's dimensioning features to your style, taste, and project needs, the settings variables allow you to customize practically everything else about AutoCAD.

Below is a list of the settings variables from AutoCAD Release 10. The appendix of your AutoCAD manual has a brief description of each of them. Some of the variables ("read only") cannot be changed. As you look through the list, you will notice that you have already set many of the variables in the course of specifying different command options. Others were set as you built up your prototype drawing features. The settings shown here are for a ½" scale prototype. Note that if your UNITS fractional display is set to 1, then increments less than 1" will read as 0 in this list. However, the various settings will really function at their fractional setting despite the 0 readout here.

SETVAR

Locating the SETVAR command
- the Root Menu under SETTINGS

How to change a SETVAR setting
1. Select SETVAR.
2. Type in the name of the variable you want to change, or type ? to see a list of all of them.
3. Type in the new setting.

```
setvar
Variable name or ?: ?

ACADPREFIX      ""                        (read only)
ACADVER         "10 c2"                   (read only)
AFLAGS          0
ANGBASE         0
ANGDIR          0
APERTURE        5
AREA            1459.5350                 (read only)
ATTDIA          0
ATTMODE         1
ATTREQ          1
AUNITS          0
AUPREC          0
AXISMODE        0
AXISUNIT        0'-0",0'-0"
BACKZ           0'-0"                     (read only)
BLIPMODE        1
CDATE           19900523.113052920        (read only)
CECOLOR         "BYLAYER"                 (read only)
CELTYPE         "BYLAYER"                 (read only)
CHAMFERA        0'-0"
CHAMFERB        0'-0"
```

```
CLAYER        "OUTLINES"               (read only)    LIMMIN       0'-0",0'-0"
CMDECHO       1                                       LTSCALE      12.0000
COORDS        2                                       LUNITS       4
CVPORT        1                                       LUPREC       0
DATE          2448035.48018160         (read only)    MENUECHO     0
DIMALT        0                                       MENUNAME     "acad"                    (read only)
DIMALTD       2                                       MIRRTEXT     1
DIMALTF       25.4000                                 ORTHOMODE    1
DIMAPOST      ""                       (read only)    OSMODE       0
DIMASO        1                                       PDMODE       3
DIMASZ        0'-0"                                    PDSIZE       0.0000
DIMBLK        ""                       (read only)    PERIMETER    17'-1"                    (read only)
DIMBLK1       ""                       (read only)    PICKBOX      3
DIMBLK2       ""                       (read only)    POPUPS       1                         (read only)
DIMCEN        -0'-0"                                  QTEXTMODE    0
DIMDLE        0'-0"                                    REGENMODE    1
DIMDLI        0'-0"                                    SCREENSIZE   47'-8",34'-6"             (read only)
DIMEXE        0'-0"                                    SKETCHINC    0'-0"
DIMEXO        0'-0"                                    SKPOLY       0
DIMLFAC       1.0000                                   SNAPANG      0
DIMLIM        0                                        SNAPBASE     0'-0",0'-0"
DIMPOST       ""                       (read only)    SNAPISOPAIR  0


DIMRND        0'-1"                                    SNAPMODE     0
DIMSAH        0                                        SNAPSTYL     0
DIMSCALE      24.0000                                  SNAPUNIT     0'-3",0'-3"
DIMSE1        0                                        SPLFRAME     0
DIMSE2        0                                        SPLINESEGS   8
DIMSHO        0                                        SPLINETYPE   6
DIMSOXD       0                                        SURFTAB1     6
DIMTAD        1                                        SURFTAB2     6
DIMTIH        0                                        SURFTYPE     6
DIMTIX        1                                        SURFU        6
DIMTM         0'-0"                                    SURFV        6
DIMTOFL       0                                        TARGET       0'-0",0'-0",0'-0"         (read only)
DIMTOH        0                                        TDCREATE     2448035.47902147          (read only)
DIMTOL        0                                        TDINDWG      0.00286065                (read only)
DIMTP         0'-0"                                    TDUPDATE     2448035.47902847          (read only)
DIMTSZ        0'-0"                                    TDUSRTIMER   0.00286447                (read only)
DIMTVP        0'-0"                                    TEMPPREFIX   ""                        (read only)
DIMTXT        0'-0"                                    TEXTEVAL     0
DIMZIN        3                                        TEXTSIZE     0'-5"
DISTANCE      9'-11"                   (read only)    TEXTSTYLE    "TITLES"                  (read only)
DRAGMODE      2                                        THICKNESS    0'-0"
DRAGP1        10                                       TRACEWID     0'-2"


DRAGP2        25                                       UCSFOLLOW    0
DWGNAME       "32-2"                   (read only)    UCSICON      1
DWGPREFIX     "C:\ACAD10\"             (read only)    UCSNAME      ""                        (read only)
ELEVATION     0'-0"                                    UCSORG       0'-0",0'-0",0'-0"         (read only)
EXPERT        0                                        UCSXDIR      0'-1",0'-0",0'-0"         (read only)
EXTMAX        17'-0",22'-0"            (read only)    UCSYDIR      0'-0",0'-1",0'-0"         (read only)
EXTMIN        0'-0",0'-0"              (read only)    VIEWCTR      15'-2",11'-0"             (read only)
FILLETRAD     0'-0"                                    VIEWDIR      0'-0",0'-0",0'-1"         (read only)
FILLMODE      1                                        VIEWMODE     0                         (read only)
FLATLAND      1                                        VIEWSIZE     22'-0"                    (read only)
FRONTZ        0'-0"                    (read only)    VIEWTWIST    0                         (read only)
GRIDMODE      1                                        VPOINTX      0'-0"                     (read only)
GRIDUNIT      1'-0",1'-0"                              VPOINTY      0'-0"                     (read only)
HANDLES       0                        (read only)    VPOINTZ      0'-1"                     (read only)
HIGHLIGHT     1                                        VSMAX        30'-5",22'-0"             (read only)
INSBASE       0'-0",0'-0"                              VSMIN        0'-0",0'-0"               (read only)
LASTANGLE     0                        (read only)    WORLDUCS     1                         (read only)
LASTPOINT     11'-1",14'-1"                            WORLDVIEW    1                         (read only)
LASTPT3D      11'-1",14'-1",0'-0"
LENSLENGTH    50.0000                  (read only)    Command:
LIMCHECK      0
LIMMAX        17'-0",22'-0"
```

Pdmode, pdsize

Pdmode and pdsize are two very important setting variables that you have not yet set in your prototype. You will need to set them before you will be able to use some of the upcoming commands.

Pdmode (point definition mode)

Point definition refers to a marker that is placed on a drawing by the DIVIDE and MEASURE commands (investigated in the next chapter). These markers identify measured divisions of the line. With the pdmode setting variable, you can choose what the marker will look like. Here is a chart showing you all of the available choices.

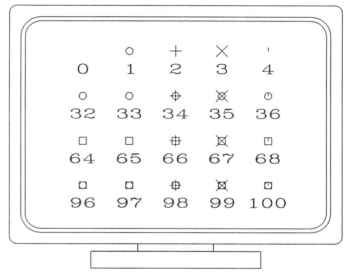

Locating the pdmode settings variable
- the Root Menu under DRAW, POINT
- the Root Menu under SETTINGS, SETVAR
- the Tablet Menu under POINT

Select EXAMPLE: from the POINT Menu to see a chart showing all of the point variations.

How to set pdmode — using POINT

1. Select SETVAR.

2. AutoCAD says: Point point:

    Select pdmode.

3. AutoCAD says: New value for PDMODE <0>:

    Type 3

pdsize (point definition size)

This setting variable controls the size of your point marker. A positive number has the effect of the points getting larger if you zoom in. A negative number has the effect of the points staying the same size when zoomed (if there is a **Regen**).

Once you have set pdmode and pdsize, type **Regen** to make them appear on your drawing. These marker points are "OSNAPable" with the OSNAP override NODe option.

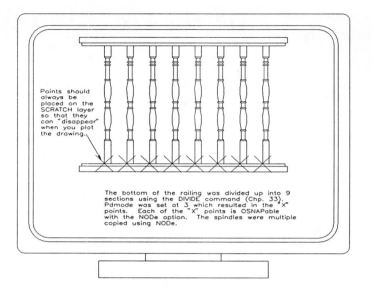

Points should always be placed on the SCRATCH layer so that they can "disappear" when you plot the drawing.

The bottom of the railing was divided up into 9 sections using the DIVIDE command (Chp. 33). Pdmode was set at 3 which resulted in the "X" points. Each of the "X" points is OSNAPable with the NODe option. The spindles were multiple copied using NODe.

PROJECT 27

SETTING VARIABLES

1. Set the pdmode and pdsize for each of your prototype drawings.

   Set pdmode to 3.

   Set pdsize to -2.

2. Be sure to save each drawing following each session.

33 EDITING YOUR WORK
PART VIII

> **FUNCTION**: These commands help you to divide up or space multiple objects in order along a line, a circle, an arc, or a polyline. Whether it is pars on a <u>LIGHT PLOT</u>, railing spindles on an <u>ELEVATION</u>, or buttons on a costume pattern, these commands function like a combination scale rule, calculator, and marker. Both commands divide an entity up but each does it a little bit differently.

DIVIDE

The DIVIDE command divides an entity equally into a *number* of divisions that you specify. That is, 5 divisions, 6 divisions, or whatever *number* of divisions. You do not care about the measurement between the spaces when you use this command.

Locating the DIVIDE command
- the Root Menu under EDIT
- the Pull Down Menu under OPTION (Release 11 and beyond)
- the Tablet Menu

Here's how DIVIDE works

To explore the DIVIDE and MEASURE commands you will need to go to a blank prototype drawing. Draw several circles and lines of different sizes in your OUTLINE layer.

1. Make your LAYOUT layer current.

2. Select DIVIDE.

3. AutoCAD says: Select object to divide:

    Pick one of your lines.

4. AutoCAD says: <Number of segments>/Block:

    <Number of segments> refers to the quantity of spaces that you want the entity divided into. If you select this option, you then give AutoCAD a number of divisions. The result will be markers drawn at each of the divisions.

    Block refers to the name of a symbol from your symbol library. If you select this option you give AutoCAD a block name (chair, PAR, etc.) as well as the number of divisions. The result will be the symbol drawn at each of the divisions.

    Type 5

    Your line has now been divided into five equal spaces. Or has it? If nothing seemed to happen, review Chapter 32 and PROJECT 27.

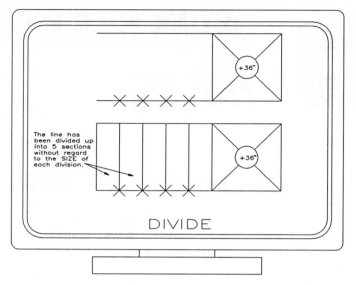

MEASURE

MEASURE divides an entity into divisions of a specific *length*. This division command will often leave one division shorter than the others at the end. You can predetermine at which end of the line the short segment will end up. Pick the end of the line where you don't want it to be at the Select objects: prompt.

Use this command when you want a line, polyline, circle, or arc divided into definite measured distances.

Locating the MEASURE command
- the Root Menu under EDIT
- the Pull Down Menu under OPTIONS
- the Tablet Menu under EDIT

Here's how MEASURE works

1. Make your LAYOUT layer current.

2. Select MEASURE.

3. AutoCAD says: Select object to measure:

Pick one of your lines.

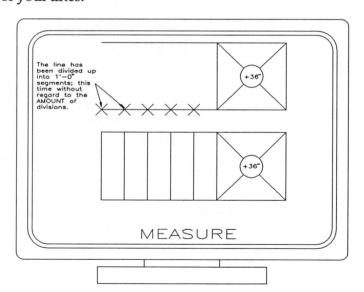

4. AutoCAD says: <Segment length>/Block:

    Type 1

Your line has now been divided into 1′ segments.

5. Now try dividing up and measuring all of the other lines and circles that you drew.

6. Draw lines from a marker on one entity to a marker on another with the OSNAP NODe option.

7. Freeze your SCRATCH layer. This will leave you with your finished drawing while eliminating the need to erase each marker.

PROJECT 28

DIVIDE, MEASURE

1. Create a PROJECT 28 drawing from your ½" scale prototype.

2. Make the OUTLINE layer current.

3. Draw one fence plank:

    a. Draw a 13′-4" long horizontal line that will be the base line of the fence.

    b. Draw a vertical line up from the left end of the base line 6′-8" high.

    c. Offset the vertical line 8" to form the other side of the first fence plank.

    d. Draw the top of the plank using **ENDpoint**.

    e. CHAMFER the top corners at 2".

4. Draw all of the remaining planks:

    a. Make the LAYOUT layer current.

    b. Divide the baseline up into 8" increments.

    c. Make the OUTLINE layer current.

    d. Set OSNAP running mode to NODe.

    e. **Multiple** COPY the first plank using the intersection of the left vertical line and the baseline as the base point.

5. Draw the two horizontal 2x4′s.

6. Use TRIM to erase the vertical lines that cross through the 2x4′s.

7. Freeze the LAYOUT layer.

8. Fully dimension and label the drawing.

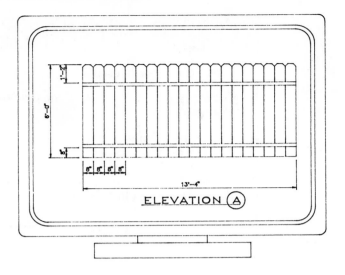

ELEVATION Ⓐ

34 SYMBOL LIBRARIES PART I

BLOCK
WBLOCK
INSERT
MINSERT
RENAME
PURGE

FUNCTION: Repetitive drawing of multiple symbols can be made quicker and easier with the use of symbol libraries. If you are a lighting designer, your symbol library will be a collection of lekos, fresnels, pars, strips, etc. For the scenic designer it will be your FLOOR PLAN chairs, tables, couches, and pianos. A symbol library can also hold ELEVATION views of doors, windows, fireplaces, and more. A computer-aided symbol library can enhance your work; any symbol can have the ability to carry lots of important information about the particular symbol. This first chapter on symbol libraries takes you through the first step — making the symbol.

BLOCK

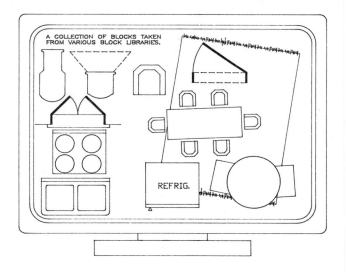

A COLLECTION OF BLOCKS TAKEN FROM VARIOUS BLOCK LIBRARIES.

REFRIG.

AutoCAD calls the symbols that you draw and then electronically store away "blocks." To store a particular symbol that you have created for future use, you first make it into a block using the BLOCK command.

Groups of blocks that are related (lighting instruments, sound equipment, furniture, etc.) can be "stored away" and made available for use at any time in any drawing. Each of these related groups constitutes a symbol library. Once a symbol has been created it is ready to use in just a couple of keystrokes.

You can create your own symbol libraries and you can buy pre-made symbol libraries that are ready to use in your drawings. These libraries include windows, bathroom fixtures, kitchen cabinets, office equipment, landscape symbols, and more. Manufacturers of these products regularly advertise their AutoCAD symbol libraries in many of the AutoCAD magazines. Two of these magazines are: *CADENCE* and *Cadalyst*.

CADENCE Magazine
Ariel Communications, Inc.
P.O. Box 203550
Austin, TX 78720-9976

Cadalyst Subscriptions
314 E. Holly #106
Bellingham, WA 98225

Locating the BLOCK command
- the Root Menu under BLOCKS
- the Tablet Menu

Making a BLOCK

Starting from your ½" prototype drawing, create a 2' x 2' chair symbol for a <u>FLOOR PLAN</u>.

Make sure that your block is being created on the layer you want it to be on forever (FURNITURE, LIGHTS, etc.). When you put a block into a drawing it will retain its color, linetype, and layer information.

A block created on layer 0 will take on the characteristics of the layer that is current at the time that you insert the block. For example, a lighting designer may want to create symbols on the 0 layer. If it is on a <u>REP PLOT</u>, there might be a layer for all instruments that are common to all shows. The layer might be white. There might be another layer for instruments that are special to show #1 in red, another for show #2 in blue, etc. As each symbol is inserted it will automatically take on the color of the show layer that is current. By plotting in color it will be easy to distinguish each show's specials from the common instruments.

1.   Select BLOCK.

2.   AutoCAD says: Block name (or ?):

Type CHAIR1

MEMO

Block names can be only eight letters or numbers long. You may want to reserve the last two spaces for code numbers. Don't name your first chair block CHAIR. When you decide that you're ready for another chair, you're stuck. Start with CHAIR1 or TABLE1 so that you have room to grow to CHAIR99 or TABLE99.

---

3.   AutoCAD says: Insertion base point:

Select a permanent "carrying handle" for your symbol. I suggest using OSNAP to pick the lower left corner of the object. If it's a lighting instrument, pick the yoke/c-clamp position.

4.   AutoCAD says: Select objects:

Window your symbol to select it.

5.   AutoCAD says: Select objects:

Hit **ENTER** to get out of this loop.

Your symbol may have disappeared but it is now stored as a block. Later you will use this same BLOCK command to make your related symbols library available at any time in any drawing. *If you need your original drawing to stay intact, make a copy of it and then BLOCK the copy!*

WBLOCK (Write Block)

You will use this command primarily to take a new symbol that you drew as part of a project and place it into an existing symbol library.

Locating the WBLOCK command
- the Root Menu under BLOCKS
- the Tablet Menu

Making the CHAIR1 block into a write block

1. Select WBLOCK.

2. AutoCAD says: File name:

   Type CHAIR1

3. AutoCAD says: Block name:

   Select from the Menu Area or type =

Your CHAIR1 symbol is now a write block — ready to transport to an existing symbol library.

INSERT

To insert a symbol WBLOCK symbol into your symbol library or to call up an entire symbol library for use in a drawing, use the INSERT command.

Locating the INSERT command
- the Root Menu under BLOCKS
- the Tablet Menu under BLOCKS

Inserting the CHAIR1 block into the drawing

1. Select INSERT.

2. AutoCAD says: Block name (or ?):

   Type CHAIR1

MEMO

The "?" option appears in these and many other AutoCAD commands. Selecting this option results in a list of data. In the case of these commands the "?" will show you a list of blocks that have been made or are available on that drawing. Hit the **F1** function key (flip screen toggle) to return to the drawing screen.

---

3. AutoCAD says: Insertion point:

   Place the symbol on your drawing.

4. AutoCAD says: X scale factor <1> / Corner / XYZ:

   Unless you want to stretch your symbol horizontally hit **ENTER**. (Stretching your chair horizontally is a fast way to make a couch symbol. You may want to do this for your next symbol creation.)

5. AutoCAD says: Y scale factor (default=X):

    Unless you want to stretch your symbol vertically hit **ENTER**.

6. AutoCAD says: Rotation angle <0>:

    Rotate your chair until it is at the desired angle. You can also type in an angle. 0 is the default and choosing that angle will place the chair at the same angle at which it was created.

    Your CHAIR1 symbol is now in place. Blocks are single entities. To edit a part of the symbol you must first EXPLODE it. You can insert a block that can later be edited by adding an "*" in front of the block name. By typing *CHAIR1 in step 2 we could easily edit parts of the block without using the EXPLODE command.

MINSERT (Multiple Insertion)

MINSERT calls up a symbol that you have stored away as a block and inserts it as an entire group of chairs, tables, or leko symbols. The group will take the form of a rectangular array.

Locating the MINSERT command
*   the Root Menu under BLOCKS
*   the Tablet Menu under BLOCKS

Inserting multiples of the CHAIR1 block into a drawing

1. Select MINSERT.

2. AutoCAD says: Block name (or ?):

    Type CHAIR1

3. AutoCAD says: Insertion point:

    Place the symbol on your drawing.

4. AutoCAD says: X scale factor <1> / Corner / XYZ:

    Unless you want to stretch your symbol horizontally hit **ENTER**.

5. AutoCAD says: Y scale factor (default=X):

    Unless you want to stretch your symbol vertically hit **ENTER**.

6. AutoCAD says: Rotation angle <0>:

    Hit **ENTER**.

7. AutoCAD says: Number of rows (---) <1>:

    AutoCAD is showing you 1 row.

    Type 7

8. AutoCAD says: Number of columns (|||) <1>: AutoCAD is showing you 3 columns.

    Type 7

9. AutoCAD says: Unit cell or distance between rows (---):

    With our 2'x 2' square chair in mind:

    Type in 4'

This will eventually result in a 2′ space between rows of chairs.

10. AutoCAD says: Distance between columns (---):

Type in 2′

The result should now appear on the screen — all chairs should be touching each other side to side and 2′ apart front to back.

The MINSERT command would also be helpful in quickly drawing identical windows in an <u>ELEVATION</u>, or perhaps an electric full of lekos on a <u>LIGHT PLOT</u>.

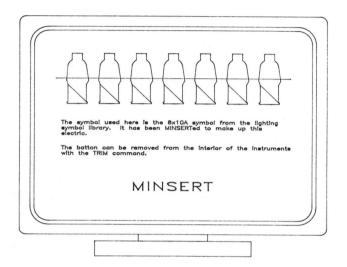

The symbol used here is the 8x10A symbol from the lighting symbol library. It has been MINSERTed to make up this electric.

The batton can be removed from the interior of the instruments with the TRIM command.

MINSERT

RENAME

This command is the one to use when you want to rename blocks, layers, linetypes, text styles, views, viewports, and user coordinate systems.

If you started your symbol library with CHAIR rather than CHAIR1, and now you have five chair symbols, you can rename CHAIR CHAIR1 with this command.

Locating the RENAME command
- the Root Menu under UTILITY

How RENAME works

1. Select RENAME.

2. AutoCAD says: Block/LAyer/LType/Style/Ucs/VIew/VPort:

   Select **Block**.

3. AutoCAD says: Old block name:

   Type in the old name.

4. AutoCAD says: New block name:

   Type in the new name. The block is now renamed.

PURGE

PURGE rids your drawing of all blocks, layers, line types, shapes, and styles in your drawing that you aren't using. The command will only work if it is the first command issued upon entering the drawing editor screen. If any other command has been given prior to the PURGE command it will not function.

Locating the PURGE command
- the Root Menu under UTILITY

How PURGE works

1. Select PURGE.

2. AutoCAD says: Blocks/LAyers/LTypes/Shapes/Styles/All:

   Select **Blocks**.

   The **All** option will show you the unused elements in all of the categories and ask you if you want to purge them.

3. AutoCAD will then list the unused block names in your drawing and ask you if you want to purge them.

   Purging your drawing of unused items will make your lists easier to understand and save memory.

MEMO

Many AutoCAD veterans feel that you really must go one step further than PURGE if you really want to make your drawing memory efficient. The trick involves WBLOCK. It is felt by some that PURGEd elements are flagged as being erased but are still a part of the data base. This in turn continues to eat up memory and slow down your drawing. The answer seems to be to WBLOCK the drawing. Type the drawing's name for File name: and select * for Block name:. This creates a more efficient file by getting rid of all of the unused PURGEable elements.

Apparently this works, even if you haven't PURGEd anything. I know of a few people who have tried this and swear by it. So next time disk space is getting tight, you might try it.

35 SYMBOL LIBRARIES PART II

> **FUNCTION**: This chapter will get you thinking about *organizing* your symbol collections. You will see how to begin arranging your symbol groups into library files. These files will then be accessible at any time on any drawing, saving you the time and trouble of ever having to draw them again.

Building a Symbol Library File

Think about a name for each of your libraries. You could name each library LIB1, LIB2, etc. Or you might try FURN1 (furniture library 1) FURN2, etc.; LIGHTS1, LIGHTS2, etc.; PLANSYM1, PLANSYM2, etc. Choose an identification system that makes sense now and will make sense to you in a year. Use a name that will grow as your libraries grow. If you find later that you have made a mistake in naming your libraries, there is always the RENAME command.

Design your symbols carefully. Start with a real object or an existing plastic symbol template. Scenic designers will most likely have at least five libraries:

FLOOR PLAN FURNITURE — This group will include chairs, sofas, rugs, pianos, refrigerators, etc. If you are working with a limited stock of furniture that you use a lot, then you will probably want to design your symbols based on the real McCoy. Otherwise you should draw generic symbols that will represent an array of periods and styles. Start with a plastic furniture template that you like and have used.

FIXTURES — This symbol group will include sinks, toilets, tubs, etc. These items come in several standard sizes so be careful about accuracy.

LANDSCAPE SYMBOLS — These include <u>PLAN</u> views of a variety of trees, shrubs, and rocks.

ELEVATION SYMBOLS — These items include <u>ELEVATION</u> drawings of windows, doors, railings, gates, etc. They can also include people, trees, and shrubs. The best way to form this collection is to add symbols to the file as you draw them in upcoming design projects. Saving these is a real timesaver. And don't forget that you can make variations by changing their X,Y orientations.

FLOOR PLAN SYMBOLS — This collection will include arches, single door swings, double door swings, window seats, casement windows, other windows, bookcases, multiple variations of size, swing, and hinge location. These symbols are another real timesaver.

LIGHTING SYMBOLS — A lighting designer's symbol library will include <u>PLAN</u> and <u>SECTION</u> views of lighting instruments as well as bases for booms and perhaps some sidearm variations.

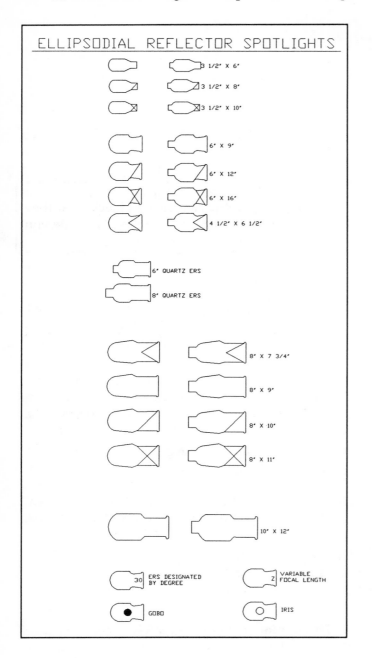

ELLIPSODIAL REFLECTOR SPOTLIGHTS

3 1/2' X 6'
3 1/2' X 8'
3 1/2' X 10'

6' X 9'
6' X 12'
6' X 16'
4 1/2' X 6 1/2'

6' QUARTZ ERS
8' QUARTZ ERS

8' X 7 3/4'
8' X 9'
8' X 10'
8' X 11'

10' X 12'

ERS DESIGNATED BY DEGREE
VARIABLE FOCAL LENGTH
GOBO
IRIS

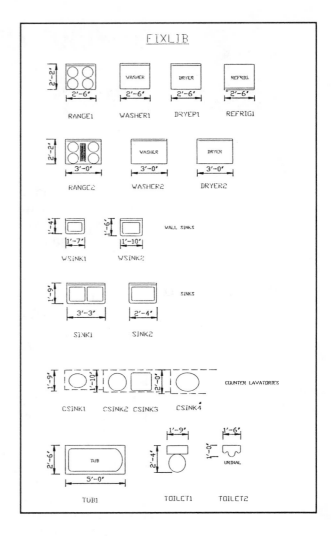

FIXLIB

RANGE1   WASHER1   DRYEP1   REFRIG1
RANGE2   WASHER2   DRYER2

WSINK1   WSINK2   WALL SINKS
SINK1   SINK2   SINKS
CSINK1   CSINK2   CSINK3   CSINK4   COUNTER LAVATORIES
TUB1   TOILET1   TOILET2

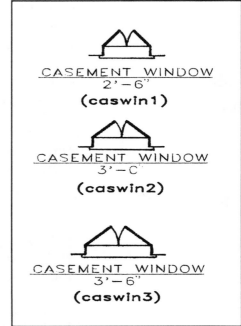

CASEMENT WINDOW
2'-6"
(caswin1)

CASEMENT WINDOW
3'-C"
(caswin2)

CASEMENT WINDOW
3'-6"
(caswin3)

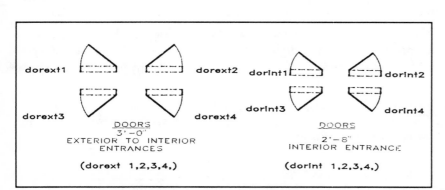

dorext1   dorext2   dorint1   dorint2
dorext3   dorext4   dorint3   dorint4

DOORS
3'-0"
EXTERIOR TO INTERIOR ENTRANCES
(dorext 1,2,3,4,)

DOORS
2'-8"
INTERIOR ENTRANCE
(dorint 1,2,3,4,)

Drawing the library file

1. Draw your symbols on a blank drawing editor screen from a prototype drawing. Use the prototype that is the most appropriate for the scale of the drawing that the symbol is most likely to be inserted into. Name your drawing FURN1, FURN2, LIGHTS1, ELEV1, etc.

2. Think about layers. If you have a separate symbol layer(s) — FURNITURE layer, SYMBOL layer, or INSTRUMENT layer — make it current when you draw your symbols. Use special layer 0 if you want your symbols to take on the qualities of whatever layer they are inserted into.

3. Your symbols must be very accurate as to the size of the objects that they represent. Have an existing template or accurate measurements beside you as you draw.

4. If your symbols require text (most <u>PLAN</u> symbols do) include that on your TEXT layer.

5. Arrange the symbols neatly in columns and rows. Draw 8½" x 11" sections in your LAYOUT layer and keep symbols together in groups contained in those rectangles. One could house chairs, another could house rugs, and another sofas, etc.

6. Use text to put the name of the library at the bottom of each 8½" x 11" section. It is helpful to have text indicating the name of each block, and dimensions to show the size of each table, rug, etc. The text and the dimensions must not be a part of the block. They are only here for reference.

Making the library drawing file

1. After the drawing of each library is completed, copy each symbol and make that copy into a block using the BLOCK command. This way your symbol will be on the drawing permanently and you will have made your block. If you make your *original* symbols into blocks, you will have to insert each one back into the drawing, one at a time.

2. When you finish each symbol library, save the drawing session. This results in a drawing (.dwg file) that houses one of your symbol libraries.

3. Repeat all of the above steps for your next symbol collection (FURN2 or LIGHTSYM, etc.).

Using your symbol library

1. Go to the drawing that will use your symbol library.

2. Select INSERT.

3. AutoCAD says: Block name (or ?):

    Type (the name of the library file you want to use)

4. AutoCAD says: Insertion point:

    Type **CTRL C** or select (CANCEL)

The library file has now been placed in your <u>FLOOR PLAN</u> or <u>LIGHT PLOT</u>. Canceling the Insertion point part of the command keeps all of the symbols from appearing at once on your drawing.

5. To make one of the symbols appear, use the INSERT command to call up a particular leko, chair, or tree and position it in your drawing.

Cataloging your symbol libraries

After making dozens and dozens of symbols, you will soon forget the look and name of most of them. The solution is to make a symbol library catalog. An organized catalog can you save you from a frustrating search for "the unknown block."

1. Plot out each of your .dwg library files.

2. Cut the paper apart at the 8½" x 11" division lines.

3. Punch holes in each sheet and put the pages together in a three-ring binder.

PROJECT 29

BUILDING A SYMBOL LIBRARY

1. Follow the steps outlined in this chapter to create your own symbol libraries.

2. Exchange library drawings with other "CADers" so that as many people as possible can share as many symbols as possible.

3. Plot all of the libraries out and make catalogs. Each catalog page should have:

    a. the name of the library file at the top or bottom of the page

    b. the block name of each symbol at the bottom or top of each symbol.

36 SYMBOL LIBRARIES PART III

> **FUNCTION**: Each of your symbols has the ability to store and supply data. Lighting symbols at the time of insertion can be encumbered with information that includes: instrument #, circuit #, lamp wattage, gel color, type of instrument, focus area, location, etc. Furniture symbols could have stock #, prop house or studio rented from, style or period, upholstery fabric, etc., inventoried in the symbol. These remarkable symbols that warehouse data are called *attributes*. The information attributed to a symbol can later be plotted out on the drawing itself or printed out as a separate list.

ATTDEF (Attribute Definition)

ATTDEF is the command you will use to define an attribute — to create a symbol that can retain information.

Locating the ATTDEF command
- the Root Menu under BLOCKS
- the Tablet Menu

Defining an attribute with ATTDEF

1. Call up the symbol drawing file from which you want to make attribute symbols (LIGHTS, FURN1, etc.).

   Let's say you want to make an attribute symbol from a block named LEKO. This attribute will yield information about color, wattage, etc. Later, when you insert the leko on your <u>LIGHT PLOT</u>, you will be prompted for the information and it can be automatically printed on your drawing and/or stored away for later extraction and assembly into an instrument schedule or hook-up sheet.

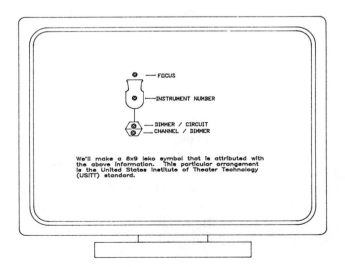

— 225 —

2. Insert your symbol (block).

3. Make your TEXT layer current.

4. Select ATTDEF.

5. AutoCAD says: Attribute modes — Invisible:N Constant:N Verify:N Preset:N Enter (ICVP) to change, RETURN when done:

> **Invisible** – Do not display the symbol but allow the information to be taken away and put in a list.

> **Constant** – All occurrences of this attribute have the same value. Not a good choice for lighting instruments as a typical fresnel symbol for instance will be used many times and have a different focus area, circuit, etc. for each occurrence.

> **Verify** – Issue extra prompts to verify a proper value.

> **Preset** – Do not prompt for this Attribute during Block Insertion.

To change the status of one or more of these variables, simply type the letter(s) and then hit **ENTER**.

Leave these options as they are.

> Hit **ENTER**.

6. AutoCAD says: Attribute tag:

The tag is to identify what sort of information this will be.

> Type FOCUS

7. AutoCAD says: Attribute prompt:

The prompt is what AutoCAD will actually ask you when you insert the block.

> Type FOCUS AREA?

8. AutoCAD says: default attribute value:

The default value will appear in brackets at the end of the prompt.

> Type number

9. AutoCAD says: Start point or Align/. . ./Style:

This positions the focus area text in relation to the symbol.

> Select **Centered**

10. AutoCAD says: Center point:

Pick where the center of the color text is to be on your LEKO block.

11. AutoCAD may say:

Height:

> Type in or drag the text height.

12. AutoCAD says: Rotation angle <0>:

> Choose the default 0.

Your first attribute definition is complete. Now attribute instrument number to the same symbol. To do so, go through all the above steps again using the information below:

tag	INSTRUMENT
prompt	NUMBER ?
default value	X

Repeat the steps as often as you need to or want to, adding information such as circuit, dimmer, channel, etc. Perhaps add the hexagonal dimmer/channel information symbol. If you want to make any of the attributes invisible on the drawing but visible in a list (hook-up sheet) be sure to change the Invisible setting to Yes.

13. Now you need to re-block the symbol.

    Select BLOCK.

14. AutoCAD says: Block name:

    Type ALEKO (for attribute leko)

15. AutoCAD says: Insertion base point:

    Pick a point on or near your leko. Perhaps this point should be where the yoke and c-clamp of the instrument are, in order to make alignment with the pipe or batten easier.

16. AutoCAD says: Select objects:

    Use a window to capture the leko and the attributes.

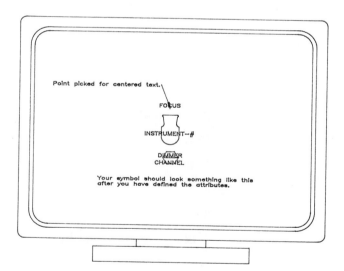

Inserting an Attribute Symbol

You will use the INSERT command to use attribute symbols in a drawing. There are two methods for entering the attribute information during the insert command. One uses the Command Prompt Area and the other uses a Dialog Box. Let's look at the Command Prompt Area method first:

Command prompt method of attribute insertion

1. Select INSERT.

2. AutoCAD says: Block name:

   Type ALEKO

3. AutoCAD says: Insertion point:

   Pick the point.

4. AutoCAD says: Enter attribute values
   CHANNEL NUMBER <NUMBER>:

   Type 87

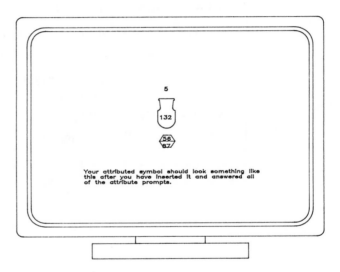

5. AutoCAD says: DIMMER NUMBER? <NUMBER>:

   Type 56

If you have more attributes for ALEKO, continue answering the prompts until you get the Command prompt. Your symbol has been inserted and the information has been automatically printed on the drawing. Now let's try the Dialog Box method.

Dialog box method of attribute insertion

1. Select SETVAR.

2. AutoCAD says: Variable name or ?:

   Type ATTDIA. ATTDIA is the setting variable that toggles the ATTribute DIAlog box ON (1) and OFF (0).

3. AutoCAD says: New value for ATTDIA <0>:

   Type 1

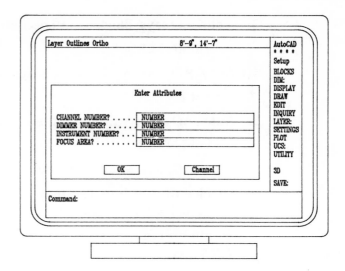

4. The next time that you insert an attribute, a dialog box will appear that shows you all of your attributes and their default settings.

    Pick any of the settings that you wish to change.

    Pick the OK box to set your choices.

Changing the Tags or Prompts

You can change the tags or prompts by preceding the block name with an * when you insert it. Use the CHANGE command to then alter your attributes. Re-BLOCK the symbol in order to keep your changes. When the BLOCK command asks for block name, use the same name. AutoCAD will say that the drawing for this block already exists — say YES in order to redefine it.

ATTDISP (Attribute Display)

ATTDISP controls the visibility of the attribute text with three options.

Locating the ATTDISP command
*   the Root Menu under DISPLAY

The three ATTDISP options are:
Normal – Displays the text according to your settings in the ATTDEF command.
ON – Overrides the ATTDEF settings and makes all text visible.
OFF – Overrides the ATTDEF settings and makes all text invisible.

ATTEDIT (ATTRIBUTE EDIT)

Using ATTEDIT is a way of editing attribute text on an already inserted symbol, while at the same time keeping its block properties.

Locating the ATTEDIT command
*   the Root Menu under EDIT
*   the Tablet Menu

Let's change the text of one of your inserted ALEKO symbols
1. Select ATTEDIT.

2. AutoCAD says: Edit attributes one at a time? <Y>

    Hit **ENTER.**

3. AutoCAD says: Block name specification <*>:

   Hit **ENTER**.

4. AutoCAD says: Attribute tag specification <*>:

   Hit **ENTER**.

5. AutoCAD says: Attribute value specification <*>:

   Hit **ENTER**.

6. AutoCAD says: Select attributes:

   Pick the attribute text that you want to change. The text *will not* turn dotted when it is picked.

   Hit **ENTER**.

7. AutoCAD says: 1 attributes selected.

   Value/Position/. . ./Next <N>:

   Select **Value**.

8. AutoCAD says: Change or Replace? <R>:

   Select **Change**.

9. AutoCAD says: String to change:

   Type the existing text.

10. AutoCAD says: New string:

    Type the change.

11. AutoCAD says: Value/Position/. . ./Next <N>:

    Hit **ENTER** to get out of this loop.

Your text has been changed and your symbol remains a block.

ATTEXT (Attribute Extraction)

One of the remarkable things about attribute symbols is that the information they contain can be taken out of the drawing and made into a form, list, or schedule. The lighting designer will want a hook-up sheet, and the scenic designer may want a list of furniture types and styles and inventory numbers.

The ATTEXT command allows you to specify what format the extracted information should be in as it leaves your drawing. Extracting this sort of information from AutoCAD is easy but requires the use of a data base program.

When your drawing is complete, invoke the ATTEXT command. With this command you will be asked to specify a file format (CDF, SDF, or DXF). You can select either individual entities or the entire drawing.

The file formats are:

CDF	=	Command Delineated Format
SDF	=	Standard (fixed field) Format
DXF	=	Drawing Interchange Format

These file formats can be read by most major data base programs. When the information is in your data base you can design the form that you want the information to be read in.

PROJECT 30

ATTRIBUTES

Where appropriate, add attributes to your symbol libraries.

37 DISPLAY TECHNIQUES PART III

FUNCTION: One of the tasks that you take for granted in pencil and paper drafting is the ability to compare drawings instantly. Let's say you're working on a <u>LIGHT PLOT</u> and you suddenly need to refer to the <u>CENTER LINE SECTION</u> of the theater. Or you're drawing <u>ELEVATION W</u> and you need to look at the <u>PLAN</u> to determine how it fits into <u>ELEVATION X</u>. CAD drawings are not instantly available to you in this way since they are stored away as electronic memory. In order to compare these drawings, you would need to save your drawing, quit, and then call up the new drawing at the Main Menu. All of this takes time — REGEN time! Plotting out each sheet while you work may be one solution, but that takes lots of time and space. This chapter explores a remedy — the SLIDE commands.

MSLIDE, VSLIDE (Make Slide, View Slide)

MSLIDE takes a sort of electronic photograph of any of your drawings. This slide can then be called up, almost instantly, while you are working on another drawing, with the VSLIDE command. The slide is identical in the way it looks to the actual drawing file from which it has been made.

It is important to note, however, that this slide is not something that you can draw on, edit, or even zoom in on. It is merely an electronic snapshot that allows you to reference and compare drawings.

Locating the MSLIDE and VSLIDE commands
- the Root Menu under UTILITY, SLIDES

Making a slide

1. Call up the drawing that you want to make a slide of.

2. Determine the composition of the drawing by using the ZOOM command if necessary.

   The majority of the time you will want to be zoomed all the way back in order to see the entire drawing. With a <u>FLOOR PLAN</u>, however, you may want to zoom in on the relatively small area of the sheet that contains the scenery itself.

3. Select MSLIDE:

   AutoCAD says:

   Slide name<name of current drawing file>:

4. Select the default by hitting **ENTER** or type in a different name for this slide (PLAN, SHEET3, ELEVA-F, etc.) The slide has now been made.

Viewing a slide

1. While in the drawing editor, select VSLIDE.

2. AutoCAD says: Slide file<name of current drawing file>:

3. Type in the name of the slide. The drawing that you want to reference should immediately appear on the screen. That's all there is to it.

4. To return to your drawing session:

    Select REDRAW.

    Make a slide of each sheet of show drawings, plots, or patterns as a matter of routine. This will ensure that every drawing will be instantly available for comparison at any time.

PROJECT 31

MSLIDE, VSLIDE

1. Make slides of several of your drawings.

2. Call up another of your drawings under option 2 (Edit an existing drawing) of the Main Menu.

3. View several of the slides that you created.

PART III
DESIGNING AND DRAWING FOR THEATER, FILM, AND TELEVISION

PERSPECTIVE RENDERINGS
FLOOR PLANS
STAGING PLANS
CL SECTIONS
ELEVATIONS
LIGHT PLOTS
SOUND PLOTS

38 DESIGNING and DRAFTING SCENERY

> **FUNCTION**: As I said much earlier, in the Introduction, it is assumed that you already know how to draft scenery and lighting. The intent of this book is to show you how to use a new technology to accomplish these same tasks, quicker and more accurately. This chapter will expose you to just such a strategy in the area of scenic design.

Developing CAD Drawing Strategies

Many new students of CAD find that the first couple of projects they do in AutoCAD could have been done in much less time had they stuck with their trusty T-squares, lead holders, and scale rules. The truth is they are right. The problem is that they have replaced their old drawing tools with a new computer, but they are relying on ingrained pencil and paper drawing skills. This mismatch will actually make the work harder than ever before and slow you down to a crawl.

Part III points you in the direction of developing new computer-aided drawing skills and strategies. A CAD program gives you bags of tricks that are not available to the pencil and paper drafter. The problem is that your old drawing repertoire has become entrenched. You will have to practice, work hard, and eventually replace those skills with new ones designed to make your drafting experience better.

As you practice and discover the strategies and advantages of CAD drafting you will eventually become as fast as you were with pencil and paper (and twice as accurate). In no time at all you will fly through a project (and your drawings will be nearly flawless). But it will take you time to begin thinking and planning out a project in a brand new way. Don't make your next deadline project your first AutoCAD assignment. Stick with pencil and paper but continue practicing with AutoCAD. Use AutoCAD for those projects that have a more leisurely schedule at first. Only when you are finally up to and past pencil and paper speed can you pack away all of your old compasses, erasers, and scale rules.

Floor Plans and Staging Plans

The FLOOR PLAN or STAGING PLAN drawing is a key to developing many of the other drawings in a complete set of CAD plans. Here is a guide for developing CAD PLAN drawing skills and planning your drawing strategy.

Theater/studio architecture

One of your very first CAD responsibilities will be to draft the FLOOR PLANS of the theaters, or STAGING PLANS of the sound stages or studios that you design in. You will find this one of the most frustrating and un-believably time-consuming experiences of your life. You see, the way that you will probably do this is to take a blueprint of the space and measure and draft from one corner to the next, to the next, etc. Hair-pulling time comes when you are finishing up the project and find that one side of the stage turns out to

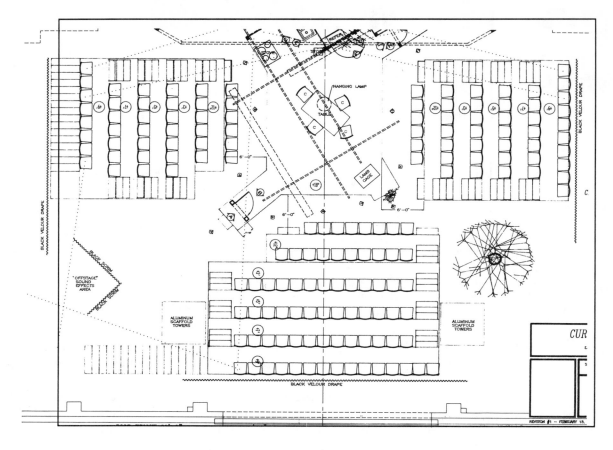

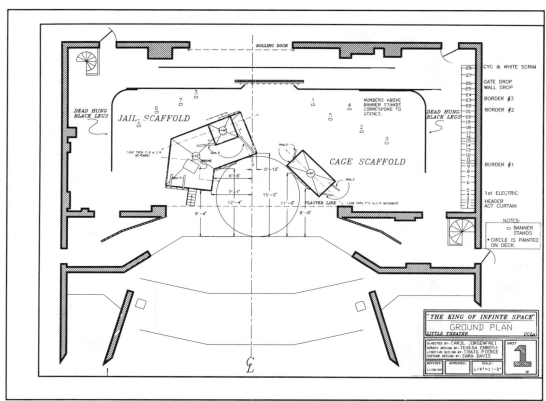

be a couple of feet shorter than the other. Well, you know that isn't true so it must be that you are doing something wrong.

The problem isn't you, it's in your blueprint. CAD measurements need to be completely accurate (or at least a planned lie). As you measure your blueprint you are measuring nooks and crannies that can only be as accurate as the scale of the drawing, the accuracy of the original draftsperson, or the steadiness and consistency of the blueline. People I know who have attempted such an assignment are — to the person — totally bewildered.

The secret is to either:

- survey and measure the space from scratch with the accuracy of CAD in mind
- have the blueprint electronically scanned
- take the smart way out and hire someone to do it for you
- or carefully plan out a close approximation of the space (lie).

The planned lie!
Here's how to go about constructing a close approximation of the space:

1. Start out by drawing the gross shape of the space. Look for a basic geometric shape that defines the outline of the building (usually a simple rectangle).

2. Draw that shape onto the blueprint using pencil and drafting machine.

3. Measure the shape and CAD draft it.

4. Go back to your blueprint rectangle and subdivide each side into a few parts that define and contain the important elements of the architecture (proscenium opening, loading door, support columns, control booths, etc.).

5. Measure these divisions on your blueprint and add them to your CAD PLAN.

6. Continue this strategy, making smaller and smaller subdivisions with each step. Soon your drawing will be complete and will be as accurate as any could be without surveying the space from scratch. I would add that if you can get as many important measurements from the actual space as possible, the better off you will be. More and more theaters and stages have such drawings on AutoCAD already. It wouldn't hurt to ask the production manager at the next job site if such a disk exists!

Use a recessive plotter pen color for the architecture. The PLAN of your set should stand out — not the stage itself. You should have a STAGE layer that will plot in yellow. Yellow doesn't blueprint or photocopy very well. Therefore, it is an excellent choice for the theater architecture.

Scanning
Scanning is another way to get an existing drawing onto your hard disk. Large format scanners read an existing blueprint and transform it into an AutoCAD drawing. It's quick but costly. If you don't have access to a firm that will do this for you, you can send your drawing off to mail order scanning services around the country. These services advertise in AutoCAD magazines.

A problem with a scanned drawing is that all of the information will be on one layer. This is quite a problem with ELEVATIONS and FLOOR PLANS but is probably not so much of a problem with just the architecture. Your prototype most likely uses only two layers for this drawing — STAGE and HIDDEN STAGE. It would be a simple matter to go through and assign these layers to each line.

A prototype plan for each stage

To avoid ever having to draw the stage architecture again, keep a prototype of each stage that you work in. Draw your stage on a prototype drawing with a new name. Drawing names might be:

> PHPROTO (Playhouse Prototype)
> LTPROTO (Little Theater Prototype)
> ST1PROTO (Stage 1 Prototype)
> STBPROTO (Studio B Prototype)

Title block

Drawing the title block must be the most tedious of all pencil and paper drafting tasks. AutoCAD can suddenly make the job of dealing with title blocks almost effortless. By drawing your title block on your prototype once, you should never have to draw it again. Your title block is a part of every drawing that you do, therefore it should be on every one of your prototypes. All that you should ever have to do is to fill in the information pertaining to a particular assignment.

All title block information can be divided into two categories: show-specific text information pertaining to a current production; and standard text information that never changes from assignment to assignment.

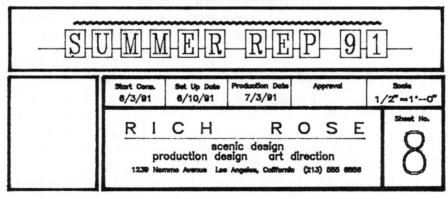

Standard information

This information will be a permanent part of your title block and should be entered onto each prototype:

- Outline(s) of Title Block
- (space for production title)
- DIRECTOR: (space for name)
- DESIGNER: Your name
- DATE: (Space for date)
- SCALE: ½" = 1'-0"
- (space for theater or stage)
- (space for approvals)
- SHEET # (space) OF (space)
- (space for any affiliation stamps)

Show-specific information

This information changes from production assignment to production assignment and will be typed into the title block on a show prototype:

- PRODUCTION TITLE
- Director's Name
- Date
- Name of theater or stage
- Sheet Number
- Number of Sheets

The best way to enter the show-specific information is with the CHANGE command. Type "XXXX . . ." wherever this type of information occurs. Put the X's in the style, size, and position that you want them to be in and save them as part of your generic block. Use the CHANGE command to transform XXXX into CURSE OF THE STARVING CLASS and Mark Taper Forum, etc., etc. This technique makes the entry of specific text simple by eliminating the time-consuming task of changing text styles and the tedious cursor/cross hair work of lining up text strings.

Keep all title block text in the TEXT layer. The lines and polylines that make up the actual block should be drawn in your OUTLINE layer.

Sightlines

If you are doing theatrical drafting then you have to deal with sightlines. In pencil and paper drafting, sightlines are drawn in a lighter than light weight line from each extreme sightline seat to the edges of the proscenium opening and beyond.

Although drawing sightlines is no problem with AutoCAD, CAD plotters don't like those "lighter than light weight" lines. My suggestion is to use AutoCAD's DOT linetype. As you can see from this example, DOT has the least impact of all of the linetypes.

Since sightlines will most likely be the only object in your drawings requiring a DOT line, you should have them tucked away in their own SIGHTLINE layer with DOT as the linetype. To keep the impact of the sightlines minimal on your drawing screen as well as your plot, use cyan for the layer color.

Drawing walls and other major scenic elements

Establishing the position of set elements or walls with AutoCAD is almost like manipulating model pieces. The entities can be pulled and pushed around to your heart's content. Hundreds of tracings and erasures for each combination are a thing of the past. Here's how to go about establishing wall position:

1. Draw in sightlines.

2. Make your LAYOUT layer current.

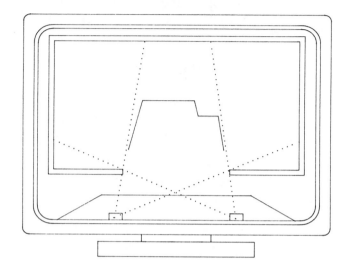

3. Draw simple single lines representing a length of wall. In other words, forget about doors, windows, etc.; just draw the simplified length of the wall.

4. Repeat for each wall length.

5. Use the MOVE command to "play" with the walls. Experiment with different positions and combinations.

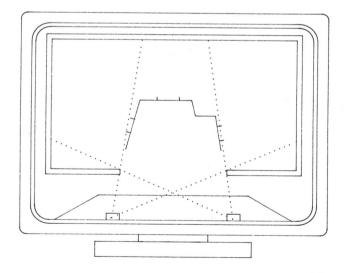

6. Once you have established the positions of all of the scenic elements, draw in the positions of all of the detail — doors, windows, columns, etc. Don't draw any of these in any great detail, simply indicate positions by drawing reveals. If you have these items already in a symbol library, you don't even have to draw them.

7. Don't bother with ERASE or TRIM or any of the editing commands — those activities would waste time. This layer will be frozen later on — it'll never be seen. Repeat the above steps for platforms and other scenic elements.

8. Make your OUTLINE layer current.

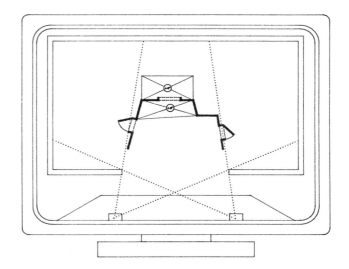

9. "Load-up" your target cross hairs with OSNAP options **INTERSECTION** and **ENDpoint**. Don't forget to separate them with a comma.

10. Select PLINE and enter a line width of 1" (more, of course, if your walls are thicker than a theatrical flat).

11. Draw right over your layout lines from end point to end point, intersection to intersection, to indicate your wall positions. This should be a fairly easy and quick process. All of the placement and fitting problems were worked out in the LAYOUT layer. This is the equivalent of tracing your rough drawings.

12. Make your HIDDENOUTLINES layer current.

13. Draw in, or insert from your symbol library, all dashed lines representing doorways, windows, etc. Use the normal LINE command for this operation. To draw lines parallel to your angled walls (in order to draw window sills, door thicknesses, etc.) use the SNAP command rotate option to rotate the Grid. Use OSNAP **ENDpoint** to select one end of the wall that you want to draw parallel to, when AutoCAD asks for base angle. Select the other end of the wall for rotation angle. The Grid will automatically turn to match the wall. Turn Ortho on to draw perpendicular lines.

14. Most of the major set element drawing work should be complete. Make your PLATFORMS layer current in order to draw those in next, over your layout lines.

15. Any layout line that would work perfectly well as the actual OUTLINE or PLATFORM, etc. layer need not be traced over. If the LAYOUT line width is okay then you should use the CHANGE command to change the layer. Avoid redrawing any line that is simply in the wrong layer.

16. Save all television "swing set" <u>PLANS</u> that are used in a <u>STAGING PLAN</u>. <u>STAGING PLANS</u> are <u>FLOOR PLANS</u> in a studio. They consist of a line of

"swing sets" representing different locations. Swing sets are the sets that are not the permanently recurring main set. All of these sets are arranged so that cameras and microphone dollies can quickly and easily get to any of the sets. A typical situation comedy configuration consists of a main camera/microphone aisle with audience bleacher on one side and a long lineup of the sets on the other side. A soap opera configuration typically has a center aisle with sets lined up along both sides of the aisle.

Most sets are used one week, stored away, and then used weeks later if the show is a continuing series, and the plot takes the characters to that locale over and over again. Other sets are repainted and repapered to represent a new location. Weeks later when the script calls for the set to repeat, the saved PLAN can be inserted into the new STAGING PLAN. With the ROTATE command you will be able to change the angle of the walls to open the set up or close it in to fit the space.

You should keep a catalog binder of your swing sets just as you do for your symbol library. In effect, your swing set library is another kind of symbol library.

Architectural drafting symbols

Door, window, and other similar architectural drafting symbols in FLOOR PLANS can be tricky to draw. I suggest that you start a library of those symbols right away. Every time you create a new one, store it away in your architectural symbol library so that you never have to go through the agony of drawing it again. An appropriate name for this library may be ARCHSYM1 or ARCHLIB1.

Remember to MIRROR symbols to get reverse door swings, etc. Don't forget STRETCH and SCALE when it comes to variations of each symbol. Store each variation in your library. The door swing in this example was stored away as a BLOCK and appears many times throughout the drawing.

Most of these symbols should be created on the layers that they would be drawn on. The door and its reveals would be on the OUTLINES layer. The dashed header lines would be on the HIDDENOUTLINES layer. The door swing arc should be on the OUTLINES layer.

Elevation markers

Elevation markers are the circles with triangular arrows that point at a scenic element. Inside the circle is a capital letter that corresponds to an ELEVATION drawing occurring later on in the plans.

Here is another drawing nuisance that can be alleviated if you assign the task to AutoCAD. When creating your markers, place them on their own ELEVMARK layer. This will give you the freedom to turn them on and off. Use your TITLES type style.

To make a marker

1. Make the ELEVMARK layer current.

2. Type an "X" in your TITLES text style.

3. Draw a circle around the letter. Don't let the circle touch the letter, but don't let it get too big either.

4. ZOOM in on your circle.

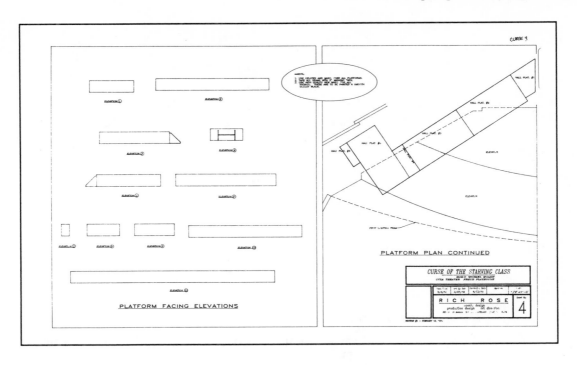

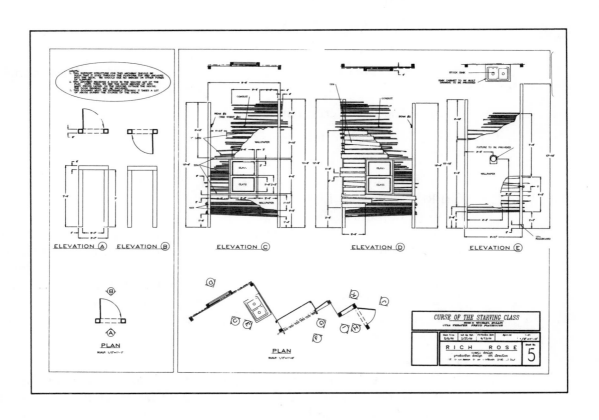

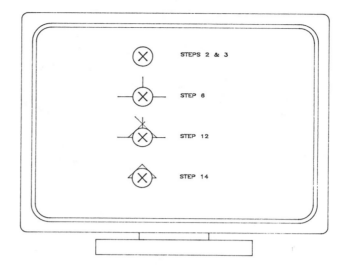

5. Turn Ortho on.

6. Draw medium length lines outward from the 9:00, 12:00, and 3:00 positions of the circle. Use the Quadrant OSNAP override.

7. Select the SNAP command from SETTINGS.

8. Select the **Rotate** option.

9. Select the default 0,0 basepoint.

10. Type 45 for the rotation angle.

11. Turn the Snap drawing aid off.

12. Using the **Nearest** OSNAP option, draw the two sides of the triangle. The middle of the lines should just touch the circle.

13. Erase the 12:00 vertical line.

14. Use TRIM to cut off the excess line length.

15. Rotate back to 0 degrees using the SNAP command.

Be sure and save this as a symbol. Block it in your prototype, your ST1PROTO, or your furniture library of symbols. You should NEVER have to draw one of these again.

When you go to insert the symbol into your <u>PLAN</u> you will be given a chance to rotate it in the proper direction. After all of your elevation marker symbols have been inserted into your <u>PLAN</u>, use CHANGE to alphabetize them. A very quick way of doing this is to select CHANGE and then, in order, pick all of the "X's" in one step. You can then change the type in all of the A-Z letters in one more step. AutoCAD automatically remembers the order in which you picked your "X's".

Furniture

Review the chapters on symbol libraries when it comes time to actually create your personal symbol library. You should create all of your furniture on a separate FURNITURE layer. This separate layer concept is important in that if you have a complicated <u>FLOOR PLAN</u> you will have the ability to plot out a <u>PLAN</u> for the carpenters that eliminates confusing clutter.

As you create new furniture and prop symbols for particular design assignments, be sure to WBLOCK them and put them in your permanent library. This is how most of your symbol "collecting" will take place. Don't hesitate to ask fellow CADers if you can copy their libraries. Most will be too glad to help you out, especially if they can steal your libraries as well.

Seating

The chairs for the rows of seats in this example were created from a chair symbol that had been in my library for about two years. I measured the actual theater seat that was going to be used for the repertory seating and found out that I needed to stretch and scale the chair to make it the right size. Once that was done, it became the newest item in my furniture collection.

The bleachers themselves were drawn pretty quickly:

1. LAYOUT lines were drawn to indicate the position of the bleacher units.

2. Switching back to the PLATFORM layer, one seating level was drawn (4' x 20') for the stage right unit.

3. Multiple COPY was then used to create the other four levels.

4. One of the audience stair units was drawn next.

5. Multiple COPY was used to create the other three units.

6. The middle four rows of chairs were MINSERTed.

7. The other two rows were then MINSERTed separately.

8. The entire unit was MIRRORed at the center line to create stage left.

9. The center stage unit was an EXPLODEd, STRETCHed, and TRIMmed version of stage right. Some additional drawing was needed for the upper level and audience escape staircase.

I think you'll agree that this is pretty far removed from pencil and paper drafting. You can see that if I had drawn the units with those old and musty traditional strategies, it would have taken two to three times as long. With AutoCAD you are drawing only one of the units and creating the other two from it.

Flown scenery

In this example from *Curse of the Starving Class*, the flown scenery consists of overhead roof structure beams (drawn in dashed lines).

The flown structure was actually created in ½" scale on another sheet in the drawings. This was done for two reasons: (a) it was decided that a ¼" scale plot wasn't sufficient to show the positioning accurately; and (b) I wanted to work out the look of the beams in ELEVATION at the same time that I worked out the positioning in PLAN. The two were inter-related in my mind.

I took the set portion of the FLOOR PLAN and made it into a WBLOCK. This was then INSERTed into a ½" prototype. Now I could draw my ELEVATIONS and work on beam placement all at the same time (in the FLY layer). Once that was completed, the beam structure was WBLOCKed and INSERTed into the FLOOR PLAN.

For traditional counterweight batten flying scenery, you might want to add a BATTENS layer and drawing to your PLAN prototype or add a BATTENS drawing to your FLY layer. Once this layer was turned on, you would see the position of every batten in the theater or studio. To indicate

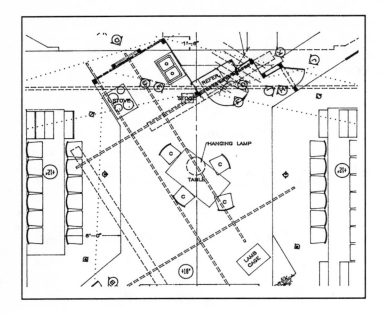

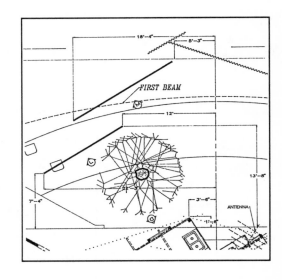

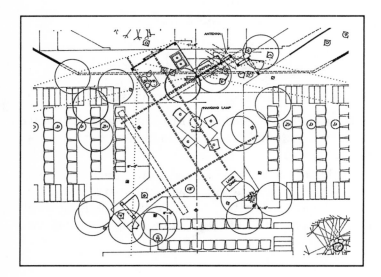

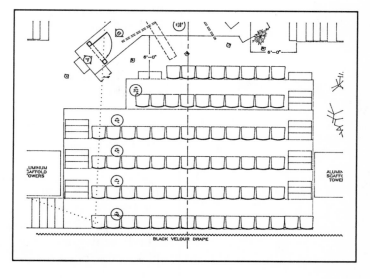

flown scenery you would draw a dashed line in the FLY layer over that batten. The batten layer would then be frozen out.

Dimensions

Review the chapters on dimensioning before dimensioning your <u>FLOOR PLAN</u> or <u>STAGING PLAN</u>. Here are some keys to dimensioning <u>PLANS</u>:

1. Make your DIMENSION layer current.

2. Have a platform height symbol in one of your libraries. Create a circle with + XX" inside of it. After the symbol has been inserted in the platform, change the "XX" text to the numeric value of the platform height; 24", 30", etc.

3. Load your cross hair target with the OSNAP overrides **ENDpoint** and **INTERSECTION**. This will make the task of dimensioning quite routine.

Fire egress

I have created a FIRECLEARANCE layer for productions where audience and scenery come in contact with each other. You can see this in this theatrical thrust configuration and you can see this in many arena configurations.

At each corner or projection of the platforming or bleachers, I drew a 3′ radius circle. This became a boundary that was not to be crossed by set or patron. This layer was for my benefit only. I used it to obtain exact positioning and configuration of the scenery. After the set was adjusted and shaped, the layer was frozen.

Draperies

The 40′ long draperies you see in this <u>PLAN</u> are from a drape in my furniture library that is about 4′ long. To create these drapes the block was inserted over and over, end to end, to build the desired length.

This particular drape symbol is made up of a series of alternating arcs placed end to end. The curved nature of this particular symbol does increase regeneration time. You might want to make your symbol out of zigzags in order to avoid those memory-eating curves.

All of my drapes are on a separate DRAPES layer so that I have the option to turn it on and off.

Meeting with the Director

This turns out to be one of the joys of the electronic <u>FLOOR PLAN</u>. Normally once I have had a chance to complete a <u>FLOOR PLAN</u>, the director and I will arrange a meeting time to look it over. Here's what used to happen with my pencil and paper drawings:

> During the meeting we discuss various issues and I take many notes about what I understand took place. I spend the next day redrafting and then call the director to reschedule a meeting. In the next meeting we talk about the improvements and the problems that are a result of my notes or misunderstandings from the previous meeting. I take more notes. This process repeats itself over the next day or so.

The electronic CAD meeting is much different and highly efficient. The director and I sit around the monitor. Together we move furniture and set pieces around. There is no mis-communication, and the PLAN is usually finished to everyone's satisfaction by the end of that meeting. As a matter of fact, I can plot out a drawing for the director right then and there. If there are revisions to be made that come up later on, they can be handled the same way.

CAD drawing creates another neat way to eliminate wasted time.

Revisions and Revision Schedules

REVISION SCHEDULE		
SHEET #	CURRENT REVISION	DATE DRAWN
1	1	FEBRUARY 18, 1989
2	0	
3	1	FEBRUARY 18, 1989
4	1	FEBRUARY 18, 1989
5	0	
6	1	FEBRUARY 18, 1989
7	1	FEBRUARY 18, 1989
8	1	FEBRUARY 18, 1989
9	1	FEBRUARY 18, 1989
10	1	FEBRUARY 18, 1989

Because drawing revisions are so quick and easy, you will find yourself doing lots of them — believe it or not! When other members of your production team find out how simple it is to do revisions on AutoCAD, they soon lose any inhibitions they had about asking you for changes — they know that you can do them in a snap! The trouble is that a whole new category of problems arises as you and the carpenters begin to drown in a sea of revision sheets. Everyone quickly loses track of which is the latest revision of each sheet.

If this becomes a problem (and it will) you may want to attach a revision schedule to your PLAN. This is a table on the TEXT layer that keeps track of all of the sheets. It tells you the latest revision number and date for each sheet of drafting.

Every time you draw a revision, you update the table on the PLAN and plot out both the PLAN and the sheet with the revisions. Be sure and confiscate all of the old PLANS.

Other Plans

FLOOR PLANS or STAGING PLANS that convey other types of specific information are effortlessly produced with AutoCAD. These drawings go into great detail explaining one facet of the PLAN. I used to make them only reluctantly back in my pencil and paper days. The repetitive tedium involved in redrawing FLOOR PLANS was the cause of much hesitation. Today, drawing with CAD eliminates the monotonous drudgery and frees you up to spend time drawing only the new information — not redrafting the entire drawing. Another important benefit is the absence of copying errors. In pencil and paper drafting, these are caused by copying and scaling up or down. There are so many ways that mistakes can be made that the mistakes *always* get made. Since AutoCAD doesn't transfer, but instead makes an exact copy of the original drawing, the result is improved accuracy. Here are some examples of other PLANS made from copies of the original FLOOR PLAN from *Curse*.

Seating riser plan

The stage carpenters requested this drawing to help them put the bleachers in place. They needed a new drawing with another stratum of dimensions. The existing PLAN had so much information that any more dimensioning would have been too confusing.

The drawing was created by freezing all of the layers that weren't involved. It was then re-title blocked and labeled.

Platform plan

I like to include a ½" scale PLATFORM PLAN in my drawings. It is an excellent source of information about platform stock breakdown and layout. I make a PLATFORM PLAN by WBLOCKing the platforms in the PLAN. The best way to do this is to turn off or freeze all of the non-platform layers. The platforms are then INSERTed into a ½" prototype.

You can make quick work of drawing the plywood tops and their "X" and dimension symbols with the ARRAY command Rectangular option. The non-ARRAYable tops can be finished off by INSERTing a platform top symbol.

As is often the case, this PLATFORM PLAN couldn't fit onto one sheet. Making another drawing that shows the excess is as elementary as INSERTing the platform block on another sheet. Label the platforms that are common to both drawings to avoid confusion and duplication.

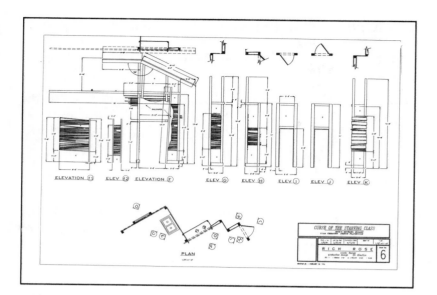

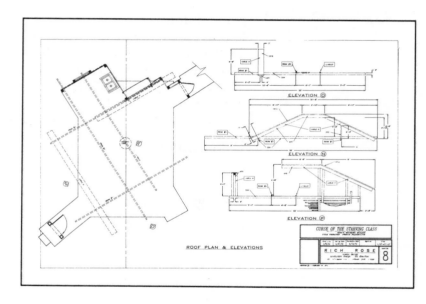

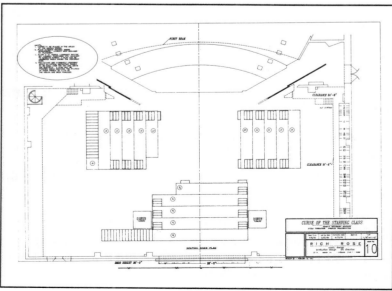

The "spillover" sheet shows that I INSERTed the drawing within a bordered area. The parts of the drawing that went over the border were merely "snipped off" using the EXPLODE and TRIM commands.

Roof plan

This drawing was started using the same WBLOCK technique used in the PLATFORM PLAN. I wanted to work out the look of the beams and roof configuration in ELEVATION as well as the placement of the beams in PLAN. After the work was completed, I took the beam configuration over to the FLOOR PLAN, assuring complete accuracy.

Tile plan

Again, the platforms were inserted from the same WBLOCK, guaranteeing complete accuracy. This PLAN helped me figure out the placement of the floor tiles and was used by the carpenters to place the tiles — an important tier of construction information that was completed in just a few minutes.

Elevations

You now have some sense of how drafting with a computer is very different from drafting manually. You can begin to distinguish between the subtle yet important strategies to approaching each method. Mastering these strategies is an important element in achieving success with CAD, as important as mastering the individual commands.

Many of the tactics that we have looked at are applicable to all types of CAD drafting — not just PLANS. Here are some new strategies that you need to understand in order to draw ELEVATIONS efficiently in AutoCAD.

Using wall plans to develop elevations

Developing ELEVATIONS can be made simple if you INSERT WBLOCK PLANS of the set walls and other elements.

1. Begin with a ½" prototype.

2. INSERT the wall PLAN in the show configuration at the bottom of the sheet.

3. Separate a wall from the PLAN for which you want to develop an ELEVATION. To do this COPY the individual PLAN wall at the top of the sheet.

4. ROTATE the wall to 0°.

5. Make the LAYOUT layer current.

6. Turn Ortho on.

7. Load your target cross hairs with OSNAP overrides **ENDpoint** and **INTERSECTION**.

8. With Ortho on, draw horizontal guidelines representing the top and bottom limits of the ELEVATION.

9. In OSNAP running mode, draw vertical lines from the PLAN above the ELEVATION representing the vertical elements.

10. Repeat the above steps for all of the ELEVATIONS that you can fit on each sheet.

11. Turn on the OUTLINES layer and draw the outlines and applied details.

12. Textures, such as the lath work in this example, can be copied over and over from one section that you have drawn. A close examination of this lath will reveal this technique. The lath was copied right over the 4 x 4 vertical supports and then TRIMmed away.

13. The window symbol could be brought from a library of such <u>ELEVATION</u> symbols. If it was created for this drawing, it should be WBLOCKed into the library for future use.

14. The last steps are to dimension and add any construction notes. Be sure to create dimensions and text in their respective layers.

15. To reference and compare this sheet with other sheets of drawings, use MSLIDE to make a slide. Use VSLIDE to do your comparisons.

Details

<u>DETAIL</u> drawings are often drawn on an entirely new sheet of drafting. If the plot scale is to be larger than ½", you will need to work on the appropriately scaled prototype. If the larger scale <u>DETAIL</u> is to be on the same sheet as the <u>ELEVATION</u> from which it originates, you must use a different strategy.

To create a larger scale drawing on a sheet intended for ½" scale, you must use the dimension variable DIMLFAC (dimension length factor). Let's say that you want to take a 3' long window drawn in ½" scale and create a <u>DETAIL</u> twice as big — a 1" scale <u>DETAIL</u>.

1. COPY the window that you want to DETAIL and put it in a blank area of your drawing.

2. SCALE it to be twice as big.

3. Alter the DIMLFAC.

In our example you are working on a ½" scale prototype and you want to make the window <u>DETAIL</u> in 1" scale. Set the DIMLFAC to .5 (review Chapters 27 and 28). This multiplies the apparent measurement by .5. Something that is 3' long in ½" scale that has been scaled to twice the size for the 1" <u>DETAIL</u> will ordinarily dimension out to 6'. But because the DIMLFAC has been set at .5, the measurement is halved before it is printed. The result is the correct 3' measurement.

4. Make the DIMENSION layer current.

5. DIMENSION the drawing.

6. Reset the DIMLFAC back to 1.

If <u>DETAIL</u> drawings are drawn from scratch (as opposed to being developed in the smaller scale <u>ELEVATION</u> and then enlarged), they should be taken back to the original <u>ELEVATION</u> to achieve the infallibility of accurate duplication.

CL Section

Like your <u>PLAN</u> drawing experience, the <u>CENTER LINE SECTION</u> will also be a baffling encounter. It always ends up being a time consuming and frustrating ordeal when you attempt to copy the hand-drafted architecture of the theater or stage to CAD. The only way out is to use one of the techniques covered in the section on <u>PLANS</u>.

Whatever method you use to transfer the architecture, make certain that you start from a prototype of the proper sheet size and desired plot scale. Once the stage has been drawn, SAVE the drawing as a <u>SECTION</u> prototype. Call it something like:

> PHCLSECT (Playhouse Center Line Section)
> LTSECPRO (Little Theater Section Prototype)
> ST1CLPRO (Stage 1 Center Line Prototype)
> or STBCLSEC (Studio B Center Line Section).

(Remember, eight letters maximum if you are using MS-DOS or you want your drawing to be read on a DOS system at some point.)

AutoCAD provides you with some tricks that can make drawing the set on the SECTION less painful than with pencil and paper. Here is one of those tricks used on this *Curse* SECTION example:

1. It was decided that rather than redrawing the set wall that had to appear on the SECTION, the already drawn ELEVATION E would somehow be used. Why draw something twice?

2. ELEVATION E was made into a WBLOCK.

3. ELEVATION E was then INSERTed into the SECTION.

4. Next, the wall was reversed using the MIRROR command.

5. The next step was to EXPLODE the wall and then use the STRETCH command to squeeze it narrower. This was necessary because we see the wall foreshortened at an angle in the SECTION.

6. You can determine the "squeeze" dimension by measuring the upstage to downstage dimension of the wall in the PLAN, and then drawing two LAYOUT layer guide lines that are that far apart on the floor line of the CL SECTION.

Another method of transferring the set is to INSERT the PLAN into this drawing:

1. Go to the PLAN and CHANGE all layers to LAYOUT.

2. SAVE the drawing under a new name.

3. Call up the CL SECTION drawing.

4. INSERT this LAYOUT PLAN:

    a. Rotate it 90°.

    b. Align the rotated LAYOUT PLAN:

        (1) vertically — line up the center line of the PLAN with the floor line of the SECTION.

        (2) horizontally — line up the edge of stage lines in both the SECTION and PLAN.

5. Draw vertical lines representing upstage-downstage wall extremes as you would in a pencil and paper SECTION.

6. Draw a horizontal line representing the tops of the scenery.

7. Fill in the appropriate detail.

A SECTION library can be a real timesaver. Such a library could include people, SECTION views of scaffold and/or other platforming systems, trees and other plants.

Save the Good Stuff! Never having to draw the same scenic element twice has got to be one of the foremost advantages that CAD brings to your work. Taking advantage of symbol libraries is central to saving time in this way.

Whenever you create a drawing that has even the most remote chance of being used again — WBLOCK it. The aluminum scaffold in the *Curse* <u>PLAN</u> is an example of this "class" of symbol. It really is from an older drawing. Elements that were created for this show include the lamb cage, the stove, and the TV antenna. You can bet that these are now in my furniture symbol library.

It's a good idea to save all of your production drawings for possible use later on. Work on the hard disk when in production. After the show has opened, make sure that your floppy disks are updated and then remove the show from the hard drive. Any scenic element that you ever draw with CAD will be instantly available to you for a new application from your file of floppies.

PROJECT 32

THEATRICAL FLOOR PLANS AND CL VERTICAL SECTION

1. Develop the following new prototype drawings:

   a. A <u>PLAN</u> prototype for each of the theaters that you regularly work in.

   b. A <u>SECTION</u> prototype for each of these theaters.

   Each prototype should include a title block with the standard information. Show-specific information should have "X's" for text in the correct size, style, etc. You will use CHANGE to customize each block for a particular production later on.

2. Add this title block to all of your other prototype drawings.

3. Draw a <u>PLAN</u> and <u>CL SECTION</u> of a theatrical set.

PROJECT 33

TELEVISION STAGING PLAN

1. Develop a <u>PLAN</u> prototype for each of the sound stages that you work in.

   Each prototype should include a title block with the standard information. Show-specific information should have "X's" for text in the correct size, style, etc. You will use CHANGE to customize each block for a particular production later on.

2. Add this title block to all of your other prototype drawings.

3. Draw a <u>STAGING PLAN</u> using the following elements:

   a. A sound stage that is 110′ x 95′.

   b. The "swing sets" provided here (shown in ¼" scale).

   c. A camera/microphone dolly aisle of 14′.

   d. An audience bleacher section that is 22′-0" x 66′-6".

4. Rotate and/or angle set walls as needed to make them fit.

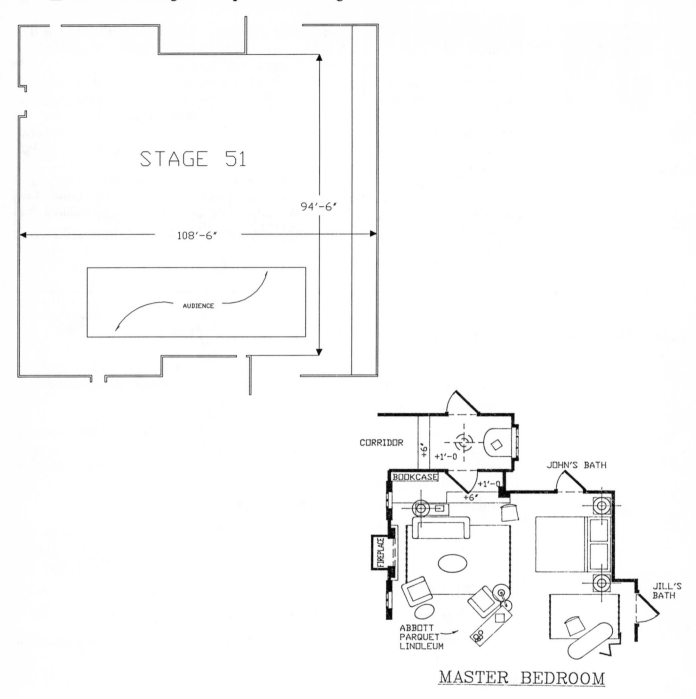

ELEVATIONS

Draw <u>FRONT ELEVATIONS</u> of the set for which you drew the <u>FLOOR PLAN</u> in either PROJECT 32 or 33. If you will be using PROJECT 33, draw the <u>ELEVATIONS</u> for one of the swing sets only.

39 3D PERSPECTIVE

FUNCTION: AutoCAD's 3D drawing capability is quite impressive. It's application in theater, film, and television, however, seems to be quite limited. Rarely do you need to call on any three-dimensional capabilities for drawing <u>PLANS</u>, <u>SECTIONS</u>, <u>ELEVATIONS</u>, or <u>LIGHT PLOTS</u>.

This chapter on 3D is included for quite a different reason. AutoCAD 3D can be a valuable resource for the scenic designer who wants to develop a sketch or rendering with highly accurate perspective. With AutoCAD 3D you start out by drawing a simplified PLAN of your set. AutoCAD then automatically generates a perspective view.

Computer-Generated Drawings

The problem with computer-generated drawings is that they have no soul, no life. They inevitably appear passionless, mechanical, and machine drawn. You, however, are only going to use the computer to generate a very unadorned "wire frame" perspective line drawing. The lines and the perspective will be highly accurate, but they will represent only the planes and general outlines of the set.

After plotting out this wire frame perspective, you can trace it onto drawing, watercolor, or marker paper in order to render a depiction of the set that is full of style and reflects the drama of the setting.

The 3D Commands

There are dozens of new commands and command options to learn with 3D. You will only be using a few of them. Here is a list of each of the ones that you will be using, accompanied by a brief description.

DVIEW (dynamic view) – Allows the computer artist to change the viewing position of the set while seeing the effects of that change simultaneously on the screen.

DVIEW OPTIONS – Provides various ways to effect changes to the viewing position.

WCS (world coordinate system) – WCS refers to the standard X,Y axis that you have become accustomed to working with up to this point. When you are in the WCS you can draw lines flat on the drawing plane of your paper only. You cannot draw lines off of the paper in the Z axis.

UCS (user coordinate system) – The UCS command gives you the ability to customize your own coordinate systems. You can have a different coordinate system on each wall of scenery that rises up vertically (or at any angle) from the floor. This allows you to easily draw lines off of the deck in any direction, including straight up and away in the Z axis. When you do this, the X and Y and Z directions no longer have anything to do with what they meant in the WCS. For instance, Y no longer means the up and down direction on your drafting paper, it means up and down the 3D scenery that is being referenced.

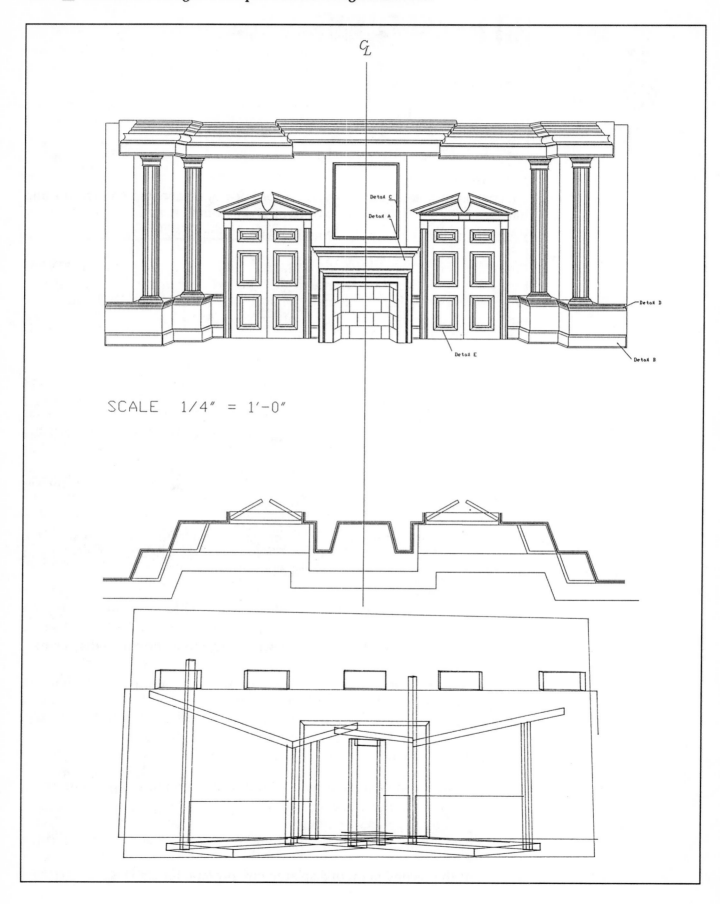

SCALE   1/4″ = 1′-0″

CAmera – The term AutoCAD uses to represent the apparent rotation of the set. It is important to realize that the object isn't rotating, rather it's the viewer or **CAmera** that is rotating around the stationary object, or changing viewing positions in the audience.

eXit – Used to "lock in" a DVIEW view and must be selected before using any drawing or editing commands in 3D. If not, all DVIEW set-up information will be lost.

3point – One of many UCS options for establishing a custom coordinate system.

Distance – Simultaneously turns AutoCAD's 3D perspective mode on and moves the viewer or **CAmera** toward or away from the set.

PAn – Pans the viewer or **CAmera** in relation to the set.

Locating these 3D command options
- the Root Menu under DISPLAY
- the Pull Down Menu under DRAW, 3D CONSTRUCTION
- the Tablet Menu under 3D/AUTOSHADE™
- UCS is found under SETTINGS in the Root Menu as well as in the 3D area of the tablet.

A 3D Prototype

Working in three dimensions can get confusing. You can actually get lost or get a false sense of where you are in the drawing. This happens because you are performing the conflicting tasks of drawing the set in a 3D world while visualizing it on a flat 2D monitor. Because of this phenomenon I recommend that you create a 3D prototype that you will start all of your 3D set drawings from.

The 3D prototype itself can be made from any of your other prototypes. You will simply add a 3D cube or box to the prototype to turn it into a 3D prototype. You will do all of your drawing inside the 3D box. This will serve as a constant reference so that you don't get lost or confused.

Your 3D box should be a little bigger than the area that your scenery usually takes up in height, length, and width. The width of the proscenium opening might serve nicely as the length of each side of the cube.

Building a 3D reference box

1. Create a 3DPROTO drawing from your HALFFRAM. Erase all title block information as well as the border. The drawing should be completely blank.

2. SAVE.

3. Make your LAYOUT layer current.

4. In your blank 3D prototype draw a rectangle that represents the area that your scenery usually takes up in height, length, and width.

5. Select COPY.

   At the Select Objects: prompt, **Window** the rectangle you just drew.

   At the <base point or displacement>/Multiple: prompt, type a displacement of:

   0,0,25′

   At the Second point of displacement: prompt, hit **ENTER**.

This is how you use the COPY displacement option. You have just told AutoCAD that the displacement is straight up off of the paper (Z axis) at 25′.

6. Select DVIEW from the tablet or from the Root Menu under DISPLAY.

    AutoCAD will ask you to Select Objects:

    Window and select the rectangle again.

7. Select OPTIONS.

8. Select **CAmera**.

    You see a Slider Bar at the side of the screen. AutoCAD is asking you to slide the diamond-shaped indicator until you have the desired rotation angle for this axis. Pick something like 15°.

MEMO

Notice that as you slide the diamond-shaped indicator, the object rotates at the same time. This real-time coordination between the slider bar and the set's movement is what dynamic view refers to.

A very complicated set rotates very poorly. Only one or two of the lines in the set will appear to rotate — the rest of it disappears. When you are rotating a complicated set, you should select only key lines or entities at the Select Objects: prompt in Step 6 above.

---

9. Another Slider Bar appears at the top of the screen. AutoCAD is asking you to slide the diamond-shaped indicator until you have the desired rotation angle for this axis. Pick something like -75°.

10. Select **eXit**.

11. You don't have a cube quite yet. Your vertical lines are missing. However, they are impossible to draw in the WCS (world coordinate system).

12. Select UCS.

13. Select 3point (Type 3).

    *   For origin point, pick the lower left corner of the front face of the cube (use ENDPOINT).

    *   For positive portion on X axis, pick the MIDPOINT of the bottom line of the front face of the cube.

    *   For positive portion of Y axis, pick the ENDPOINT of the upper left corner of the front face of the cube.

    The coordinate icon should now reflect your input.

14. Now draw the four vertical lines that will complete the cube. Draw one and then copy with the Multiple option. Don't forget OSNAP.

15. Select WCS (or UCS WORLD).

16. Return to the PLAN view of your cube.

    Type PLAN or select it from the tablet.

17. SAVE.

Your 3DPROTO prototype drawing is now complete.

Creating a 3D perspective wire frame set drawing

1. Create a new drawing from your 3DPROTO drawing.

2. Make your OUTLINES layer current.

3. Draw your set in <u>PLAN</u>. Draw only the simplest lines. Don't draw doors, windows, or other detail. Start your set at the downstage edge of the cube using OSNAP **NEArest** and finish the same way if possible.

4. Select COPY.

   At the Select Objects: prompt, use **Crossing Window** to select the set you just drew.

   At the <Base point or displacement>/Multiple: prompt, type a displacement value of: 0,0,18′.

   At the Second point of displacement: prompt, hit **ENTER**.

   The set lines that represent the top limits of the set should now be displayed floating 18′ above the stage floor.

5. Select DVIEW.

   AutoCAD will ask you to Select Objects:

   Window and select the rectangle and your set.

6. Select OPTIONS.

7. Select **CAmera**.

   Pick something like 15°.

8. Another Slider Bar appears at the top of the screen.

   Pick something like -90°.

9. Select **eXit**.

10. To be able to draw in the vertical lines of the set you will need to get out of the WCS.

11. Select UCS.

12. Select 3point.

    • For origin point, pick the lower left corner of the front face of the cube (use ENDPOINT).

    • For positive portion on X axis, pick the MIDPOINT of the bottom line of the front face of the cube.

    • For positive portion of Y axis, pick the ENDPOINT of the upper left corner of the front face of the cube.

    The coordinate icon should now reflect your input.

13. You can now draw and Multiple-COPY the vertical lines of the set walls.

14. To see the set in true perspective mode, select DVIEW. Next **Window** or **Crossing Window** your set and cube.

15. Select OPTIONS.

16. Select **CAmera**.

- Pick something like 10° for the vertical rotation.

- Pick -90° for the horizontal rotation.

Adding perspective and detail

1. Select Distance. A new slider bar appears that indicates the distance multiple. You will most likely have to select 16x. You will then probably need to select 16x again. The set will most likely finally appear but it will be quite far away. Slide the slider bar until the set almost fills the screen.

2. To center the set, select the **PAn** option from the Screen Menu Area.

3. **eXit**.

4. Your set is now in 3D perspective (and the word vanishing point didn't even come up once!). Fine tune your view now:

   - use DVIEW **CAmera** to rotate the set some more

   - use Distance to bring the set closer or move it back

   - ERASE the cube

5. If you want to you can draw on any of the walls to add doors, windows, or other sorts of detail. You must make a UCS for any wall that you want to add detail to. Pick the lower left corner of the wall for the origin point, the bottom MIDPOINT of the wall for the X axis, and pick the MIDPOINT or ENDPOINT of the wall for the Y axis. Then draw away! It's quite simple and accurate.

6. If you have drawn the ELEVATIONS for your set, you can bring them into the drawing and "hang" them right onto your wire frame. To do this:

   a. Make each ELEVATION that you want to hang on your wire frame into a WBLOCK.

   b. Make sure that the insertion point is a corner that exists in both the ELEVATION and the wire frame of the wall.

   c. Establish a UCS for the wall you are about to import.

   d. Use the INSERT command to bring the ELEVATION into the drawing.

   e. Use OSNAP to place the wall accurately.

   You can't draw on the walls or import ELEVATIONS in perspective mode. To turn perspective mode off select PLAN (from the tablet or type it in). To get back to a non-perspective 3D view, return to step 5.

   Use Ortho to help you draw all of your vertical and horizontal lines.

   You can save the various UCS's that you define for each wall by using a UCS dialog box. (For Release 11, select UCS CONTROL. For Release 10, select UCS DIALOG. Then select MODIFY UCS.) It is available from the SETTINGS Pull Down Menu. To create and save a UCS with this technique:

   - at the dialog box select Define new current UCS

   - select the name box and give each UCS a name that relates to the wall (WALL1 or WALL2, etc.)

   - select Origin, X axis, plane (this is the same as 3point)

- define the UCS as you would had you selected 3point.

To alternate between the different walls for purposes of adding detail, go back to the main UCS dialog box and put a check in the box that makes that wall's UCS current.

7. The last step is to plot out your perspective wire frame and then transform it into a fully developed sketch or rendering on the appropriate paper.

PROJECT 35

COMPUTER-ASSISTED PERSPECTIVE SKETCH

1. Develop a simple wire frame perspective from a <u>FLOOR PLAN</u>.

2. Define at least two UCS's using the Modify UCS dialog box.

3. Draw some detail on each of these walls (window, door, etc.).

4. Plot out your perspective view.

5. Transfer your plot to watercolor or marker paper to create a full color the-atrical rendering.

40 DESIGNING and DRAFTING LIGHTING

> **FUNCTION**: The symbol-intensive nature of <u>LIGHTING PLOTS</u> makes lighting design and AutoCAD natural partners. Because of this, <u>LIGHTING PLOT</u> generation is the most fully developed, second party supported, and most popular theatrical AutoCAD application. AutoCAD's facility with attribute symbols works to the advantage of the lighting designer. Using a data base or another specialty program, you can create hook-up sheets and instrument schedules with just a few key strokes.

Memory

Designing the <u>LIGHT PLOT</u> is memory intensive. A <u>LIGHT PLOT</u> is a compact drawing that is full of information. Lighting symbols are made up of zillions and zillions of curves that take a lot of mathematical calculations and therefore a lot of time to draw. They also have lots of text, more so than scenic or pattern drafting. Although you can use a 286 based computer for this task you are better off with AutoCAD 386™ and a 386 machine. The 80386 computers have disk caching and enough memory for all of the drawing to fit into RAM. Time won't be taken up with long waiting periods filled with disk accessing. In a <u>LIGHT PLOT</u> this typically takes the form of the 80286 computer reading what's on the first electric, drawing it, going to the second electric, putting the first electric back on disk, drawing the second electric, putting it away, and then getting the information for the third electric from the disk, etc., etc., etc. Each of these operations is done while you wait and wait and wait. Operations that can be done in memory, as opposed to this disk information swapping, are faster.

A large <u>LIGHT PLOT</u> will take ten to fifteen minutes just to generate on the screen from the Main Menu of a 286 computer with 1 megabyte of memory. You can practically take a coffee break whenever a REGEN occurs during a drawing session on one of these computers. Lighting designers really should have computers with as much sophistication as they can afford. A 30 MB hard disk is recommended on a 386 IBM format machine.

Designing Lighting Symbols

The drawing of <u>LIGHT PLOTS</u> is quite repetitive. For instance, a design for an industrial automobile show by designer Bob Heller has electrics filled with PAR 64's. The symbol consists of:
- the lighting instrument itself
- the channel #
- the color
- type of PAR 64 (medium, wide, narrow)
- instrument #

This symbol and similar symbols representing other lighting instruments fill the entire plot. Once a lighting instrument symbol library has been created, a plot can almost be generated with only the INSERT, MINSERT, and COPY

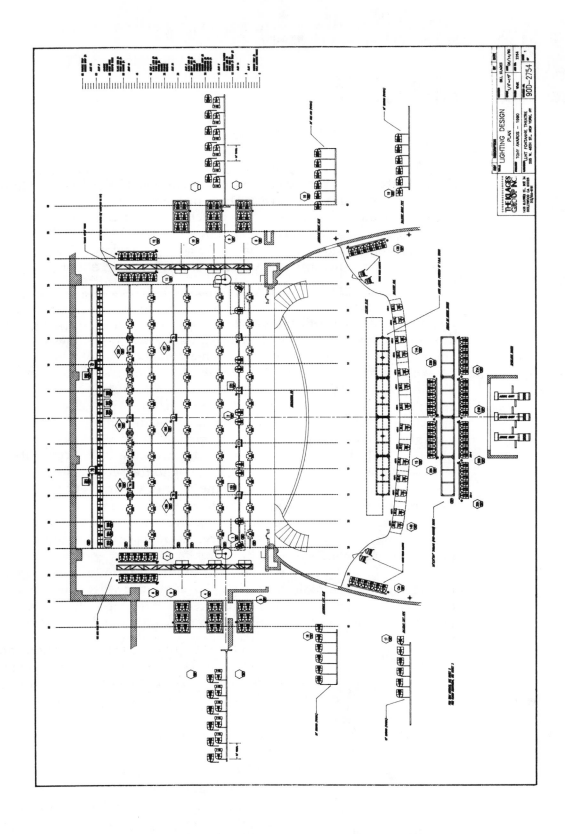

commands. Some batten drawing, set <u>PLAN</u> information, and a little text are almost all you need to complete the drawing.

A good symbol library can start with the basic United States Institute for Theater Technology (USITT) instrument symbols, including:

- ERS's
- fresnels
- standard theatrical strip lights
- scoops

You will then need to augment this library with symbols for the state of the art lighting instruments and pieces of equipment that are used in rock and roll and industrial shows as well. These include:

- Vari-lights
- MR 16 strip lights
- 8′ box truss sections
- box truss variations with the instruments facing in other directions

Box trusses are used extensively in touring rock and roll and industrial shows. Each truss contains 6 PAR cans. It is hung, struck, and stored as a unit. This self-contained unit travels intact from venue to venue. Therefore, the truss symbol contains 6 PAR symbols as part of the unit.

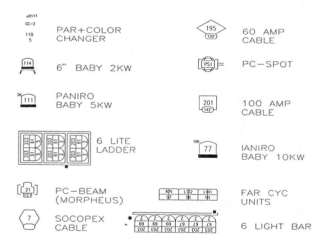

Plan out in advance where you want different text information categories to appear in relation to your symbol. The USITT has very definite guidelines as to what form this information should take. However, it doesn't take the complexity of rock and roll and industrial show touring into account. An example of such a plan includes:

- channel or circuit text above the instrument
- dimmers text above the instrument
- purpose text below the instrument
- instrument number inside the instrument

When the instrument is rotated away from the orientation in which the initial BLOCK was made, the alignment described above is no longer in effect. The text is rotated, making it difficult to read because of its non-horizontal orientation, as well as the fact that the text may have rotated right over another instrument or its attribute text. This is a small problem with attributed instrument symbol INSERTion. A way to get around this is to create four BLOCKS for each symbol. Each variation has the instrument turned 90° with the text information maintaining a horizontal orientation throughout the design.

A similar problem occurs when you MIRROR booms. The text will also MIRROR. The text must be ERASEd and re-entered. These sorts of problems are more frequent in rock and roll and industrial designs where symmetry is more common. Theatrical lighting designs tend to be much less symmetrical.

MEMO

AutoLISP® (AutoCAD's programming language) routines are a way of getting around these and similar sorts of problems. What follows here is only one of hundreds of LISP routines that AutoCAD users have developed to solve various problems. The AutoCAD® forums on such services as Compuserve have many user solutions to all sorts of problems. There may be an answer from someone in another profession for a problem similar to one that you might be having. You will soon develop a wish list of lots of features that you would like customized to your needs. Networking with other users on such a service can be very helpful.

Text rotation LISP routine

Pre-eminent lighting designer Bill Klages has gotten around the text rotation problem by writing an AutoLISP program that works with your Auto-CAD program. This program guarantees a satisfactory text rotation regardless of the instrument position or insertion rotation angle. Mr. Klages' Tony Awards light plot featured on the first page of this chapter was drawn using this program.

```
;----------------------------------------------------------
; ROTEXT.LSP                              annotated version
; function to rotate attribute text
; William M. Klages                       5/4/90
;
;----------------------------------------------------------
(defun c:rotext ( / ss1 emax vtest edata enext count mode)
  (graphscr)
  (setvar "CMDECHO" 0)
  (setq mode (getvar "OSMODE"))                 ;save osnap setting
  (setvar "OSMODE" 8)                           ;osnap to node
  (princ "select instruments to rotate text...")
  (setq ss1 (ssget)                             ;selection set of instruments
        count 0                                 ;counting variable
        emax (sslength ss1)                     ;number of instruments
  ); setq
  (if (/= ss1 nil)                              ;loop
    (progn
      (while (< count emax)
        (setq ename (cdr (assoc -1  (entget (ssname ss1 count)))))
              enext (entnext ename)
              edata (entget enext)
              vtest (cdr(assoc 0 edata))
        ); setq
        (while (/= vtest "SEQEND")              ;step through entity data
          (if (= vtest "ATTRIB")
            (progn
              (setq edata (subst  (cons 50 (+ PI (cdr  (assoc 50 edata))))
                                  (assoc 50 edata) edata))
                                                ;rotate attribute text 180deg
              (entmod edata)                    ;modify data
            ); progn
          ); endif
          (setq enext (entnext enext)           ;step through entities
                edata (entget enext)
                vtest (cdr(assoc 0 edata))
          ); setq
        ); endwhile
        (entupd ename)                          ;update entity
        (setq count (1+ count))                 ;next member of selection set
      );endwhile
    ); progn
  ); endif
  (setvar "OSMODE" mode)                        ;reset osnap
); defun
```

Using lighting symbols

INSERT lighting symbol BLOCKS like you would any other library symbol. First INSERT the library and then call up the individual symbols as you need them (review Chapter 35). It is a good idea to have Ortho and Snap on when working with lighting instruments. Lighting instruments are usually at 1'-6" intervals. Having Snap on and set to 18" makes the placement of the instruments quick and uniform. Ortho keeps the instruments lined up along the same batten.

When the <u>PLOT</u> is complete, you may find that you need to go back and put in (or take out) an instrument or two. This requires that you do some instrument renumbering. The CHANGE command is helpful for this task. Rather than ERASE and renumber each of the instruments, the CHANGE command allows you to renumber almost automatically. After selecting the CHANGE command, pick each of the instrument numbers that needs to be altered — in order. Next, cycle through the command options until you get to New text:. At that point you can type in the string of new numbers one at a time, separated by hitting the **ENTER** key. Using this technique, you do not invoke the CHANGE command for each renumbering task. You call it up only once, saving lots of time and effort.

These symbol-filled <u>LIGHT PLOTS</u> are quite large and filled with lots of tiny bits of information. One piece of information usually relates to another piece of information in some remote area of the drawing. The solution doesn't lie in zooming out all the way either. A ZOOM **All** view doesn't give you a good sense of the design, since the parts are too tiny to read. Somehow you need to find out if all areas are being covered adequately. Are instruments pointed in the right direction?

The solution is in two parts. One part is to plot your drawing out every so often. Take the time to examine it at length on your drafting table. In this way you can check over all of the detail in a scale larger than your 12" monitor permits. It is very important to be able to see all of the drawing at once. Preliminary plots are the only way to get a sense of how distances, positions, and angles are working.

The second part of the solution is the slide feature. Make slides of zoomed-in key areas of the <u>PLOT</u>. These slides can be a handy quick reference tool that allows you to see certain areas of the <u>PLOT</u> while avoiding REGENs.

Layers

If you use large format photocopy as your reproduction method, you will find that green and yellow don't copy well. Yellow copies a little better than green. You can use this to your advantage in drawing a <u>LIGHT PLOT</u>. Many lighting designers will draw the set in green so that it recedes and becomes less important than the instruments. This is quite important. If the set and the instruments had to compete for visual attention the <u>PLOT</u> would become unreadable. To some degree a similar effect can be achieved with blueline copies as well.

A repertory design plotted in color can be very handy to the master electrician responsible for instrument plugging at every changeover. The nature of a <u>REP PLOT</u> requires that too many instruments share too few electrical circuits. Instruments that are common to all shows can be plotted in one color on one layer. Instruments that are special to a "show A" can be plotted on another color on another layer. Instruments special to a "show B" can be plotted on yet another color on another layer, and so on. At changeover the M.E. can look at the <u>PLOT</u> and use color as a quick guide for plugging or unplugging these instruments into or out of circuits.

Here is a suggestion for layers that the lighting designer might use to supplement the layers suggested in Chapter 11.

SET	Basic PLAN outlines drawn in green.
ELECTRICS	The battens that contain the instruments.
COMMON	The instruments that are common to all shows in a <u>REP PLOT</u>.
SHOW A	The instruments that are in show A only.
SHOW B	The instruments that are in show B only.
SHOW C	The instruments that are in show C only.
SHOW D	The instruments that are in show D only.
BOOMS	Used to draw boom, shin-buster, and tree positions.

AutoCAD-Based Lighting Programs

Lighting design is an area of entertainment design in which several companies have put out design programs that use AutoCAD. These programs have built-in features that tackle problems particular to the needs of the <u>LIGHTING PLOT</u>. Some of these features include automatic TRIMming of the batten through the instrument and instrument schedule generation without the need for a separate data base program. Other features incorporate automatic re-numbering when an instrument is inserted or removed. These programs take the nearly automated job of developing a <u>LIGHT PLOT</u> on AutoCAD and make it even more streamlined.

These programs are available from theatrical supply companies and are often advertised in *Theater Crafts* and *Lighting Dimensions* magazines.

Lighting Instrument Schedule Programs

There are many programs designed to take your instrument information and manipulate it to your specifications in order to make any number and style of hook-up sheets, instrument schedules, dimmer patch sheets, etc. These programs are completely independent from AutoCAD.

One such program is LIGHT WRITE™, available from ROSCO theatrical supply company. Besides formatting the information to your specifications, some of these programs can analyze your data and then tell you what and how much color to buy, or how much of each size to cut, etc.

LIGHT WRITE™ asks you to choose from a directory of design formats: theatrical plays, dance, industrial shows, etc. It will also prompt you for the name of the show, number of dimmers, and wattage capacity of the dimmers. Armed with all of this preliminary information, the program will let you know when you are getting close to overloading your dimmer capacity as you assign focus, circuit, dimmer, etc. to each instrument. Circuit and dimmer reports can quickly tell you how much cable and how many dimmers, circuits, two-fers, etc. you need in any area of the <u>PLOT</u>. These reports are available whenever you ask for them. However, the program does a lot of error checking as you are entering the information. It will let you know when you are overloading a circuit the instant you plug that 3K fresnel into a 2K dimmer. It will also warn you about dimmers in more than one circuit, circuits that are in more than one dimmer, overloading of electrical service legs, etc. The list goes on and on and the program is very, very fast.

After your instrument information is loaded into the program you have a number of ways to look at different types of information. You can look at specific instruments to see what they have been assigned to do, or you can look at entire electrics to see what is on them. You can survey the types of instruments that you are using in your <u>PLOT</u> as easily as you can list all of the instruments that use a certain color. Any or all of the information can be changed in a few keystrokes in this program. If you decide to change all of your sidelight from one color to another for example, it is a simple matter for this program to handle. Other features include automatic saves every thirty minutes, and the ability to completely customize the printout formats. If half of lighting design is paperwork, programs such as these can lighten your load considerably.

PROJECT 36

LIGHTING

1. Develop or insert your previously developed lighting instrument library into a <u>FLOOR PLAN</u> prototype drawing that will become a <u>LIGHT PLOT</u> prototype drawing.

2. Add the layers suggested in this chapter as needed.

3. Draw all of the permanent lighting positions on the ELECTRICS layer.

4. Save your new prototype.

5. Create a new PROJECT 36 drawing from the PROJECT 32 or 33 drawing.

6. Draw the important <u>FLOOR PLAN</u> information on the SET layer, or insert the entire <u>PLAN</u> drawn in that project.

41 DRAWING THE SOUND PLOT

FUNCTION: The process of developing the schematic of the sound design is one that is enhanced by the computer. With the many text editing features and layering capabilities available with AutoCAD, what can be a confusing and frustrating task is made much smoother.

Adapting CAD Features to Sound Design

DRAWING SYMBOLS — AutoCAD's ability to draw the shapes that define speakers, amplifiers, etc. works quite well here. The POLYGON command can be used to draw many of these symbols, or the regular LINE command can be used. **Multiple** COPY, of course, can be used to place replicas of any of the symbols.

TEXT FEATURES — Different font styles and sizes are used to denote different aspects of the design. One style for speakers, another for tape decks, etc.

COLOR — The sound designer can use color to her or his advantage since multiple copies are kept to a minimum. This is quite unlike multiple copies of scenic shop drawings where individual color plots would be out of the question. Use color to help identify the different components as well as the patch paths.

EDITING — Changes, mistakes, and additions are easily accomplished using AutoCAD's editing commands. This process is similar to the scenic designer or lighting designer who pushes and pulls and otherwise changes the symbols around on the drawing quite effortlessly.

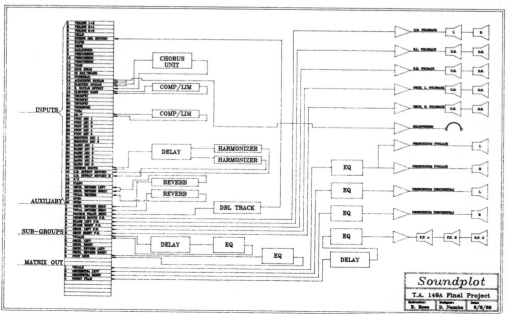

42 A LAST WORD

Over my many years of teaching AutoCAD to Theater and Film/Television students and professionals, I have seen two strong patterns emerge in the habits and abilities of my students. One of the foremost of these was what I call the "now what?" syndrome. In this scenario the student said to me at the end of the quarter, "I really enjoyed the class but how can I use AutoCAD in the theater?" — followed by a thud as I hit the institutional green linoleum tiles.

This, of course, is the reason I wrote this book. With more generic publications, the novices had to be nudged to the brink in order to make the creative and intellectual leap necessary to apply a general purpose (non-theatrical) text to the process of solving very specific, entertainment-related drawing problems. The pattern that emerged was that, rather than a successful landing, too many were spiraling into the gorge. Once there they carried the scars of frustration and impatience that made it impossible for them ever to climb out — back to the T-square for them. The idea behind this book was that if I could build a bridge between the computer skills and the real life creative issues of theater and film/television design, then many more people would make the connection. This book takes the very first line drawing project and turns it into a true life problem — a <u>FLOOR PLAN</u>.

The other strong trend was the "here today, gone tomorrow" syndrome. This roughly translates into the students' consummate mastery of ideas explored later on in the course, yet an almost complete deficiency in awareness of the preceding fundamentals. As I write this paragraph today my graduate students, while working on their final projects, are discovering the joys of TRIM **Crossing** and FILLET 0 as if they were experiencing them for the very first time. I am a model of motivation and support as they learn to use the command which I have apparently been keeping secret from them these many weeks. All the while I am grinding my teeth in frustration behind the facade of my supportive smile.

My advice to the reader is to not be fooled into thinking that just because you have finished these many pages that you are in any way a CAD master. It is only after you have triumphed over the earlier, as well as the later, concepts that you will ever be able to achieve the requisite speed and accuracy that orchestrate to make computer-aided drawing and design a much more efficient instrument than the pencil and paper. *Review* the earlier chapters and I *promise* you that you will discover pages seemingly written in disappearing ink that only now make themselves accessible to you. Review the words as well as the projects and you will verifiably be on the way to becoming an ace.

One more thing. The concepts and commands in this book have only touched on AutoCAD's capabilities. Take the time to discover the *AutoCAD Reference Manual* that came with your software. Its pages will reveal to you aspects of AutoCAD that will build on and enrich your newly acquired skills.

INDEX